Ecological Aspects of Development in the Humid Tropics

Committee on Selected Biological Problems
in the Humid Tropics

Division of Biological Sciences

Assembly of Life Sciences

National Research Council

NATIONAL ACADEMY PRESS
Washington, D.C. 1982

NOTICE: The project that is the subject of this report was approved by the Governing Board of the National Research Council, whose members are drawn from the Councils of the National Academy of Sciences, the National Academy of Engineering, and the Institute of Medicine. The members of the committee responsible for the report were chosen for their special competences and with regard for appropriate balance.

This report has been reviewed by a group other than the authors according to procedures approved by a Report Review Committee consisting of members of the National Academy of Sciences, the National Academy of Engineering, and the Institute of Medicine.

The National Research Council was established by the National Academy of Sciences in 1916 to associate the broad community of science and technology with the Academy's purposes of furthering knowledge and of advising the federal government. The Council operates in accordance with general policies determined by the Academy under the authority of its congressional charter of 1863, which establishes the Academy as a private, nonprofit, self-governing membership corporation. The Council has become the principal operating agency of both the National Academy of Sciences and National Academy of Engineering in the conduct of their services to the government, the public, and the scientific and engineering communities. It is administered jointly by both Academies and the Institute of Medicine. The National Academy of Engineering and the Institute of Medicine were established in 1964 and 1970, respectively, under the charter of the National Academy of Sciences.

This study was supported by funds from the U.S. Agency for International Development, through a contract (CX-0001-0-0013) with the National Park Service.

Library of Congress Cataloging in Publication Data

National Research Council (U.S.). Committee on
  Selected Biological Problems in the Humid Tropics.
  Ecological aspects of development in the humid tropics.

  Bibliography: p.
  1. Ecology—Tropics.   2. Land use—Tropics—Planning.   3. Underdeveloped areas—Environmental policy.   4. Environmental policy—Tropics.   5. Nature conservation—Tropics.   6. Conservation of natural resources—Tropics.   7. Human ecology—Tropics.
  I. Title.
  QH84.5.N373 1982   333.73'0913   82-3620
  ISBN 0-309-03235-0   AACR2

Available from:

NATIONAL ACADEMY PRESS
2101 Constitution Avenue, N.W.
Washington, D.C. 20418

Printed in the United States of America

Preface

This report is to be seen within the context of a comprehensive effort by the U.S. Agency for International Development Office of Forestry, Environment, and Natural Resources, through an agreement established in 1979 with the National Park Service, U.S. Department of the Interior, to review existing technical information on environmental protection and natural resource management and to organize it in a manner that AID missions and developing countries can use effectively in project planning and execution. The overall project envisions three phases: (1) a series of four review papers designed to assess the state of the art on selected environmental and natural resource issues in developing countries; (2) a number of case studies undertaken in cooperation with a host country institution to document alternative approaches to regional resource planning and to introduce new ways of thinking about environmental issues; and (3) some half-dozen "design aids" emphasizing methods for identifying development opportunities within the context of a given river basin, watershed, or other geographic system.

In response to a request for assistance from the Office of International Affairs, National Park Service, the Committee on Selected Biological Problems in the Humid Tropics was formed in May 1980 to prepare the first of the review papers, that dealing with the humid tropics. It is the aim of this report to indicate the chief patterns through which people utilize the humid tropics, to provide a concise description of humid tropical ecosystems, to focus in particular on what the Committee sees as critical aspects deserving special attention—renewable natural resources, germplasm resources, agriculture, forested lands, soil, and surface water—and to comment briefly on regional development as seen from an ecological perspective. In this connection, it must be noted that the term ecology is used throughout the report in its essentially biological context—the interrelationships of living organisms with their environment; it does not as here used encompass social, economic, or political issues.

Jay M. Savage, *Chairman*
Committee on Selected Biological
Problems in the Humid Tropics

Acknowledgments

The Committee wishes to acknowledge the assistance of the following persons:

Agency for International Development

LIDA L. ALLEN	DANIEL J. DEELY	ALBERT C. PRINTZ
GEORGE BELT	WILLIAM M. FELDMAN	MICHAEL RECHCIGL
MICHAEL D. BENGE	JAMES C. HESTER	WILLIAM D. ROSEBOROUGH
JEROME J. BOSKEN	HAROLD M. JONES	JANE E. STANLEY
NORMAN M. CHAPIN	MOLLY M. KUX	FRED W. WHITTEMORE
DANIEL F. CREEDON	JOHN L. MALCOLM	FRANK ZADROGA
	ROBERT O. OTTO	

National Park Service

VERNON C. GILBERT	KYRAN D. THELEN
HUGH BELL MÜLLER	JEFFREY B. TSCHIRLEY

Other Affiliation

RICHARD P. AXLER, University of California
DALE BOTTRELL, University of California
FRANCESCO DI CASTRI, UNESCO
PETER FREEMAN, Consultant
CARL GALLEGOS, International Paper Company
HENRY E. GRUPPE, International Institute for Environment and Development

GARY HARTSHORN, Tropical Science Center
HUGH M. ILTIS, University of Wisconsin
WAAFAS OFOSU-AMAAH, International Institute for Environment and
Development
GORDON H. ORIANS, University of Washington
JOHN C. PRISCU, University of California
PRISCILLA C. REINING, American Association for the Advancement of
Science
ROBERT E. RICKLEFS, University of Pennsylvania
S. JACOB SCHERR, National Resources Defense Council
KEVIN TALBOT
GARY H. TOENNIESSEN, Rockefeller Foundation
FRANK H. WADSWORTH, Institute of Tropical Forestry
THOMAS M. YUILL, University of Wisconsin

Contents

ix

Summary and Recommendations

Humid tropical ecosystems, especially lowland forests and wetlands, represent a very important underexploited resource for tropical countries. Increasing population pressures and rising expectations indicate that conversion of these ecosystems to other uses will intensify during the remainder of the century. Although conversion frequently results in short-term increases in food production or economic gain, long-term, sustained-yield systems have seldom been achieved with current technology. Thus short-term gains are often obtained at the risk of severe, long-lasting environmental damage.

The ecology of these ecosystems is but poorly understood. Although there is some knowledge with which to minimize adverse impacts, the often-repeated assertion that it is adequate as a basis for internally sustainable agriculture, forestry, and fishery systems in the humid tropics is clearly unjustified. Substantial additional research and an ongoing technological application of new discoveries derived therefrom are required if development in the humid tropics is to achieve long-term benefits with minimal damage to the environment.

On the other hand, it is clear that the approximately 1.5 billion people who will be added to the population of tropical countries between now and the end of the century (90% of the world's total increase) will have heightened expectations and requirements for food, shelter, and other essentials. Attention will almost certainly focus on unoccupied lands as a source of economic betterment. As a result, rapid and extensive development will and must take place if even the currently inadequate standard of living of most countries is to be maintained.

Clearly the dilemma that faces both the economic planner and the ecologist as it relates to the humid tropics is not an easy one. The realities of the situation make it necessary to implement development strategies that are based on inadequate knowledge. The central issue is how to apply current knowledge in providing for short-term economic gain without irreversibly precluding the opportunity to attain additional knowledge and technological advancement as a basis for wise long-term utilization. The situation requires that reasonable caution be exerted in applying current knowledge, so as to minimize adverse environmental effects. To do so acknowledges that current humid tropic development projects are buying time to permit the achievement of long-term, environmentally balanced strategies and new technologies.

The Committee discerns three major divergent approaches to utilization of humid tropic resources in the short term. Advocates of these approaches agree that no one of them can completely meet the economic and environmental requirements of sustained yield, and that in most instances some mix is inevitable. They may be summarized as follows:

• Retain intact substantial parts of humid tropical ecosystems to serve as parks and reserves, as scientific repositories for study, as natural sources of germplasm, as food sources for aboriginal people, and as means for facilitating maintenance of air and water quality and for erosion control. Within this approach, human use would be restricted to tourism, recreation, scientific investigation, game harvesting, and collecting, gathering, and removal of certain forest products. This approach has limited short-term economic yield, but it affords excellent long-term environmental protection and makes possible programs leading eventually to maximum sustained yield.

• Utilize substantial parts of the natural ecosystem to produce lumber, pulpwood, plywood, and fuel, emphasizing such management practices as selective cutting, underplanting, shelterwood forestry, limited clear-cutting, and human-assisted regeneration and reforestation.

• Convert extensive areas that are already deforested, and selectively deforest others, to increase food production through applications of new agricultural technologies developed in the humid tropics. Emphasis here is on conversion of land to increased agricultural use and on use of fertilizers. Under this approach, human impact would be substantial, involving maximum modification of the ecosystem to produce short-term economic yields. The long-term environmental effects would be maximal, and long-term economic gains would depend on continued application of fertilizers and development of new technologies.

The Committee believes that each of these approaches merits consideration as applied to a given tropical country in the context of its past history of forest use and the current status of a specific development site. Given the state of knowledge, some mixture of the three is probably the route of choice for any given region, provided options for other strategies are held open. With these considerations in mind, the Committee makes the following general and specific recommendations.

GENERAL RECOMMENDATIONS

1. Ecological information and environmental considerations must be an integral part of development project planning; they must be given equal weight with agricultural, economic, and engineering factors from the outset of project design.

2. Development agencies must encourage and support ecological research that will provide essential knowledge for finding new technologies that, in turn, lead to environmentally balanced, long-term strategies for development.

3. On-going assessments of project-induced changes in the environment are essential; such feedback will aid in minimizing difficulties in subsequent projects. Further, mid-project evaluations allow shifts in course, should special constraints arise.

4. Conservation of natural areas in the vicinity of a development site should be an integral part of a project plan; these areas provide a background against which to assess environmental changes and preserve options for future development.

5. Careful attention must be paid to the contribution of natural ecosystems in sustaining long-term development in tropical countries. Projects that appear economically sound in the short term may actually be economically burdensome over time because of initially unrecognized environmental costs. Holistic planning is one way of identifying wise alternatives for economic growth and development.

6. Planning can be made much more effective by expanding and improving natural resources evaluation. Information on climate, soils, vegetation, wildlife, and water resources is essential to environmentally sound planning and facilitates wise selection among project options.

7. Considerations of technology development and transfer merit inclusion in all agricultural and forestry projects. Too often, development projects in the humid tropics concentrate their resources on roads, infrastructure, and marketing systems, essentially ignoring technology or assuming that it is available and readily transferable. When projects fail from an

economic and ecological point of view, it is often due to lack of such technology. Ideally, each project should use available technology, but should include a research component designed to test and validate such issues as land-clearing methods, choice of cropping or silviculture methods, species used, fertilization requirements, and crop–pasture–tree rotations. In addition, a strong technology transfer component is essential to training new settlers or local farmers in how to farm any new areas, as well as to providing information to technical and political leaders.

8. Development agencies must strengthen communication linkages in search of maximum dissemination among tropical countries of information on results of natural resources research, on project successes and difficulties, and on technological innovation. Opportunities for direct communication between tropical country counterparts should be enhanced.

SPECIFIC RECOMMENDATIONS

1. Because nations with limited capital are the ones that can least afford to underutilize or degrade the products and services offered by natural ecosystems, accelerated research is needed in ways to replace short-rotation shifting agriculture with alternative farming systems. Development strategies should encourage new farming systems based on diverse crops and improved germplasm. Additional research is also required in ways to improve agroforestry and animal–crop combinations.

2. Many tropical American fruits have not diffused to tropical Asia and Africa; the converse is also true. Hence, development agencies should develop and support a worldwide network for studying, acclimating, and distributing fruit crops. Rigorous pathogen control is essential in any such germplasm movement.

3. Since annual crops, pastures, or permanent crop systems should be sufficiently productive and stable to facilitate continuous use of cleared land and minimize further forest clearing, modern soil management technology should be used. Such technology should be interspersed with unmodified areas in a mosaic pattern in order to avoid the undesirable ecological effect of vast cleared areas.

4. To the extent possible, clearing primary forest to make land available for agriculture should be avoided; instead agricultural development should be encouraged in secondary forest.

5. Because human demands on humid tropical lands and their predominantly forest ecosystems are increasing, it is urgently necessary to formulate design criteria for agroforestry systems. As background, information on traditional agroforestry and food production methods in the

region should be cataloged and evaluated before this valuable empirical knowledge is lost.

6. A major effort should be devoted to the development of projects aimed at forest regeneration and utilization of degraded lands for forest production.

7. Because many humid tropical ecosystems have very high potential for long-term yield of forest products, it is essential to develop and test ecologically sound practices for achieving sustainable yield from the harvest of natural forests and for ensuring efficient plantation management.

8. Because humid tropical wetlands are very fragile, and limited in extent, they should be vigorously protected from development and pollution. Careful maintenance of their water regime is vital, because they serve as a buffer between land and water, as well as a nursery area for coastal and riverine fisheries.

9. Because implementation of these recommendations requires substantial knowledge and appreciation of the complexities of the ecology and productivity of the humid tropics, development agencies would do well to strengthen current programs and design new ways to provide planners with basic background in this area. Seminars, workshops, short courses, or other means should be used to increase the awareness of tropical country personnel and their host country counterparts concerning the unique properties of these systems and the potentials for environmentally sound management.

1

"Development" of the
Humid Tropics

THE ISSUE

Two questions are essential:

- How, and to what extent, can humid tropical ecosystems, which have existed for millennia, meet current demands without undergoing unacceptable degradation?
- To what extent can our knowledge of human tropical ecosystems guide utilization, delineate knowledge gaps, and array policy choices that will on the one hand minimize environmental stress and on the other provide increased food, fuel, fiber, and forage?

Ideally, planners seek to provide maximal sustainable benefits to the current generation, all the while maintaining conditions that make it possible to meet the needs and aspirations of the future. To be effective in the long term, development must be consonant with sound ecological principles. Otherwise, short-term expediency will take precedence, at risk of severe environmental and human trauma (UNESCO, 1978). And because humid tropical ecosystems are but poorly understood, the tendency is to apply temperate-zone ecology and to employ imported technology. This, in turn, runs the risk of unpredictable environmental difficulties, especially so because most projects involve substantial intensification of land use (Dickinson, 1981).

In the humid tropics, intensified land use incurs special risks because

7

the ecosystems that characterize the region are highly diverse and complex. Because each ecosystem is unique, each has a different level of benefits and environmental costs when subjected to increased utilization. For example, as annual rainfall increases from 2,000 to 8,000 mm, the obstacles facing agricultural development are aggravated by faster leaching potential and a higher incidence of parasitism and disease. As a consequence, the denser human populations in the humid tropics tend to occur in zones of lesser rainfall, where there are also more fertile soils, higher rates of net food production, and greater potential for recovery from disturbance.

A further factor that complicates matters is the use of technologies dependent on fossil fuels to open land for human settlement. These "new" lands foster human population growth and rising expectations that, coupled with the increased use of machines, severely stress the natural environment. For example, fossil fuels make it possible to replace traditional hand clearing of land with clearing by machine. True, the new technology clears more land per unit of human effort than does a shifting cultivator, but the negative environmental impact is greater because:

• Soils are often compacted.
• Leaching and erosion rates increase.
• Soil fertility is rapidly depleted.
• Productive capacity on a given site soon tends to decline.
• Recovery is much slower than under conditions created by hand clearing.

The economic condition of a country is determined by traditional factors—supply and demand, wages and prices, distribution of income, distribution of food and goods, and the like—within the context of the natural environment. All too frequently the role of the environment within the system is taken for granted; if considered at all, it is usually regarded as an externality. The rationale for this assumption is that natural services and goods have value only after they enter the market system or when in short supply. Such an approach to the economics of the environment has two obvious shortcomings. First, it places no value on natural goods or services; second, when these goods and services become limiting—and thus valuable in economic terms—it is usually too late. By this time, the natural resiliency of the ecosystem may well have been exceeded and the exploitation irreversible (Lugo and Brinson, 1978).

Natural ecosystems support human enterprises. Air and water quality, productivity of coastal fisheries, fertility of soils, the multiplicity of products and services that emanate from tropical forests, the buffering from floods—these are attributes of natural ecosystems. When these are removed from a region, economic and social depression often follow, though people do not always attribute it to changes in the natural ecosystem.

The following concerns relate to the issue of humid tropical development:

- the need for reliable, ecologically sound information on constraints to development
- the recognition that current ecological knowledge is limited and must be applied with caution
- the need to expand research on tropical ecology as a basis for long-term development planning
- the recognition that because humid tropical biotas and ecosystems are highly diverse, knowledge and technologies may have but limited transferability from one area to another
- the appreciation that the diversity of agricultural use as reflected primarily in shifting agricultural systems, if replaced, must be by systems that are also compatible with climate and soils
- the recognition that forest management is site-specific and that its success depends on an *in situ* human infrastructure that has a strong research component
- the need to expand knowledge on tropical soils and their potential uses
- the realization that water resources development has an impact on many other ecosystems

VIEWPOINTS

There are at least three points of view on how best to utilize humid tropical resources, in the next two decades, with minimal irreversible environmental damage. Each has strong advocates, but no single course of action can meet the economic and environmental requirements of tropical countries. Thus a mix of these possibilities is inevitable, assuming significant areas are maintained essentially intact to provide a buffer to change, assure environmental quality, and preserve significant options for later generations.

The three positions are:

- To retain intact most of the humid tropics not now heavily utilized by humankind as parks, preserves, and reserves; scientific repositories for study; natural germplasm and genetic resources banks; and space and food preserves for aboriginal peoples.

Under this option human uses would be restricted to tourism, recreation, scientific investigation, game and fish harvesting, and collecting, gathering, and removal of some forest products. This approach provides small short-term economic yield, excellent long-term environmental protection, and a low but sustained yield. Economic benefits increase with time as human population densities increase and the needs for tourism and recreation become more extensive. Finally, this course reserves maximum options for the future.

• To utilize substantial parts of the natural forest areas for lumber, pulpwood, plywood, fuel, and other forest products. Emphasis here is on intensive well-managed production, selective cutting, underplanting, shelterwood, limited clear-cutting, harvesting of forest products other than timber, and human assisted or natural regeneration and reforestation. In this case, human interventions center on harvesting wood products and ensuring continual regrowth of trees. This approach has excellent potential for short-term and long-term economic yields (sustainable) and for environmental protection. Additionally, it is applicable to small, family oriented operations as well as to major commercial development. It balances economic and environmental values and leaves open many future options. Unfortunately, current technology is inadequate to ensure sustained yield over the long term (25 or more years). Advocates of this course of action believe that future technical development will increase and make possible sustained yields.

• To convert extensive areas already deforested, and selectively to clear others, to provide increased food production through application of new agricultural technologies developed in the humid tropics. Emphasis is on conversion of land to increased agricultural use by applying fertilizers. In this instance human impacts will incur substantial modification of the environment to produce short-term economic gains. The complementary long-term environmental effects are greatest of the three approaches, and long-term economic gains necessitate continued fertilization and the development of new technologies, including new or improved crops and livestock.

Each of these approaches must be evaluated on its merits in terms of a particular tropical country, its history of forest use, the status of a specific development site, and the country's regional development plan. In the current state of knowledge, a mixture of all three is probably the best for any given region, provided options for alternative use remain open and periodic assessments are made of the gains and difficulties as projects are carried forward.

PATTERNS OF UTILIZATION

Over time, man has used the humid tropical forests in diverse ways (Payne, 1975). Some are characteristically preindustrial; others have emerged during the past two decades and will likely accelerate in the foreseeable future.

1. *Hunting and Fishing:* Wildlife and freshwater fishes have served as protein sources for those living on the margins of, or in, the forests from prehistory to the present. In some areas today it is estimated (UNESCO, 1978) that 50%–65% of the protein available to rural populations is still derived from forest wildlife and fisheries.

2. *Hunting, Fishing, and Food Gathering:* Hunting, fishing, and food gathering represent an ancient style of forest life still practiced by aboriginal peoples and by those in some areas of very low population density.

3. *Extraction of Forest Products:* Such natural forest products as rubber, chicle, Brazil nuts, cacao, and hearts-of-palm are removed from the forest for sale. Occasional removal of trees for housing materials or boat construction and gathering of firewood are also typical of preindustrial cultures that exploit the forest without serious impact on it.

4. *Migratory Shifting Agriculture:* Involves agricultural crops grown on cut-and-burn-prepared fields cleared within the forest. After a few growing seasons, each farmer moves to a new area and clears new fields, abandoning the old. Small livestock (poultry, pigs, etc.) and domestic vegetable and fruit gardens contribute to the food supply. This system is effective at the subsistence level, provided population densities are low.

5. *Sedentary Shifting Agriculture:* Where deforestation is extensive, where population densities are increasing, or where it is possible to produce marketable foods, this life-style tends to replace migratory shifting systems. Villages with permanent residences are established. Crops are raised on plots that are allowed to go alternately fallow and that do not return to primary forest before being put back into production. The shifting cultivators commute on foot to their plots. This is now the commonest form of shifting agriculture.

6. *Intensive Continuous Subsistence Agriculture:* Typically utilizes alluvial and other high-base status soils for cropping (primarily irrigated paddy rice), aided by draft cattle or buffaloes. Forests are wholly removed, and slopes are often terraced to increase production. Very high population densities are supported by these means; indeed, productivity has generally doubled in the last decade as a consequence of improved rice production technology.

7. *Commercial Plantation Farming:* The development of extensive areas for such monocultures as banana, cacao, sugar cane, oil palm, rubber, and pineapple has been accelerated by mechanization, fertilization, and chemical pest and disease control. Typically, virgin forests or areas previously under shifting agriculture are converted for this purpose.

8. *Livestock, Pastures, and Meat Production:* Although sedentary shifting and intensive subsistence agricultural systems often include forage or small pastures for livestock, humid tropical areas have not until recently been regarded as suitable for major livestock production. During the last 15 years, primarily in response to FAO encouragement and the generally rising price of beef in industrial countries, millions of hectares have been converted to pasture for beef production.

9. *Extractive Forest Industries:* Involves extensive exploitation of natural forest products for distant export markets. Many items formerly harvested on a limited basis for food or local use are now removed in large quantities, as for meat, skins, plummage, the pet trade and biomedical laboratories, and for fuelwood and charcoal.

10. *Commercial Lumbering:* Covers an array of practices from selective removal of high-value cabinet woods to clear-cutting for lumber, plywood, or pulpwood. Mechanization makes deforestation of extensive areas feasible and economically profitable, at least in the short term. But the logistical difficulties and ecological penalties of lumbering in the humid tropics are often overwhelming (Zobel, 1979).

11. *Commercial Forest Plantations:* A few areas where native forest have been removed have been reforested with a monoculture of growing nonnative species (customarily pines, eucalypts, or *Gmelina arborea*). They are ecologically simplified and therefore easier to manage and regenerate than would be a multispecies system, but only about 1% of the area of the humid tropics is so used at present (Lanly and Clement, 1979).

12. *Water Impoundments:* Construction of dams in humid tropical areas for hydroelectric power or irrigation is predicated upon the abundance of water in humid tropical forest environments, but at the cost of drowning previously undisturbed forest.

13. *Mining, Drilling, and Road Building:* The removal or modification of topsoil and vegetation in exposing mineral resources and in constructing roads have typically localized, but significant, impacts. Less directly, opening of new roads frequently leads to population influxes and further deforestation.

14. *Parks and Reserves:* The preservation of natural landscapes, and of organic diversity and recreational opportunity, including controlled hunting and fishing, represents a special, limited exploitation of natural ecosystems.

15. *Colonization:* Large-scale resettlement of people from rural or urban centers onto new land, for economic or political reasons, is relatively new. Because much unoccupied land in humid tropical areas is undisturbed forest, colonization usually increases forest removal (Goodland, 1980).

16. *Urbanization:* The growth of large, dense populations in urban centers and in newly established cities in the humid tropics during the remainder of the century seems inescapable. Increased immigration from rural to urban centers indicates that urbanization will accelerate as time goes on (Edington and Edington, 1977; Abdalla, 1980).

ENVIRONMENTAL CONSTRAINTS

The undisturbed tropical evergreen forest forms an extremely complex ecosystem characterized by great species richness and multiple pathways of energy flow and nutrients. Although the system is highly stable under the environmental conditions and fluctuations to which it is adapted, it cannot resist sudden, massive environmental perturbations, especially those produced by human interventions. Until about two decades ago, these interventions had minimal impact because human exploitation under conditions of high rainfall and excess water availability is difficult.

That these interventions promise to be even more severe during the remainder of the century is amply documented (UNESCO, 1978; Barney, 1980; NRC, 1980; U.S. Interagency Task Force on Tropical Forests, 1980). Points to keep in mind are:

- The extent of humid tropical forests has been reduced by 15% since the early 1960's.
- At least 50% of the deforestation results from shifting cultivation, which provides, at best, marginal subsistence for 200 million people.
- Wasteful logging and relogging practices make minimal use of the available forest trees, at the same time increasing deforestation and destroying potential agricultural sites (Zobel, 1979).
- Reforestation and natural regeneration plans are too limited to have significant effect in counteracting forest destruction in some areas.
- Most agricultural replacement systems prove more unstable and less productive than anticipated, and the economic benefits purchased by removing the forest have fallen far short of expectations.
- Atmospheric changes, locally and in terms of worldwide carbon dioxide and water cycles, are a cause of concern as deforestation increases.
- The overall impact of deforestation poses a serious threat to local, regional, and global environments and to socioeconomic stability.

- Current knowledge is adequate to slow this disastrous course.
- Current knowledge remains *inadequate* to assure the wise utilization of the resources of humid tropical forests and development of stable alternative uses of forest lands.

When population is at low density and its members engage in such activities as hunting and food gathering, or administering a national park or reserve, the effect on natural ecosystems is minimal. Because of the low density, harvesting and trampling are limited and local. Ecosystem recovery can keep pace with human demands and impacts on the ecosystem are hard to discern. But because humans will ordinarily congregate in certain places and because they prefer certain species over others, one could assume some changes in species composition and abundance.

More dense human concentrations are made possible by shifting cultivation, a mode of land use that involves cutting and burning of the natural forest and planting and harvesting of preferred agricultural crops. Although the impact of this activity is intense at a scale of several hectares, because shifting cultivators rotate plots in periods that exceed 20–30 years, the damage is diluted. Furthermore, shifting cultivators normally do not cut all the trees and do not interfere with the structure of roots and soil, thus facilitating recovery of the ecosystem. Only if cultivators concentrate excessively or if land is limiting are rotation times shorter and the damage to the forest ecosystem proportionately higher.

Still higher population densities can be sustained through more permanent agriculture. The term agroforestry refers to agricultural systems wherein trees are part of the system, such that the resulting agricultural plots resemble a forested landscape. Abundant variations are possible, and, although proven workable in practice, these systems have not been studied in much detail. Because trees remain as part of the ground cover and because agroforestry schemes usually involve fairly dense cover of crops, these new ecosystems maintain much of the stability that characterized the original forest. There is a shift in species composition towards those that are of direct use to humans, and higher net yields to humans are possible. The main cost is that mineral cycles are more open, which may lead to soil erosion, particularly in the early phases.

Forestry in the tropics is mostly extractive, with but little emphasis on regeneration. Done improperly, the harvest imposes tremendous damage to the trees left behind. Soils can also be damaged by heavy machinery or by skidding logs over fragile terrain. Impacts are evidenced by soil erosion, poor stand regeneration, poor stocking of usable species, slowed forest regeneration, and a less productive landscape. The opportunity for continuous use of the site is diminished in proportion to the carelessness of the harvest operations.

Under intensive agriculture, the risk of soil erosion, water quality deterioration, and loss of wildlife (particularly if chemical pesticides are used) is introduced. These difficulties reflect the very open nature of an agricultural field, in which substantial human and technological inputs must be maintained in order to maximize net yields from a few species.

Water works bring about dramatic changes in water and soil quality and affect ecosystem structure and function both locally and regionally. Because water is important to the transport of materials and organisms, by manipulating water flows one manipulates the structure and function of ecosystems both close by and far from the point of manipulation. Changes involve species composition, complete elimination of certain ecosystems, and, by less complex ones, many of which are dominated by species noxious to humans.

The intensive human agglomerations typical of mining operations and colonization or urbanization projects bring about profound alterations of the landscape. These activities have the potential of altering water, air, and soil quality, as well as altering the structure and function of the ecosystems involved. Too, they not infrequently disrupt aboriginal and tribal groups that have long been adjusted to the undisturbed environment.

The Committee recognizes that the economic value of the lands, forests, and other natural communities in the humid tropics is substantial. It also recognizes that conversion of these ecosystems can produce prompt, but ephemeral, economic profits for the very short term (5 years), and that this potential has generated intense pressure for development. In the longer term, many of these economic gains are counterbalanced by the inability of current technology to accomplish sustained yields and the high risk of substantial environmental damage. For these reasons, proposed development projects in the humid tropics must be very carefully evaluated, with maximum awareness of the complexity of environmental impacts. Unless management is ecologically oriented, any activity other than minimal utilization runs the risk of long-term negative effects, effects that may be mitigated if proper attention is given to ecological principles in development planning.

In the chapters that follow, the Committee attempts to discuss the unique characteristics of humid tropical ecosystems and their location in the tropics (Chapter 2), and to treat in detail selected ecological aspects of development by way of illustrating how ecological knowledge can help to assure its success (Chapters 3-8).

The ecological issues selected for further analysis are associated with:

management of germplasm and species diversity (Chapters 3–4), tropical agriculture (Chapter 5), forestry (Chapter 6), soil management (Chapter 7), and water resource management (Chapter 8). Appendixes are provided to furnish further detailed data. Each section provides information on factors that should be evaluated before a development project is undertaken, suggests under what circumstances project initiation is contraindicated, and offers alternative management strategies applicable to humid tropical sites. Such management implies utilization of the environment in ways that contribute substantially to human welfare while minimizing adverse effects (Edington and Edington, 1977). It also implies conservation of parts of natural ecosystems as sources of environmental products and services, for example, as national parks and reserves, and as a reservoir of genetic resources.

AN ECOLOGICAL VIEW OF REGIONAL DEVELOPMENT

Tropical forests are increasingly being subjected to development pressures that require the attention of land managers and policymakers. Sometimes the new ecosystems thus formed are well suited to human needs; at other times they are not. Solutions to the difficulties that arise cost time, effort, and money and must be undertaken promptly. It is imperative that the negative aspects of development be identified, their effects on tropical ecosystems cataloged and understood, and alternative strategies sought in order to minimize them. The principles here set forth apply generally, because, even though different ecosystems have different degrees of fragility and stresses are of different quality and intensity, the responses of ecosystems to stressors follow predictable patterns (Lugo, 1978). In fact, these are by their very nature ecosystem issues; efforts toward their resolution must address ecosystem levels of function and organization (Jansson and Zuchetto, 1978).

To analyze regional impact, one must know what kinds of ecosystems make up the region and how they interact. A conceptual model of the region should be formulated by way of gaining a perspective of the situation with and without an array of development projects. From the model, one can then infer a number of important ecological concepts that are applicable. These concepts are addressed below and include coupling of ecosystems, relationship between stress and stressors, transient and steady-state conditions, ultimate state of a region, and value of natural ecosystems. The overriding consideration in attempting regional analysis is that the landscape is a living unit and that changes in one sector will affect (in positive or negative ways) other sectors.

REGIONAL MODELS AS TOOLS

Figure 1-1 is a simplified model of a regional system. The symbols are those of Odum and Odum (1976). The solid lines represent the flows of energy and matter; the dotted lines illustrate flows of dollars. The box symbolizes the boundaries of a particular region or country. The circles represent the external forces that drive the systems. Both natural ecosystems and managed systems are driven by natural forces, but people impose additional forces on managed systems. Both types yield products and services that people use or export. People manage the landscape and import energy in a wide variety of forms (shown as "people-inputs"); they export goods and services and produce wastes. Wastes and human-induced impacts stress managed and natural ecosystems, thereby reducing their productive potential; they also stress people themselves. The "balance of payments" can be thought of as the difference between inputs and exports.

If now the flow of people-inputs is related to the flow of products and services from natural and managed systems by some constant, then an increase in people-inputs leads to the exploitation of natural ecosystems and permits increases in human populations. Without using energy and

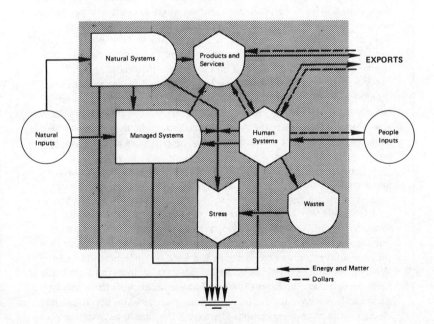

FIGURE 1-1 Conceptual model of a region or country.

resources, human activities cannot be sustained. Thus, the energy and re-source-use policy of a country bears directly on the population density that the environment can "carry."

Carrying capacity (see "Ecological Concept" on p. 109) is the state of a region wherein the flows of money, energy, and matter are at their optimal, such that the maximum useful value is derived from the inputs without long-term damage to natural ecosystems.

Carrying capacity is determined by the ability of the natural ecosystem to handle people-inputs. The ratio between people-inputs, or purchased

---

ECOLOGICAL CONCEPT

SUCCESSION

Succession is a process of ecosystem change. Ecosystems are continuously changing from "immature" to "mature" stages. Immature or young stages result after an ecosystem is disturbed by a natural or human factor. Mature stages are those later stages of succession when the ecosystem achieves a certain degree of balance or steady state. A succession is called a secondary succession when the changes occur in areas that have been disturbed; it is termed a primary succession when it occurs in areas where ecosystems have not been present before (e.g., a new rocky substrate or a new area exposed by the sea or a glacier). Obviously, secondary successions reach maturity more rapidly than primary successions, because they start with a substantial source of biotic and soil materials.

Successions may be under the control of external factors such as fires, salinity, and drought (termed allogenic successions), or under community control as is the case of isolated bogs (termed autogenic successions). Allogenic successions are the most common successions. People are allogenic factors that take advantage of the properties of successional systems.

In general, young ecosystems have a higher net primary production, lower species diversity, open mineral cycles, and higher yields. For these reasons, they are favored by people. Mature systems are more species-diverse, have lower yields, and have high gross primary productivity, but they also have high maintenance respiration. They are not easily managed; but they are favored for their recreational and aesthetic values, and they provide indirect services to people in the form of environmental quality. Whereas mature ecosystems achieve long-term stability and maintain themselves (at least until an allogenic disturbance disrupts them and triggers another secondary succession), young ecosystems are constantly changing and require continuous attention if they are to be maintained in a given stage.

energy, and natural-energy inputs is a useful index for determining the degree to which the carrying capacity of a country or region is dependent on external supplies of energy. The higher the ratio the more dependent is the region on external sources. However, with increasing human activity the capacity of local ecosystems to match external inputs diminishes.

Coupling of Ecosystems

The lines of the model in Figure 1-1 represent flows of matter, money, and energy. Obviously, all sectors are closely interrelated or coupled such that changes in one system are certain to affect another. Natural ecosystems are coupled to natural sources of energy (four are shown in the model). This energy drives the natural ecosystem, which is the only sector that can process and convert it into yields and services without human interventions (Westman, 1977). Natural ecosystems in Figure 1-1 are shown as having two outflows that couple them to human systems (through products and services) and to managed systems. In evidence of the coupling to managed systems is the dependency of managed systems on water and soils derived from the natural sector, which dependency is critical for sustained yield of the forestry and agricultural sectors.

Natural ecosystems are also linked to human systems through the negative effects of wastes and other human impacts that stress the natural ecosystem; at times, in small doses, they help the natural sector, e.g., the beneficial effect of sewage on the growth of trees in wetlands and some degraded soils (Hornick *et al.*, 1979; Reppert *et al.*, 1979). The production of heat couples all sectors with the atmosphere. Imports and exports also have impact on natural ecosystems, because, as a result of these exchanges, greater or lesser demand is placed upon them.

Thus, the sectors of a given region form a tight network of interactions that makes up a countrywide ecosystem. One sector cannot get ahead of another without causing an impact. The sector with the slowest developmental capacity inherently limits growth. If, then, plans for the development of any sector are to be sustainable they must address the issue of countrywide impacts. It is futile to focus on environmental issues, or social issues, or agricultural issues without first considering the overall regional issues.

Stress and Stressors

Interventions in the energy, money, or matter flow of a system can be considered as a source of stress. Stress is defined as a drain of potential energy, matter, or money flow in the system. The external force that causes the stress is termed the stressor. The two are distinct. Thus, population growth is viewed by many as a source of stress, whereas in reality it is but a response to external forces—the stressors. Stressors may be natural or human-induced, but regardless of their nature they levy a cost on ecosystem survival—a cost that must be met from the energy, matter, or money reserves of the system. When the cost exceeds the reserves of the system, the system collapses. Yet, a stressor does not always impose a drain on ecosystem reserves; at certain intensities, it may elicit a positive response, as in application of sewage to wetlands.

Knowing how a given ecosystem responds to stressors of different kinds and intensities is critical for management and environmental planning, because a stressor may be beneficial to a system under certain conditions but negative under others. In addition, the stressor may act on various sectors of an ecosystem and its impacts may be more or less intense, the intensity depending on which sector it attacks (see Chapter 8 on forested wetlands). The opportunity for mitigation also depends on which sector of an ecosystem the stressor acts upon (see Figure 8-6).

TRANSIENT AND STEADY-STATE CONDITIONS

Development may be defined as the intensification of human energy, matter, and money flows through a region. When resources are diverted to a region, the process of change or ecological succession (see "Ecological Concept" on p. 18) is set in motion. Systems undergoing change are termed transient systems. They will move to a different stage in response to any further change in the external forces that impinge upon them. For example, aquatic weeds are transients that invade bodies of water in the tropics following nutrient enrichment, changes in hydroperiod, or changes in water flow. This system of weeds will flourish so long as the transient condition of nutrient-rich still waters continues. As nutrient concentrations, water flows, or hydroperiod change, the weed species disappear and another set of species becomes predominant under the new complex of environmental conditions. But if the weeds are simply killed or harvested, without substantial change in the environmental conditions, they will reinvade and reestablish themselves.

A steady state is reached when the components of a system are in harmony with the external driving forces and when these forces remain either constant or pulsate at predictable intervals. These systems do not change appreciably in function or appearance over time.

Ultimate State of a Region

A central issue of development is deciding what should be the ultimate state of the region in question. We recognize that many natural ecosystems progress through various transient stages into steady states characterized by longevity, high energy flow per unit area, high diversity and complexity, and so on. Those engaged in planning tend to speak of long-term stability, happiness, and improved quality of life for people as among the central objectives of development. Development is a process of change that leads to transient systems. But precisely because they are transient, any given set of living conditions that is established becomes a short-term happening in a continuous process of change. Knowing how and when to stop is perhaps the most critical problem in the development, granted neither of the two extremes—100% developed lands or 100% lands left untouched—is satisfactory. Development, to be realistic, must seek a balanced steady state between the two extremes.

Two things are clear: (1) to reach a steady state, external energy input must itself remain constant (as long as energy sources are changing, the regional subsystems may also change); (2) unending growth is thermodynamically impossible. Thus a steady-state society is the only long-term solution available, and the longer we wait to implement it, the fewer alternatives we will have. But steady state does not mean zero change, because steady states may pulsate. The key to understanding steady state is to recognize that energy and resource use adjusts to a supply of energy and resources that does not expand. The efficiency or ingenuity with which these supplies and energy resources are utilized by people has no limits, providing ample room for continuous development of the human culture.

Carrying capacity may be temporarily exceeded in a given locality when additional supplies of materials, energy, and money become available. However, the long-term carrying capacity of a region is limited by the ability of its natural ecosystem to process available natural-energy resources. Development of a region may exceed this local carrying capacity by concentrating resources from other regions.

Value of Natural Ecosystems

The full value of natural ecosystems cannot easily be measured by the traditional market system, which tends to measure the value of human activity rather than the inherent value of products and services from the natural sector.

Odum (1978) pointed out that one shortcoming of the market system with respect to evaluating natural resources is that it values a natural product on a basis that does not represent its true value in terms of the ecosystem that produces it. Depending, for example, on the conditions of the market at a given time, the presumed value of such ecosystem products or services may fluctuate widely, even though the absolute cost to the ecosystem to produce them remains constant. Another shortcoming of the market-system approach is that the natural ecosystem is often evaluated on the basis of one or two functions that are readily identifiable as "useful," rather than on the multiplicity of functions performed (see p. 203).

To the extent that market-system evaluations influence the thinking of developers and government agencies, natural ecosystems are converted to other uses without due regard for the implications of that conversion. Determining the value of natural ecosystems is a critical research priority.

PRIORITIES FOR REGIONAL DEVELOPMENT

Judicious development of tropical lands requires a clear understanding of the functions and limitations of the large-scale ecosystems in which it will take place (Figure 1-1). Care should be taken to identify the nature and intensity of coupling mechanisms in the large regions that are most affected by development enterprises. The intensity of external subsidies must be modulated so that they do not become stressors to the local ecosystems. Development schemes must consider and incorporate the value of natural ecosystems; above all, they should include steady-state scenarios or end points at which development activities turn into activities to maintain quality. These precautions, if heeded, will ensure that local carrying capacity is enhanced, not diminished, in the long term.

Priority areas of ecological research that would contribute to a better understanding of regional development in the humid tropics include:

- studies of the relationships between the external driving forces of development and the responses of the tropical ecosystems to these forces
- innovative studies to determine the value of natural environments
- studies on the responses of tropical ecosystems to stressors
- comparative studies of the carrying capacity of contrasting humid tropical environments
- regional studies on ecosystem coupling mechanisms
- development of planning models to facilitate a transition from orderly growth to steady-state alternatives, using ecological, economic, and energic information

SUMMARY

Development is here defined as the intensification of the flow of energy, matter, and money through a region. Developmental activities set in motion processes of change (succession) in natural ecosystems. In large regions, different types of ecosystems are coupled and interdependent. Thus, analysis of the impacts of development at a regional scale requires ecosystem-level scrutiny. This is best accomplished by devising models of regional or countrywide systems and using them to facilitate data collection and to analyze ecosystem-level interactions and change.

Because ecosystem structure and functioning (including human systems) are highly sensitive to changes in external driving functions and because development involves the manipulation and change of these functions, it is important to evaluate impacts in relation to them. The intensity of development that is possible in a region is dictated by (1) the carrying capacity (the state of development when the flows of money, energy, and matter are at rates that support the maximum amount of useful value without causing long-term harm) and (2) the capacity of the natural environment to absorb stress and match human needs.

It is proposed that end points of development be determined that will avoid long-term degradation of the environment's carrying capacity. Slowing the rate of development of a region (to achieve a steady state) need not mean stagnation, because substantial human efforts may then be dedicated to improvement and maintenance of the quality of life, which go well beyond merely the initial development of lands.

REFERENCES

Abdalla, I. S. 1980. The rural exodus: who is leaving and why. Ceres 13:13–20.

Barney, G. O. 1980. The global 2000 report to the President. A report prepared by the Council on Environmental Quality and the Department of State. U.S. Government Printing Office, Washington, D.C. 766 p.

Dickinson, J. 1981. Una perspectiva ecológica sobre el desarrollo. Interciencia 6(1):30–37.

Edington, J. M., and M. A. Edington. 1977. Ecology and environmental planning. Chapman and Hall, London. 246 p.

Goodland, R. J. 1980. Indonesia: environmental progress report. Paper presented at ninth annual conference on Indonesian studies, August 1980. Center for South and Southeast Asian Studies, University of California, Berkeley.

Hornick, S. B., J. J. Murray, R. L. Chaney, L. J. Sikora, J. F. Parr, W. D. Burge, G. B. Willson, and C. F. Tester. 1979. Use of sewage sludge compost for soil improvement and plant growth. ARM-NE-6. U.S. Department of Agriculture, Science and Education Administration. 10 p.

Jansson, A. M., and J. Zuchetto. 1978. Energy, economic and ecological relationships for

Götland, Sweden—a regional systems study. Ecol. Bull. 28. Swedish National Science Research Council, Stockholm. 154 p.

Lanly, J. P., and J. Clement. 1979. Present and future natural forest and plantation areas in the tropics. Unasylva 31:12-20.

Lugo, A. E. 1978. Stress and ecosystems. Pages 62-101 in J. H. Thorp and J. W. Gibbons, eds. Energy and environmental stress in aquatic systems. U.S. Department of Energy Symposium Series, CONF-771114. National Technical Information Service, Springfield, Virginia.

Lugo, A. E., and M. M. Brinson. 1978. Calculations of the value of salt water wetlands. Pages 120-130 in Wetland functions and values: the state of our understanding. American Water Resources Association, Minneapolis, Minnesota.

NRC (National Research Council). 1980. Research priorities in tropical biology. National Academy of Sciences, Washington, D.C. 116 p.

Odum, H. T. 1978. Energy analysis, energy quality, and environment. Pages 55-87 in M. W. Gilliland, ed. Energy analysis: a new public policy tool. Selected Symposium 9, American Association for the Advancement of Science. Westview Press, Boulder, Colorado.

Odum, H. T., and E. C. Odum. 1976. Energy basis for man and nature. McGraw-Hill, New York. 297 p.

Payne, W. J. A. 1975. The role of domestic livestock in the humid tropics. Pages 143-155 in The use of ecological guidelines for development in the American humid tropics. IUCN Publ., New Ser. 31. International Union for the Conservation of Nature and Natural Resources, Morges, Switzerland.

Reppert, R. T., W. Sigles, E. Stakhiv, L. Messman, and C. Meyers. 1979. Concepts and methods for wetlands evaluation. Res. Rept. 79-RI. Institute for Water Resources, U.S. Army Corps of Engineers, Fort Belvoir, Virginia. 109 p.

UNESCO (United Nations Educational, Scientific, and Cultural Organization). 1978. Tropical forest ecosystems. A state-of-knowledge report prepared by UNESCO/FAO/UNEP. Natural Resources Research XIV. UNESCO, Paris. 683 p.

U.S. Interagency Task Force on Tropical Forests. 1980. The world's tropical forests: a policy, strategy and program for the United States. Publ. 9117. Department of State, Washington, D.C. 53 p.

Westman, W. E. 1977. How much are nature's services worth? Science 197:960-964.

World Bank. 1981. Economic development and tribal peoples: human ecologic considerations. Office of Environmental Affairs, World Bank, Washington, D.C. 103 p.

Zobel, B. 1979. The ecological impact of industrial forest management. Res. Rept. 52. Cartón de Colombia, Calí. 11 p.

2
Humid Tropical Ecosystems

The idea of the ecosystem as an interactive and integrated unit formed by the combination of the physiochemical (abiotic) environment and its biotic community (microorganisms, plants, and animals) is fundamental. In the many studies of mature ecosystems, it has become clear that a complex series of systems has evolved that establishes dynamic equilibrium within the constraints of the abiotic environment. For this reason, a mature ecosystem has the capacity to adjust to the impact of normal fluctuations in climate, nutrient supplies, and other factors and thereby maintain organization and function. In addition, the ecosystem has the resiliency to overcome instances of severe damage that affect relatively small areas and to bring itself back to a balance over a relatively short period of time. It has been further held by some that the many levels and kinds of interactive relations among the components of complex ecosystems promote their self-regulating and self-maintaining functions. Thus, when relatively minor modifications and utilization of humid tropical ecosystems at low human population densities occur, it can be anticipated that the disturbance will be minor. Large-scale human utilization, however, may well override the regulatory function of the system's components and lead to serious, long-term damage.

THE HUMID TROPICS: DEFINITION AND DISTRIBUTION

For the purposes of this study, the humid tropics are defined as those areas of the earth's land surface where the mean annual biotemperature in the lowlands is greater than 24°C and where annual rainfall equals or exceeds potential evaporative return of water to the atmosphere.

In general, the humid tropics correspond to tropical areas that originally supported broad-leaf evergreen forests and the humid component of vegetation above timberline. As for lowlands, this definition includes all areas receiving a total annual rainfall in excess of 1,500 mm. These areas are frost-free and usually have no more than 2 dry months (precipitation <100 mm per month) per year.

NATURE OF THE TROPICS

The geographic and climatological concept of the "tropics" is of a region lying mostly between the Tropics of Cancer and Capricorn, where relatively large amounts of solar radiation reach the earth's surface throughout the year. As a result, seasonal fluctuations in temperature at any given locality are minimal, and there is no distinct winter season. Because of the unequal distribution of land and water on the earth's surface, complexity of physiography, the impact of prevailing winds and marine currents, and the role of local atmospheric conditions, the outer boundaries of the tropical zone are best defined by temperature characteristics. Although a number of systems have been suggested for delimiting the zone (Nieuwolt, 1977), a scheme involving reduction of temperature data to sea level equivalents best defines the regions that by consensus are regarded as tropical and support vegetation, soil, animal life, agriculture, and patterns of economic development characteristically tropical.

According to this approach (Holdridge, 1967), the tropical region includes all areas where the mean annual biotemperature (BT) in the lowlands (or where reduced to sea level) is greater than 24°C, where

$$\text{BT}° = \frac{\text{the sum of unit period temperatures °C}}{\text{number of unit periods (days, weeks, etc)}}.$$

As an example, in calculation of BT° for Iquitos, Peru (107 m above sea level), the mean monthly temperatures for January through December are: 25.2°, 25.7°, 24.6°, 25.0°, 24.2°, 23.5°, 23.4°, 24.6°, 24.6°, 25.1°, 25.8°, 25.5°. Thus,

$$\text{BT}° = \frac{297.2°}{12} = 24.8°\text{C}.$$

In this formula, all values below 0°C and above 30°C are recorded as 0°, since it is assumed that plant growth does not occur below 0°C or above 30°C. In most cases, the BT for tropical areas corresponds to the mean annual temperature as calculated from climatic data. Only at lowland sites, in latitudinally peripheral deserts, and at extremely high altitudes will the two values differ substantially. In the first two cases, the BT will be lower than the mean annual temperature; in the last, it will be higher. The tropical region defined in this way is outlined on the accompanying map (Figure 2-1).

Within the tropical region, the primary differences in temperature are related to elevation, with an average mean annual biotemperature reduction of 5°–6°C per 1,000-m increase in elevation, subject to considerable variability as determined by local atmospheric conditions. The upland and montane sites included in the region, although having temperatures lower than those typical of lowland areas, are indubitably tropical as regards high solar radiation throughout the year and little seasonal temperature fluctuation. For this reason, Quito, Ecuador, at an elevation of 2,818 m (BT = 13°C) has a tropical climate just as much as does Madras, India, at an elevation of 7 m (BT = 25.5°C).

In general, seven major temperature-limited altitudinal zones may be recognized in the tropical region (Figure 2-2). The boundaries between the zones are at mean BT's of about 24°, 18°, 12°, 6°, 3°, and 1.5°C. Mean annual BT's for the various zones are as follows: lowland, greater than 24°C; lower montane, between 12° and 18°C; montane, between 6° and 12°C; sub-Alpine (or sub-Andean), between 3° and 6°C; Alpine (or Andean), between 1.5° and 3°C. Areas having an annual BT of less than 1.5° have permanent snow. Although the mean annual isotherm of 24°C may occur locally at an elevation as great as 800 m, in most tropical areas the boundary between lowland and premontane zones lies near an elevation of 500 m. For this reason, the accompanying diagram (Figure 2-2) uses the latter elevation for the upper limit of the lowland zone. Generally, each altitudinal zone above the lowland sector extends over approximately the same vertical distance regardless of locale: premontane, 1,000 m; lower montane, 100 m; montane, 1,000 m; sub-Alpine, 500 m; and Alpine, 500 m. For accuracy, the location of any site by zone should be determined by temperature data (e.g., with a BT = 13°C, Quito, Ecuador, at 2,818 m lies at the upper limit of the lower montane zone). In practice, especially where there are relatively few weather stations to provide data, the zones may be interpolated from altitudinal data as long as temperatures at several sites are known.

It should be noted that the elevations at which the temperature-defined zones occur decrease with increasing latitude. Near the northern and southern margins of the tropical region, the lowland zone will have a vertical extent of only about 100 m, and the lower margin of each higher zone will be displaced downward. Again, accurate temperature data are the best bases

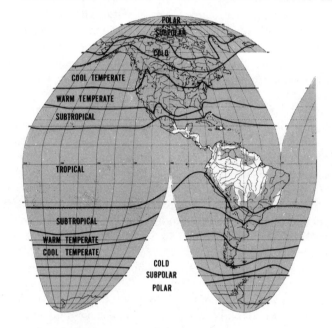

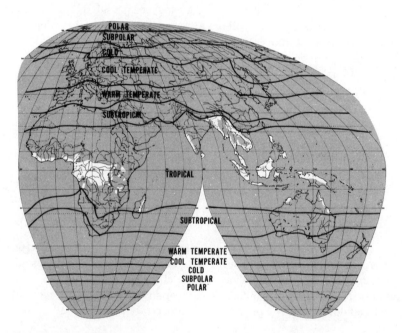

FIGURE 2-1 Geographic distribution of humid tropical areas (top, Western Hemisphere; bottom, Eastern Hemisphere).

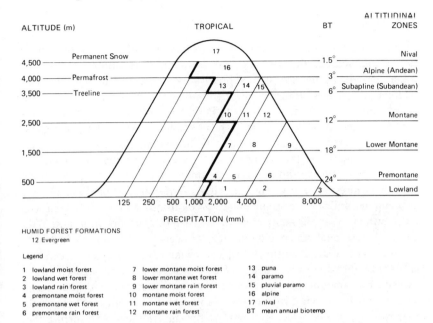

ALTITUDE (m)   TROPICAL   BT   ALTITUDINAL ZONES

PRECIPITATION (mm)

HUMID FOREST FORMATIONS
12 Evergreen

Legend

1	lowland moist forest	7	lower montane moist forest	13	puna
2	lowland wet forest	8	lower montane wet forest	14	paramo
3	lowland rain forest	9	lower montane rain forest	15	pluvial paramo
4	premontane moist forest	10	montane moist forest	16	alpine
5	premontane wet forest	11	montane wet forest	17	nival
6	premontane rain forest	12	montane rain forest	BT	mean annual biotemp

FIGURE 2-2   Temperature, rainfall, and altitudinal extent of principal humid tropical bio-climates and their associated plant formations. The dark zig-zag line indicates where the per-year potential evapotranspiration equals annual precipitation. This line marks the ecologically lower limit of available water to support humid tropical vegetation.

for determining the zone in which any site occurs, especially near the periphery of the tropical region.

Two other points are worth mentioning for tropical upland and montane situations. Because of the uniform solar radiation and re-radiation conditions at high elevations, the treeline lies near the BT of 6°C. Outside the tropical region, the treeline corresponds to the zone of permanently frozen subsoil (permafrost) whose lower or southern limit is at a BT of 3°C. In the tropical region, the sub-Alpine zone is devoid of trees and supports a series of distinctive vegetations dependent on rainfall. Under humid conditions, a complex herbaceous vegetation mixed with grasses—when best developed including arborescent shrubs—is typical. These formations closely resemble one another in vegetational aspect and include the *puna* and *paramos* of the Andes and similar plant associations in the African equatorial mountains, in New Guinea, and in tropical Asia. Finally, between this last-mentioned zone and the level of permanent snow, an Alpine tundra vegetation is found in the permafrost belt on the highest tropical mountains.

THE HUMID TROPICS

Because isolation and temperature are relatively uniform at any tropical site, differences in the amount and temporal distribution of available water, principally in the form of precipitation, account for regional and seasonal differences. Rainfall varies from 0 mm per year in several tropical lowland deserts (e.g., in northern Peru) to 11,600 mm (in the premontane forest region of Assam). In tropical situations, complexity of vegetation is correlated along a gradient with increasing precipitation (Figure 2-3). For example, in the lowlands desert, scrub and thorn woodland formations occur where rainfall totals less than 500 mm per year; broad-leaf deciduous forests occur where rainfall exceeds 500 mm per year (Figure 2-3) and are replaced generally by evergreen forests where rainfall exceeds 2,000 mm per year. In many areas of the eastern Amazon Basin and West Africa, transitional semideciduous forests occur where rainfall is 1,500–2,000 mm per year. Essentially tropical lowland broad-leaf evergreen forests are found where the amount of precipitation per unit area equals or exceeds the amount of water (potential evapotranspiration) that could evaporate from the land surface (evaporation) plus the amount that would pass through plants before evaporating through the leaves (transpiration) if water were available all year. In other lowland sites, potential evapo-

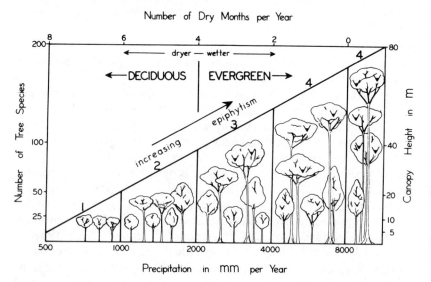

FIGURE 2-3 A gradient or ecocline of mean annual precipitation for the tropical lowland zone indicates that with increasing precipitation, in general, the complexity of the forest increases through increased diversity and ecological stratification.

transpiration (evaporation plus transpiration) per unit area exceeds precipitation. At higher elevations, because atmospheric temperatures are
lower, the amount of evapotranspiration is lower per unit time, and less
rainfall is required at cooler temperatures to maintain humid conditions.

In the lowland zone (Figure 2-3), areas receiving a total annual rainfall
in excess of 1,500 mm are included in the humid tropics; in the premontane and lower montane belts, the humid tropics include all areas having
in excess of 1,000 mm of precipitation per year. In the montane zone, all
areas having a rainfall in excess of 500 mm are included. Sub-Alpine and
Alpine areas with more than 250 or 125 mm of rainfall per year, although
covering very small areas on tropical mountains, are also included in this
definition.

Countries with territories lying within the humid tropics are named in
Table 2-1.

The tropical lowland evergreen forests are of special concern to ecologists, conservationists, and development agencies (IUCN, 1975a,b; Brown
et al., 1980; NRC, 1980a,b; Soulé and Wilcox, 1980) who regard them as
environments that hold out prospects for significant new human activities
and economic development during the remainder of the twentieth century.
At the same time many tropical humid upland and montane evergreen
forests are also likely to be affected by comparable pressures. Furthermore, many gaps in ecological knowledge, and obstacles to utilization and
conservation, are similar for lowland and higher elevation tropical broad-
leaf evergreen forests. For these reasons, this report treats the humid
tropics as a whole, although it emphasizes forest ecosystems, especially in
the lowlands. It is essential in this context to recognize that the humid
tropical regions contain an extremely diverse set of environmental conditions, habitats, plant and animal species, and biotic communities.

HUMID TROPICAL BIOCLIMATES, VEGETATION, AND SOILS

BIOCLIMATES

The primary matrix of an ecosystem is a unity provided by the mutually
reciprocal interactions among the climate, vegetation, soil, and associated
organisms. Any change in one of these factors produces changes in the
others.

Of the approximately 125 principal world bioclimates, 38 occur in the
tropical region, and 19 of these are represented in the humid tropics (Holdridge, 1967). If the 3 tropical humid tundra bioclimates are considered as
one, the 17 bioclimates previously indicated (Figure 2-2) may be briefly

TABLE 2-1   Countries and Major Islands Having Territories That Lie Within Humid Tropical Bioclimatic (or Life) Zones

Country	Land Area[a] (10^6 ha)	Humid Tropical (%)	Other (%)
Africa			
Burundi	2.8	32	68
Cameroon	47.5	35	65
Central African Republic	62.3	25	75
Congo	34.2	100	
Equatorial Guinea	2.8	100	
Gabon	26.8	85	15
Ghana	23.9	30	70
Guinea	24.6	95	5
Ivory Coast	32.2	40	60
Kenya	58.3	18	82
Liberia	11.1	90	10
Malagasy Republic	58.7	—	—
Mauritius	0.2	—	—
Mozambique	78.3	—	—
Nigeria	92.4	10	90
Rwanda	2.6	35	65
Sao Tome	0.1	100	
Sierra Leone	7.2	100	
Tanzania	94.0	5	95
Togo	5.6	33	67
Uganda	23.6	10	90
Zaire	234.5	85	15
Asia			
Brunei	0.6	100	
Burma	67.8	—	—
India	215.3	—	—
Indonesia	190.4	95	5
Kampuchea	18.1	35	65
Laos	23.7	—	—
Peninsular Malaysia	13.1		
Sabah	7.6	100	
Sarawak	12.5		
Papua New Guinea	46.2	100	
Philippines	30.0	36	64
Sri Lanka	6.6	25	75
Thailand	51.4	20	80
Viet Nam	33.3	25	75
Central America			
Belize	2.3	15	85
Costa Rica	5.1	93	7
Dominican Republic	4.9	—	—

TABLE 2-1 *(Continued)*

Country	Land Area[a] (10^6 ha)	Humid Tropical (%)	Other (%)
El Salvador	2.1	—	—
Guatemala	10.9	—	—
Haiti	2.8	—	—
Honduras	11.2	—	—
Mexico	98.6	—	—
Nicaragua	13.0	30	70
Panama	7.6	100	
Puerto Rico	0.9	—	—
South America			
Bolivia	109.9	8[b]	92
Brazil	851.2	45	55
Colombia	114.0	72	28
Ecuador	28.4	55[b]	45
French Guiana	9.1	100	
Guyana	21.5	70	30
Peru	128.5	56[b]	16
Suriname	16.3	85	15
Trinidad	0.5	90	10
Venezuela	91.2	57[b]	43
Oceania			
Australia	253.9	—	—
Fiji	1.8	—	—
New Caledonia	1.9	—	—
New Hebrides	1.5	—	—
Samoa	0.3	—	—
Solomon Islands	2.8	—	—

[a]These estimates are based on limited climatic data. SOURCES: Persson (1974), Brown *et al.* (1980). (Table prepared by Sandra Brown.)
[b]Data do not include desert, desert scrub, puna, paramo, and tropical tundra life zones, which account for about 5% of tropical South America.

characterized. Since mature vegetation on mature soils typical for a particular regimen reflect bioclimatic features, the names of the bioclimates— or life zones, as they are called by Holdridge (1967)—take their names from these mature plant associations. Representative localities for several bioclimates are provided in Table 2-2.

A. Lowland bioclimates—mean annual biotemperature greater than 24°C
  1. Lowland moist forest—mean annual precipitation 1,500–4,000 mm; no more than 4 months with less than 200 mm of precipitation (Figures 2-4, 2-5)

TABLE 2-2   Typical Humid Tropical Bioclimatic Sites[a]

Localities	Altitude (m)	Bioclimate
Africa		
Campo, Equatorial Guinea	27	Lowland moist forest
Monrovia, Liberia	15	Lowland moist forest
Victoria, Cameroon	20	Lowland wet forest
Debundscha, Cameroon	10	Lowland rainforest
Entebbe, Uganda	1,500	Premontane moist forest
Luwingu, Zambia	1,462	Premontane moist forest
Asia		
Calicut, Kerala, India	9	Lowland moist forest
Colombo, Sri Lanka	13	Lowland moist forest
Rangoon, Burma	5	Lowland moist forest
Kuala Lumpur, Malaysia	18	Lowland moist forest
Tarum, Java, Indonesia	7	Lowland moist forest
Padang, Sumatra, Indonesia	7	Lowland wet forest
Sandoway, Burma	9	Lowland wet forest
Bogor, Java, Indonesia	240	Lowland wet forest
Cherrapunji, Assam, India	1,318	Premontane wet forest
Darjeeling, W. Bengal, India	2,268	Premontane wet forest
Pangerango, Java, Indonesia	3,023	Montane rainforest
Latin America		
Belem do Para, Brazil	10	Lowland moist forest
Manaus, Brazil	45	Lowland moist forest
Iquitos, Peru	106	Lowland moist forest
Rio de Oro, Venezuela	75	Lowland wet forest
Quibdo, Colombia	30	Lowland rainforest
San José, Costa Rica	1,200	Premontane moist forest
Cajamarca, Peru	2,810	Lower montane moist forest
Mucuchies, Venezuela	3,000	Montane moist forest
Paramo de Mucuchies, Venezuela	4,221	Tundra and wet paramo

[a]Few weather station data are available for very high rainfall and montane sites in the humid tropics. This is further evidence that settlement of these areas has not proved productive and that habitats in these bioclimates cannot be readily utilized by humans. Almost all major human population centers in the tropics are in bioclimates that support dry plant formations, where potential evapotranspiration exceeds precipitation.

2. Lowland wet forest—mean annual precipitation 4,000–8,000 mm; no more than 2 months with less than 200 mm of precipitation

3. Lowland rainforest—mean annual precipitation more than 8,000 mm; no months with less than 200 mm of precipitation

B. Premontane bioclimates—mean annual biotemperature between 18° and 24°C

FIGURE 2-4   Typical aspect of lowland moist forest in Panama. (Courtesy, W. John Smith)

FIGURE 2-5 Buttressed tree trunk typical of lowland forest trees. This adaptation compensates for shallow root systems. (Courtesy, W. John Smith)

4. Premontane moist forest—1,000–2,000 mm mean annual precipitation; 2–4 months with less than 100 mm of precipitation
5. Premontane wet forest—2,000–4,000 mm mean annual precipitation; no more than 2 months with less than 100 mm of precipitation
6. Premontane rainforest—more than 4,000 mm of precipitation; no months with less than 100 mm of precipitation (Figure 2-6)
C. Lower montane bioclimates—mean annual biotemperature between 12° and 18°C
7. Lower montane moist forest—1,000–2,000 mm mean annual precipitation; 2–4 months with less than 100 mm of precipitation
8. Lower montane wet forest—2,000–4,000 mm of precipitation; no more than 2 months with less than 100 mm of precipitation
9. Lower montane rainforest—mean annual precipitation more than 4,000 mm; no months with less than 100 mm of precipitation
D. Montane bioclimates—mean annual biotemperature 6°–12°C
10. Montane moist forest—mean annual precipitation 500–1,000 mm; 2–4 months with less than 50 mm of precipitation

11. Montane wet forest—mean annual precipitation 1,000–2,000 mm; no more than 2 months with less than 50 mm of precipitation
12. Montane rainforest—mean annual precipitation more than 2,000 mm; no months with less than 50 mm of precipitation

E. Sub-Alpine (Sub-Andean) bioclimates—mean annual biotemperature 3°–6°C
13. Sub-Alpine moist grassland (puna)—mean annual precipitation 250–500 mm; 2–4 months with less than 50 mm of precipitation
14. Sub-Alpine wet dwarf shrubland (paramo)—mean annual precipitation 500–1,000 mm; no more than 2 months with less than 50 mm of precipitation (Figure 2-7)
15. Sub-Alpine rain dwarf shrubland (pluvial paramo)—mean annual precipitation 1,000–2,000 mm; no months with less than 50 mm of precipitation

F. Alpine bioclimates—mean annual biotemperature 1.5°–3.0°C; varying amounts of annual precipitation between 125 and 1,000 mm

G. Nival bioclimate—mean annual biotemperature below 1.5°C; zone of permanent snow and ice

FIGURE 2-6 Premontane rainforest, Guatemala. (Courtesy, Robert Ricklefs)

FIGURE 2-7   Wet paramo, Colombia. (Courtesy, Robert Ricklefs)

VEGETATION

Each of these major tropical bioclimates is characterized by a distinctive vegetation when undisturbed and supports a unique community of plant and animal species. Differences among the formations are generally correlated with features of temperature and precipitation as follows:

- At any given mean annual biotemperature, complexity, species diversity, stratification, height of vegetation, productivity, and degree of epiphytic development increase with increasing precipitation.
- At any given latitude at sites with similar ratios of potential evapotranspiration to precipitation, complexity, diversity, stratification, height of vegetation, and productivity decrease with elevation.
- At any given latitude, the treeline lies at a mean annual biotemperature of 6°C.

Within any of the recognized plant formations, a series of distinctive plant associations may occur, the order of occurrence depending on differences in local atmospheric conditions, soils, or water table. The primary plant association for any of the humid tropical bioclimates is characterized by the physiognomy (structure and life forms), complexity, species diversity, organization, and stratification of its vegetation. The actual kinds of plants (genera and species) that occur in the primary association will differ from place to place, but the distinctive features of the vegetation remain the same. For example, the lowland wet forests of Zaire, Brazil, and Malaysia resemble one another closely as to the features of vegetation, but the genera and species of plants found in these forests are almost entirely different, and none of the tree species are shared. Other associations within the same bioclimate occur where local atmospheric conditions (e.g., prevailing winds and rain shadow), edaphic conditions (different soils or slope), or hydric conditions (e.g., water table level and flooding) modify the combination of physical factors that produces the primary association. They, too, may be recognized by vegetational characteristics.

Humid tropical vegetation covers about 1,500 million ha, or about 31% of the tropical region and 10% of the world's land area. The largest expanse occurs in tropical America, which has 45% of the world's humid tropics, followed by Africa (30%) and tropical Asia (25%). Most of this vegetation is in the lowland zone; about 10% occurs in premontane formations, 5% in lower montane formations, 2% in montane formations, 1% in sub-Alpine formations, and less than 1% in higher elevation bioclimates. Some typical humid tropical bioclimate sites are indicated in Table 2-2. The typical vegetation for these areas may be characterized as follows:

Tropical lowland forest (moist, wet, and rain) formations These closed-canopy forests consist of a large number of broad-leaf evergreen tree species (60–400 species per km^2; 40–100 per ha) that have three or four tree stories. The canopy is at a height of 30–60 m with scattered emergent trees up to 100 m high. Many trees have large buttresses and smooth-barked, columnar boles. Thick-stemmed woody, climbing plants (lianes) are common, as are epiphytes. Cauliflory—flowers and fruit borne on short stalks attached to the main trunk or larger tree branches—is very common.

Two important hydric associations occur within the same bioclimate. One is the freshwater swamp forest, which has a simple structure (one story) and contains one to five species (often palms) that have an open canopy at 3–12 m. The other is the brackish water mangrove forest, which is similar to swamp forest in structure and number of species but may have a relatively tall closed canopy (15–50 m).

Tropical premontane forest (moist, wet, and rain) formations These closed-canopy forests consist of a large number of broad-leaf evergreen tree species (40–110 species per km^2; 26–48 per ha) that have two or three tree stories. The canopy is at a height of 20–40 m with a few emergents sometimes 50 m high. Tree buttresses are small or absent. Often many climbers are present, but few are thick-stemmed woody species. Epiphytes are abundant; cauliflory is rare.

The driest formation within this series (premontane moist forest) has been significantly modified by people. The premontane zone usually lies between 500 and 1,500 m in elevation and is excellent for coffee and tea culture, as well as for other agricultural activities.

Tropical lower montane forest (moist, wet, and rain) formations These closed-canopy forests consist of 25–50 tree species per km^2, 15–40 species per ha; two tree stories. Canopy height is 10–30 m, with no obvious emergents. There are usually no large buttresses, very few climbers, abundant epiphytes, and no cauliflory.

In some areas of poor soils, forests with a single dominant tree species occur.

Soils

It is not surprising to find that the soils of the humid tropical region are extremely variable. A quantitative system for classifying soils has been developing (Soil Survey Staff, 1975) that is similar to plant taxonomy in the sense that only properties that can be measured quantitatively are included. The Food and Agriculture Organization (FAO) has incorporated available information into the World Soil Map (scale of 1:5 million). A common legend for the entire world is now available from FAO and is really convertible into soil taxonomy units. Table 2-3 shows the distribution of soil orders and major suborders in the humid tropical regions of America, Africa, and Asia according to soil taxonomy. Table 2-4 shows the nomenclature equivalents in other classification systems used in the humid tropics. The following sections describe and characterize the major features of humid tropical soils.

Acid Infertile Soils: Oxisols and Ultisols

The most abundant soils of the humid tropics belong to the Oxisol and Ultisol orders, which together cover almost two-thirds of this region. Oxisols are deep, generally well-drained red or yellowish soils, with excellent granular structure and little contrast between horizon layers.

The technical definition (which refers to the presence of an oxic horizon of low-activity clays) indicates that these soils are low in available nutrients and are acidic. Consequently, most of the physical properties of Oxisols

TABLE 2-3 Geographical Distribution of Soils of the Humid Tropics (Data Expressed in Millions of Hectares)[a]

Soil Order and Suborder	Humid Tropics Total	Humid Tropical America[b]	Humid Tropical Africa[c]	Humid Tropical Asia[d]
Oxisols	525	332	179	14
Ultisols	413	213	69	131
Inceptisols				
Aquepts	120	42	55	23
Andepts	12	2	1	9
Tropepts	94	17	19	58
TOTAL	226	61	75	90
Entisols				
Fluvents	50	6	10	34
Psamments	90	6	67	17
Lithic	72	19	14	39
TOTAL	212	31	91	90
Alfisols	53	18	20	15
Histosols	27	—	4	23
Spodosols	19	10	3	6
Mollisols	7	—	—	7
Vertisols	5	1	2	2
Aridisols[e]	2	—	1	1
TOTAL	1,489	666	444	379

[a]Based on dominant soil in FAO maps (scale of 1:5 million).
[b]From Sanchez and Cochrane (1980) plus recent adjustments.
[c]From FAO (1975) and Dudal (1980).
[d]From FAO (1977, 1978). Includes 46 million ha of the humid tropics of Australia and Pacific Islands.
[e]Saline soils only (Salorthids).

are excellent, but their chemical properties are poor. In other classification systems, Oxisols are also known as Ferralsols, Latosols, and (incorrectly) Lateritic soils.

About two-thirds of the Oxisols of the humid tropics are located in tropical America, mainly in the areas geologically affected by the Guyanan and Brazilian shields in the Amazon Basin, mostly east of Manaus. Oxisols are also found on the Pacific coast of Colombia, but few Oxisols exist in other humid tropical regions of the Western Hemisphere.

Oxisols in humid tropical Africa are concentrated in Cameroon,

TABLE 2-4 Translation of Soil Taxonomy Terminology Used in the Humid Tropics into Other Classification Systems

Soil Taxonomy[a]	FAO Legend[b]	1938 USDA System[c]	French[d]	Brazilian[e]
Oxisols	Ferralsols	Latosols	Sols ferraltiques, fortement desaturés, typiques ou humiféres	Latossolos, Terra Roxa Legítima
Ultisols	Acrisols Dystric Nitosols	Red Yellow Podozolics	Sols ferralitiques, lessives	Podzólico Vermelho-Amarelo
Inceptisols	(various)	(various)	Sols peu evolues	Solos com horizonte B
Aquepts	Gleysols	Low Humic Gleys	Sols hydromorphes	Solos hidromorficos
Andepts	Andosols	Andosols	Andosols	—
Tropepts	Cambisols	Brown Forest	Sols brunifiés	Solos com horizonte B incipiente
Entisols	(various)	(various)		
Fluvents	Fluvisols	Alluvials	Sols mineraux bruts	Solos aluviais
Psamments	Arenosols and Regosols	Regosols	Regosols	Regosols, Areias Quartzisosas
Lithic phases	Lithosols	Lithosols	Sols lithiques	Litossolos

Alfisols	Luvisols Eutric Nitosols Planosols	Eutric Red Yellow Podzolics, Terra Roxa, Planosols	Sols ferrugineaux tropicaux, lessives	Podzólico Vermelho–Amarelo equivalente eutrofico; Terra Roxa Estruturada, Planossolos
Histosols	Histosols	Peat, Bogs	Sols organiques	Solos orgánicos
Spodosols	Podzols	Podzols	Podzols	Podzols
Mollisols	Rendzinas Phaeozems	Rendzinas Chernozems		Brunizems
Vertisols	Vertisols	Grumusols	Vertisols	Grumusols
Aridisols (saline)	Solonchaks	Solonchaks	Sols halomorphes	Solonchak

[a] Soil Survey Staff (1975).
[b] Dudal (1980).
[c] Baldwin et al. (1938), Cline et al. (1955).
[d] Aubert (1965).
[e] Costa de Lemos (1968).

Gabon, central Zaire, eastern Madagascar, Liberia, and Sierra Leone. Oxisols are not extensive in humid tropical Asia but are found in Kalimantan, other Indonesian islands, Malaysia, the Philippines, and Thailand; they make up about 3% of the soils of humid tropical Asia.

Ultisols of the humid tropics are similar to Oxisols in morphology but exhibit a marked increase of clay content with depth, which is absent in Oxisols. Ultisols, therefore, are usually deep, well-drained red or yellowish soils, somewhat higher in weatherable minerals than Oxisols but still acid and with low fertility. Their physical properties are less favorable than those of Oxisols, and many of them occupy steep slopes, which makes them more subject to erosion. Ultisols were formerly known as Red Yellow Podzolics and are also known as Acrisols.

Ultisols are the predominant soils of the Amazon Basin roughly west of Manaus and in well-drained areas of the Amazon not affected by the two ancient geologic shields. They are also the dominant soils of the Atlantic coast of Central America and humid coastal Brazil.

Ultisols are also the most abundant soils of humid tropical Asia (Dent, 1980), occupying most of Malaysia, Sumatra, Kalimantan, Sulawesi, and Mindanao. In humid tropical Africa, Ultisols are abundant in the eastern Congo Basin bordering the lake region in the forested zones of Sierra Leone, in Ivory Coast, in parts of Liberia, and in a thin forested coastal strip from Ivory Coast through Nigeria.

In practice, these two soil orders can be considered together; they encompass most of the "red" soils of the humid tropics. Their main limitations are chemical: high soil acidity; aluminum toxicity; deficiency of phosphorus, potassium, calcium, magnesium, sulfur, zinc, and other micronutrients; and low effective cation-exchange capacity, which last indicates a high leaching potential. Also, Oxisols and Ultisols with clayey topsoils exhibit high capacity to immobilize phosphorus, but this constraint is less important in those soils with sandy or loamy topsoils. The organic matter content of Oxisols and Ultisols is adequate (Sanchez, 1976). Their physical properties are generally excellent, but some Oxisols have low water-holding capacity, and some Ultisols that have pronounced increase in clay, with depth, are very subject to erosion.

The danger of laterite formation after clearing Oxisols and Ultisols is slight (Sanchez and Buol, 1975; Buol and Sanchez, 1978; Moormann and Van Wambeke, 1978). In the Amazon, only 6% of the region has soft plinthite in the subsoil; this material is capable of hardening into laterite if exposed by erosion, but most of these soils occur in flat, poorly drained topographical sites. Hardened laterite of geologic origin occurs in scattered areas in the humid tropics where it serves as excellent roadbuilding material. In such areas as the Peruvian Amazon, which is essentially

---

ECOLOGICAL CONCEPT

CATION-EXCHANGE CAPACITY AND PHOSPHORUS SORPTION
(FIXATION)

The two most common soil orders in the tropics, Oxisols and Ultisols, which together make up 63% of the world's humid tropical soils, are inherently difficult for agriculture. This is not, as has been generally assumed, because they will turn into lateritic rock on being cleared; very few will. Rather, they tend to have low cation-exchange capacities and high potential for immobilizing phosphorus.

Cation-exchange capacity is a measure of a soil's ability to retain such positively charged ions (cations) as Ca^{++}, Mg^{++}, K^+, and Al^{+++}. Thus, a soil with a low cation-exchange capacity has only a limited ability to retain these essential plant nutrients in solution. Under the high rainfall conditions of the humid tropics, water percolating down through the soil washes away these elements, ultimately carrying them to the ocean. Mineral removal by groundwater is called leaching.

Phosphorus sorption (often called phosphorus fixation, but then too easily confused with nitrogen fixation) is the conversion of soluble forms of phosphorus into slowly soluble ones upon reaction with soil constituents. Under the acid conditions of Oxisols and Ultisols, phosphorus or the negatively charged phosphate ion has a strong tendency to combine with iron and aluminum to form highly insoluble compounds. This process is so rapid that a very high percentage of phosphorus fertilizer applied to such a soil may become immobilized and unavailable to plants. Eventually, however, it does become available.

If properly managed, Oxisols and Ultisols can be productive (see Chapter 7). They must receive fertilizer supplements that are judiciously applied. After cation applications, plant mineral uptake and growth speed up to compensate for losses through leachings; after phosphorus additions, uptake competes with immobilization. There are vast areas of Ultisols in temperate regions (e.g., southeastern United States, California, southeastern China) that are successfully managed for sustained agriculture.

---

devoid of these laterites, low-cost roads are definitely inferior to those of the state of Pará in Brazil, where laterite outcrops occur.

Young Soils: Inceptisols and Entisols

The third most widespread soil order of the humid tropics is made up of the Inceptisols. These are young soils of sufficient age to show A, B, and C horizons. There are three major kinds of Inceptisols in the humid tropics:

Aquepts (poorly drained); Andepts (well drained, volcanic origin); Tropepts (well drained, of nonvolcanic origin). Many of the 100 million ha of Inceptisols in humid tropical Asia are devoted to lowland rice production. With the exception of acid sulfate soils or catclays, most of the wet Inceptisols are of moderate to high fertility and support dense human populations.

Similar areas of Aquepts or wet Inceptisols occur in the older alluvial plains along the major rivers and inland swamps of the Amazon Basin. Of the total of 42 million ha of Aquepts in the Amazon, about half are *varzeas* with good potential for intensive cultivation. The rest are mainly in freshwater palm swamps called *aguajales* in Peru.

In humid tropical Africa, there are considerable areas of wet Inceptisols, locally known as "hydromorphic soils." They have been traditionally avoided because of human disease hazard, many of which are no longer relevant. Moorman and Greenland (1980) have suggested that these soils have a significant potential for rice production, because Asian lowland rice technology can be adapted to them.

Inceptisols of volcanic origin, called Andepts, are important in volcanic regions of the Philippines, Java, Sumatra, other Indonesian islands, and Papua New Guinea, as well as in parts of Central America, the Caribbean, and the humid tropical Andean region. In humid tropical Africa, these soils are important in Cameroon and in the highlands of Central Africa around the lakes region. In general, Andepts are fertile and have excellent physical properties, but their main shortcoming is high phosphorus-fixation capacity. Andept regions are generally densely populated. Their existence in the Amazon is limited to the Coca region of Ecuador, where intensive migration is taking place.

Well-drained nonvolcanic Inceptisols, called Tropepts, occupy about 49 million ha in humid tropical Asia, but are not extensive in humid tropical America or Asia. Many of these soils are used for lowland rice production in Asia. Inceptisols occupy only 16% of the humid tropics.

Entisol is the fourth most extensive soil order in the humid tropics, covering about 200 million ha or 14% of the zone. Entisols are soils of such recent development that they do not show a significant degree of horizon differentiation. This order includes well-drained young alluvial soils (Fluvents), acid infertile deep sands (Psamments), and many shallow soils of steep regions or near rock outcrops, called Lithosols in the FAO legend and indicated as lithic in Table 2-3.

Young alluvial soils not subject to periodic flooding are among the best soils of the world. Humid tropical Asia is blessed with about 25 million ha of Fluvents along the major river valleys. Most of these soils are under intensive lowland rice production. The extent of such soils in humid tropical America and Africa is unfortunately less—about 6 million ha in the

Americas and 10 million ha in tropical Africa; they are found along river systems. These are excellent soils and deserve high priority in development schemes. Most Fluvents are already cultivated and in any case account for only 2.7% of the humid tropics.

Psamments, or deep sandy Entisols, are very different soils, usually very acid and even of lower fertility than the Oxisols and Ultisols. Psamments cover 90 million ha of the humid tropics. The largest expanses are in the western part of the Congo Basin in Zaire, in western Central African Republic, in the headwaters of the Tapajós River in Brazil, and in scattered areas around the Rio Negro Basin in Brazil and Venezuela. In tropical Asia, deep sandy areas occur in Kalimantan and Sumatra. The agricultural potential of these soils is very limited and their erodibility high. Clearing of Psamments in the humid tropics is not generally to be recommended.

Shallow soils over bedrock, called Lithosols in the FAO legend, cover about 68 million ha of the humid tropics, mostly on steep slopes. Although the fertility of some of these soils is high, their limited depth poses major constraints to agricultural development. Shallow soils are common in mountainous regions; they are also found in such other areas as the Cachimbo region of central Amazonia.

High Base Status Soils: Alfisols, Vertisols, and Mollisols

Contrary to common belief, there are considerable areas of well-drained soils with moderate to high fertility in the humid tropics. By definition, base status is the proportion of calcium + magnesium + potassium + sodium in the exchange complex of the soil. High base status is good; low base status is bad, because it implies a high level of aluminum. Soils of the orders Alfisols, Vertisols, and Mollisols are high in such bases as calcium and magnesium and therefore are of higher fertility than the dominant Oxisols and Ultisols.

Many Alfisols look much like Ultisols and Oxisols, being similar in color and other morphologic characteristics, but they have high base content and are therefore not acid or inherently infertile. Most Alfisols of the humid tropics cannot be separated from Oxisols or Ultisols without chemical analysis. Most are deep, well drained, and red or yellowish. These Alfisols are called *Terra Roxa Estruturada* in Brazil and Luvisols and Eutric Nitosols in the FAO legend; many have previously been described as Latosols.

Alfisols occur in "spots" in areas dominated by Oxisols and Ultisols along the Amazon Basin. *Terra Roxa Estruturada* soils and other Alfisols occur near Altamira, Porto Velho, and Rio Branco in Brazil; in parts of the high selva of Peru; in the humid coast of Ecuador; and in the cacao-growing region of coastal Bahia in Brazil. Many Alfisols combine the desirable physical properties of Oxisols with excellent chemical properties. In humid tropical Asia, Alfisols of the *Terra Roxa* type are found in several areas of the Philippines and Java. In humid tropical Africa, they are confined to parts of Cameroon and southern Nigeria, where they are mapped as Eutric Nitosols.

It should be emphasized that a completely different kind of Alfisol is very widespread in the forest zone of West Africa, which has a long dry season. These Alfisols (called Oxic Plinthustalfs) have sandy gravelly surface layers underlaid by gravelly materials or plinthite. Although the chemical properties are favorable, they can become acidic when fertilizers are applied; this is so because of their low buffering capacity. These Alfisols therefore have poor physical properties and poor chemical properties as well. Their management has been well studied by the International Institute for Tropical Agriculture (IITA) (Lal, 1975; Greenland and Lal, 1977). These Alfisols are the dominant soils of the forested zone of West Africa from Ivory Coast to eastern Nigeria.

Vertisols are heavy clay soils that shrink and crack with changes in moisture content. They are generally well supplied with nutrients, except for nitrogen and phosphorus. Vertisols are not abundant in the humid tropics, but are found in the high selva of Peru, the Guayas Basin of Ecuador, the lakes region of easternmost Zaire, and Java. These soils are also called Grumusols.

Mollisols are highly fertile soils typical of the temperate grasslands, where they are also known as Chernozems and Rendzinas. They occur in small patches in the humid tropics, usually associated with limestone parent materials. Unfortunately, many of them occur in steep slopes that make cultivation difficult. When found in flat to rolling topography, Mollisols are excellent agricultural soils.

Alfisols, Vertisols, and Mollisols, together with the previously described Andepts, Tropepts, and Fluvents, constitute the best soils of the humid tropics in terms of native fertility. Their aggregate extent, however, is only about 221 million ha or 15% of the humid tropics. The distribution of these good soils varies from 7% in humid tropical America to 33% in humid tropical Africa. The difference in human population between these two regions is to a great extent a consequence of these differences.

Organic Soils: Histosols

Histosols are organic soils that are also known as peats or bogs. Their occurrence is minor in humid tropical America and Africa, but they cover 24 million ha of humid tropical Asia, primarily in Sumatra, Kalimantan, and peninsular Malaysia. A review of Histosols in Southeast Asia is available (Andriesse, 1974). Organic soils are difficult to manage because they subside upon drainage and cultivation and are deficient in micronutrients, particularly copper. Those that have mineral matter within 1 m of the soil surface are less difficult to manage than the deep organics. Preference should be given to crops that tolerate waterlogging, such as rice, taro, and sago palm. At present there is no known technology for managing deep organic soils (IRRI, 1980).

Tropical Podzols: Spodosols

Spodosols, also known as Podzols, Ground Water Podzols, and Giant Tropical Podzols, are derived from coarse sandy materials and are found in clearly definable spots throughout the Amazon away from the floodplains. Native forest vegetation is different from that found in Oxisols and Ultisols. It is called "campinarama" in Brazil. The RADAM project recently identified large areas of Spodosols along the headwaters of the Rio Negro (Projecto RADAM-Brasil, 1972-1978). The presence of Spodosols largely accounts for the coffee color of this river; water passing through Spodosols characteristically carries suspended organic matter. Spodosols are also abundant in southern Kalimantan and are the main soils of Bangka and Biliton islands in Indonesia. Since they are infertile and very susceptible to erosion, Spodosols are best left in their natural state. The Spodosols have received more scientific attention than is consistent with their extent (2.2% of the Amazon, 1% of the humid tropics). Nevertheless, research on tropical Podzols reported in the international literature (Klinge, 1965, 1975; Stark, 1978; Sombroek, 1979) should be kept in perspective; under no circumstances can it be extrapolated to the dominant Oxisols and Ultisols.

Generalization About Humid Tropical Soils

Certain broad generalizations can be made in comparing the humid tropics of America, Asia, and Africa (Table 2-5). Acid infertile soils of the orders Oxisols and Ultisols cover the largest area in all of humid tropical regions, but their relative importance is greater in Latin America (82%) than in Africa (56%) or Asia (38%). The inverse occurs with moderately fertile to fertile high base status soils, which cover as much as 33% of humid tropical Asia, 12% of humid tropical Africa, but only 7% of humid tropical America. Most of these soils in Asia are already under intensive cultivation; therefore, the potential for expansion is very limited. Three broad kinds of soils that pose severe management difficulties, the acid

TABLE 2-5   General Distribution of Main Kinds of Soils in the Humid Tropics, Calculated from Table 2-3

General Soil Grouping	Humid Tropical America (%)	Humid Tropical Africa (%)	Humid Tropical Asia (%)	World's Humid Tropics (%)
Acid, infertile soils (Oxisols and Ultisols)	82	56	38	63
Moderately fertile, well-drained soils (Alfisols, Vertisols, Mollisols, Andepts, Tropepts, Fluvents)	7	12	33	15
Poorly drained soils (Aquepts)	6	12	6	8
Very infertile sandy soils (Psamments, Spodosols)	2	16	6	7
Shallow soils (lithic Entisols)	3	3	10	5
Organic soils (Histosols)	—	1	6	—
TOTAL	100	100	100	100

sands, the shallow soils, and the organics, occur in somewhat similar proportion in the three regions, except for the greater importance of organic soils in Asia and the deep sandy soils in humid tropical Africa.

In summary, the distribution of soils of the humid tropical regions of the world follows a pattern of dominance of acid infertile soils. The smallest proportion of reasonably fertile, well-drained soils is in Latin America and the largest in Asia (Table 2-5). On the other hand, the humid tropics of Latin America have the lowest proportion of the "problem soils" (acid sands, shallow soils, and organics) (5%), and Asia has the highest (22%). The situation in humid tropical Africa falls somewhere between humid tropical America and Asia.

ECOSYSTEM ORGANIZATION AND FUNCTIONING

The organization of a humid tropical forest provides a unique setting for life. The interrelationship between climate, vegetation, soil, and fauna creates a holistic unit where no one element can be significantly modified without affecting the others. The vegetation itself provides protection to the soil by absorption and deflection of radiation, precipitation, and wind. The forest also creates its own special local climate by absorbing and deflecting radiation on its canopy surface and decreasing wind velocity. In addition, the forest provides shelter and required growth conditions for plants, animals, and microorganisms.

The soil in the forest receives its organic materials primarily from continuous leaf fall, the recycling of materials from dead plants and animals, and rainfall. The soil contains and is dependent on a whole host of soil organisms (primarily bacteria, fungi, protozoa, nematodes, arthropods, earthworms, and burrowing vertebrates) for maintenance and continued fertility.

The forest derives its energy from solar radiation through the process of photosynthesis. It is dependent on the many alternative channels of energy flow through the system as regulated by consumer organisms to ensure that nutrients are released from the bodies of living creatures and returned to the nutrient pool. The fauna depends on the forest and soil for food and shelter while ensuring the return of nutrients to the soil and directly contributing to the maintenance of soil fertility.

The primary ecological features of an undisturbed humid tropical ecosystem are discussed below and will center on an undisturbed tropical lowland moist forest, since it is this kind of ecosystem that occupies the greatest area of the humid tropics and remains relatively unexploited. Figure 2-8 presents a generalized profile of such a closed-canopy, broad-leaf evergreen forest.

ECOLOGICAL CONCEPT

PRIMARY PRODUCTION

The absorption and incorporation of solar energy per unit of land area by green plants and other autotrophs is called primary production. Autotrophs are organisms that produce their own food by the process of photosynthesis (= fixation of light energy). The rate of production, referred to as productivity, is expressed in such units as energy stored per unit of ground area per unit of time, or kilocalories per square meter per year. Ecologists distinguish between gross primary production (GPP) and net primary production (NPP). GPP includes photosynthesis and the energy used in that process for cellular respiration of plants. NPP is the part of the energy fixed by plants that goes into growth and reproduction. Cellular respiration uses energy to maintain the organism so that it can carry out normal metabolic processes.

Primary production by plants is the principal food resource for most other organisms, such as herbivores and decomposers (bacteria and fungi). It is determined primarily by light, temperature, water, nutrients, and carbon dioxide, and it is highest where light, warmth, moisture, and key nutrients are abundant, e.g., swamps, marshes, and moist tropical forests.

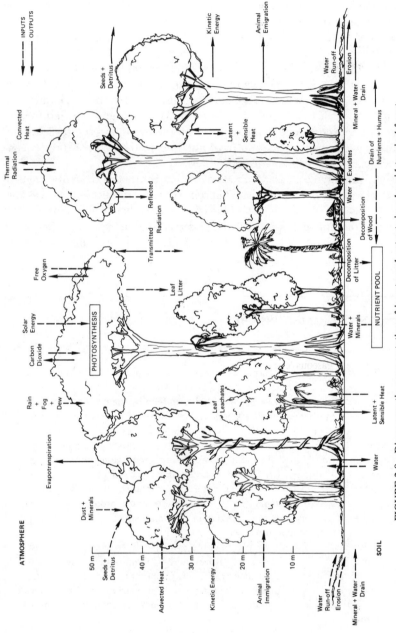

FIGURE 2-8 Diagrammatic representation of inputs and outputs in a humid tropical forest.

The environmental features characteristic of this kind of ecosystem are as follows:

- mean annual biotemperature 24°-28°C; diurnal variation 9°C; diurnal variation inside forest about 1°C
- annual insolation at canopy level 2,900 kcal/cm^2
- annual insolation at ground level averaging 130 kcal/cm^2

ECOLOGICAL CONCEPT

BIOGEOCHEMICAL CYCLES

This term refers to the cycling of chemical elements in the biosphere through special pathways from environment to organisms and back again to the environment. "Bio" refers to living organisms; "geo" to nonliving components of the earth; and "chemical" to the elements. The principal process by which these elements remain in balance at any location is through recycling. The two main types of biogeochemical cycles are: (1) the gaseous cycle, involving air or water, and (2) the sedimentary cycle, involving earth crustal processes. These cycles obtain for most elements found in the earth's crust.

For each substance, the cycle operates at different rates and along different pathways. For example, gaseous cycles pass through the atmosphere, but many differ in their passage through the ocean or the land. In general, gaseous cycles are fairly fast, because the atmosphere has a rapid turnover, particularly for gases at low concentrations. Sedimentary cycles tend to be slower because of the slow rates associated with such processes as erosion, sedimentation, and movements through the deep earth's crust.

There is also a scale dimension to biogeochemical cycles. At a macrolevel, some cycles may be described for the biosphere as a whole; examples are the rock cycle, which involves uplifting of continents, volcanism, and other such processes. On a microscale, one could describe the cycle of an element within a forest stand; such a cycle might include leaf growth, leaf fall, decomposition, and so on. Because of the differences in scale of time and space, it may appear from a human perspective that some cycles are imperfect—either too slow or too fast.

The important point is that the biosphere is a dynamic system, its biogeochemical cycles responsible for transporting materials and energy throughout the system. The net effect is the maintenance of conditions conducive to life at the scale of an organism or the planet.

- mean annual precipitation 3,000 mm; a dry season of 2 months with less than 2,000 mm precipitation per year
- ratio of potential evapotranspiration (PET) to actual precipitation (P) less than 1
- mean daily relative humidity 60%–70% diurnal, 95%–100% nocturnal
- Deep, well-drained red or yellowish soil of the acid infertile type, with high potential aluminum toxicity; a deficiency of phosphorus, potassium, calcium, magnesium, sulphur, zinc, and other micronutrients; and high leaching potential, but with good physical properties

In this environment, where there is abundant solar radiation and water, the dominant biotic aspect is the green plant component and high primary production.

ECOLOGICAL CONCEPT

SPECIES DIVERSITY

Species diversity includes two concepts: (1) the number of species present and (2) the evenness of numbers of individuals (or biomass) among those species. The sheer number of species present in an area is called species richness. Thus, an area with 50 plant species is said to be "richer" than an area of the same size in another place that has only 10. The issue becomes more complex, however, if the site with 50 species has 951 individuals of 1 species and only 1 individual of the 49 other species, whereas the 10-species site has 100 individuals of each species. In this case, the 10-species site might be considered the more "diverse," because an observer at the 10-species site would have a good chance to observe individuals belonging to all 10 species and would probably see roughly equal numbers of each species, whereas an observer at the 50-species site would regard it as containing essentially 1 dominant species. Lowland tropical species diversity tends to be high both in having many species in a unit area and having relatively uniform numbers of individuals. As a consequence of the large number of species, the number of individuals of any species is often small, especially for such large organisms as trees, so that spatial distance between individuals of the same species may be very great. It is this characteristic of tropical forests that makes selective harvest of all but the most valuable timber species difficult. Fortunately for the timber industry, some monospecific stands and low-diversity forests do occur in the lowland tropics, often in such "stressed" environments as swamps. These tend to be heavily exploited.

The variety of plants and animals in the forest is remarkable. For example, in an area of 10 km^2 from 300 to 750 different tree species may occur, whereas as many as 1,500 species of higher plants have been found in a similar-sized area—up to 600 on a single hectare (UNESCO, 1978). Although trees are the most obvious and the principal component of the biomass in the forest, many kinds of woody-stemmed climbers (lianes), herbaceous plants, shrubs, and small palms contribute to its species richness and complexity. The buttresses on many trees (Figure 2-5), stilt-roots (especially on the many palms), and abundant strangler trees and vines are characteristics. Similarly, numerous epiphytic plants (e.g., ferns, orchids, bromeliads) rest on the boles of the tall trees and in the branches and foliage of the canopy. These forms are often called air-plants. Some truly parasitic plants may also be present, and it is estimated that a significant part of the biomass of the forest canopy is composed of plants that use the tree branches as growing sites (Klinge *et al.*, 1975).

In a typical area of 10 km^2, one will find about 125 species of mammals, 400 species of birds, 100 species of reptiles, 60 species of amphibians, and 150 species of butterflies. Much higher figures have been recorded for several of these groups at particular sites (UNESCO, 1978). Population densities for most forms are low, and large mammals and snakes are infrequently encountered. The species numbers and densities of the many insect groups can only be guessed at (42,000 species per hectare is one recent estimate). In one study on this type of forest, 800 ants belonging to 50 species were taken from 1 m^2 of leaf litter (Janzen, 1981). Many species of small litter and soil organisms (especially nematodes, mites, and springtails) are also found.

The forest itself tends to be stratified into three tree canopies, or layers. The living canopy of treetops bound together by climbing plants, lianes, stranglers, and epiphytes forms the upper zone, typically reaching a height of 40–50 m, although occasional giant emergent trees stand above the canopy. The density of the canopy trees is 30–40 per hectare. A second layer (understory) reaches a height of about 30 m and characteristically has 80–160 trees per hectare. A third stratum of small trees, 5–20 m high, often dominated by palms, typically has 400–500 trees per hectare.

A fourth zone is represented by herbaceous shrubs that reach heights of 2–3 m. A fifth, the ground layer, consists of a sparse cover of tree seedlings, broad-leaf herbs and ferns, and possibly a few grasses. The floor of the forest may be divided into the thin leaf-litter layer (a sixth) and the soil biota (a seventh).

Differences in response to light, temperature, and moisture gradients from the canopy to the forest floor significantly influence the stratification of vegetation. Many epiphytes, for example, are characteristically associated

ECOLOGICAL CONCEPT

BIOMASS (=LIVING WEIGHT)

This term refers to the total amount of living matter present at a given time in a biological system, usually expressed as dry weight per unit area (biomass density). The components of a particular ecosystem—plants (autotrophs) and animals and decomposers (heterotrophs)—or the various trophic levels exhibit a characteristic biomass or standing crop.

The term biomass, or standing crop, should not be confused with productivity, which is the amount of biomass fixed in a given time. Biomass may bear little relation to productivity, because portions of some plants or animals may have been produced in a previous season or year. Rather, it is the weight present at any one moment, whereas productivity is a continuous process, although measured as the amount of food manufactured per unit of time (day, month, year).

In agricultural ecosystems, which are seasonally herbaceous, the standing crop at the end of the year is about the same as that year's net primary productivity. Because it is easier to measure biomass than to measure productivity, many people mistakenly use biomass as a measure of production in these ecosystems. The huge biomass of tropical moist forests (see table below) is not equivalent to their annual productivity (which happens to be high), because that biomass probably took hundreds of years to accumulate. When the forest is cut to "take advantage of such high productivity," the regrowth of an equivalent amount of biomass may take a very long time. The table below also clarifies the role of animals in the forest. Although animals play vital roles in the ecology of the forest, and indeed receive considerable scientific attention, their biomass is trivial.

Habitat	Plant Biomass (t/ha)	Animal Biomass (t/ha)
Tropical moist forest in the Amazonian *terra firme*	298	0.210
Mangroves in Puerto Rico	130	0.064
Tropical wet forest in Panama	284	0.073

with the different tree strata. As for animals, differing adaptations and requirements for food and shelter are reflected in marked differences among the major vertical zones; for example, ground-foraging birds or parrots that live in the canopy only. Much of the species richness, heterogeneity, and complexity of a humid tropical forest stems from stratification and the complexity of organization that it affords.

Photosynthesis provides the energy to this system, but availability of nutrients is also critical. Without nitrogen, phosphorus, sulphur, potassium, calcium, iron, zinc, and other micronutrients, the carbohydrate fixed in photosynthesis cannot be adequately utilized.

In these forests the essential mineral nutrients are primarily bound in the biomass. For example, since much of that biomass is plant material, especially wood and leaves, the nutrient pool in Oxisols and Ultisols is relatively small. Potassium, calcium, and magnesium are typical of this situation, but more than 70% of the ecosystem's nitrogen and phosphorus reserves are in the topsoil (Sanchez, 1979). Nutrients are added to the soil primarily through the breakdown of leaf litter and other decaying plant materials (mostly wood); animal wastes and carcasses also contribute. Because of the constant high temperatures and humidity, decomposition rapidly releases the nutrients into the pool. Although some nutrients are lost through leaching, most are rapidly recycled back into the growing plants. For these reasons, the leaf-litter layer is thin, and there is but limited soil nutrient storage in Oxisols and Ultisols.

The transfer of energy from plants to animals and microbes is an aspect of the organization of forests that has received considerable attention from scientists. These energy transfers constitute the food web of the forest and are responsible for supporting the impressive structural and functional diversity of these ecosystems. In general, the energy transfer through the food web follows three main pathways: (1) a grazing food chain based on living plants; (2) a grazing food chain based on dead plant parts; and (3) the detrital food chain based on plant detritus and microbes.

GRAZING OF LIVE PLANTS

The consumption of green leaves by herbivores is the most commonly known food chain. This food chain provides our meat and milk and is easily observed. In spite of its obvious importance, the grazing of living tissue consumes only about 10% of the net primary productivity of an ecosystem. Most theories about energy transfer in ecosystems are based on this type of food chain. From these studies it has been shown that:

• The food chains tend to be short (2-5 links), because energy is dissipated at each transfer point.

• About 10%-15% of the energy available in one link is transferred to the next.

• Biomass decreases with increasing trophic level.

• Such high-level consumers as leopards, snakes, or human beings tend to be generalist feeders, whereas herbivores tend to specialize.

GRAZING OF DEAD PLANT PARTS

Most of the net primary productivity of the ecosystem is transferred to the litter component of the system. The 90% of the net primary productivity that enters this pathway may be grazed by organisms living on the forest floor, or it may enter the detrital and microbial food chain (see below). Between 5% and 20% of the available litter enters the grazing food chain. Thus this food chain is about equal to, or slightly more important than, the one based on living plant parts. The relative importance depends on the ecosystem. In the tropics, because more litter is produced and because processes are faster and there is more diversity of organisms, this food chain is much more significant than in temperate or boreal systems. However, the phenomenon was first described for temperate ecosystems. In fact, much of the basic work on the subject has been conducted in the old fields of the southeastern United States.

ECOLOGICAL CONCEPT

SECONDARY PRODUCTION

This term refers to the utilization for growth, maintenance and reproduction, and transfer through the animal (heterotroph) community of energy originally produced by green plants (autotrophs). Secondary production is partitioned, at least for purposes of discussion, into energy flows through the various trophic levels. A simplified way of presenting this energy flow through an ecosystem is to divide secondary production into consumer levels such as primary, secondary, tertiary, and so on. Primary consumers are herbivores; all higher levels are carnivores.

In reality, a neat division into trophic levels may not be apparent, because one animal may feed on others at different levels, or one organism may have different life stages (e.g., larvae, adults) that may occupy different trophic levels. Ecologists, therefore, find the calculation of secondary production in complex natural systems very difficult.

Microbial and Detrital Food Chain

This is by far the most important food chain in most ecosystems. Most of the energy and materials flow through this pathway because only microbes can deal with the chemical composition of lignin and cellulose. Dead plant and animal parts are thus subjected to the action of fungi and bacteria that transform these tissues into minerals, carbon dioxide, and water. In the process, protein-rich microbial tissue is formed. Many organisms consume microbes, and thus begins a food chain based thereon.

Ecological Significance of Food Chains

The three food chains just discussed are webbed together and interdependent. Without larger organisms, microbes could not function efficiently because the large organisms fragment plant tissues and improve the surface/volume relationship. Similarly, without microbes other organisms could not survive because microbes make possible the recycling of minerals, contribute to the maintenance of primary plant productivity, and produce protein-rich tissues that form part of the food supplies of larger organisms.

Many studies have demonstrated that the organization of these food chains is related to the role that species diversity plays in the regulation of homeostasis in the system. Other studies have postulated that certain aspects of the organization and energy flow patterns through these food chains can be used to characterize tropical ecosystems as different from temperate ecosystems.

The complexity of the food webs ensures a small but constant return of nutrients to the soil, where they are almost immediately taken up by the vegetation. Without the damping effect of the complex food web, larger and irregularly timed amounts of nutrients would be added to the soil, with a substantial loss to leaching.

Role of Leaf-Litter Organisms

Figure 2-9 shows the role of leaf-litter amphibians and reptiles (the herpetofauna) in a tropical forest community. It highlights the regulatory aspects of consumers in maintaining an even flow of organic matter and nutrients through the system. Four major pathways recycle nutrients into the pool available for plant growth: (I) the animal excretion pathway, where at the lowest level litter material must be eaten and the waste excreted before microorganisms and fungi may decompose it; (II) the microbial decomposition pathway, where fragmented litter materials may be decomposed; (III) the pathway where symbiotic organisms convert materials directly to the

ECOLOGICAL CONCEPT

FOOD WEBS, TROPHIC LEVELS, AND STABILITY

A food web comprises a group of species interdependent for energy. In their simplest form these interdependencies yield a food chain composed of a linear array of species, each eating the one preceding it, and that one alone. In fact, simple food chains may never be found in isolation in nature, but close approximations occur in species-poor arctic ecosystems. Such an example would be the sequence from algae in the ocean, through an algae-eating fish, then sea lion, to polar bear. Food chains and webs involve the passage of energy across trophic levels (literally levels of "nourishment") and are always based on organisms such as a green plant that can use raw materials (nutrients in the soil solution and gases) and solar energy to make food. These primary producers are eaten by herbivores ("plant-eaters"), which may then be consumed by carnivores ("meat-eaters"). For reasons of ecological efficiency few food webs involve more than five or six trophic levels; because some energy is lost as heat at each step, there is seldom sufficient available to support an additional level.

The situation is more complex when organisms operate at several trophic levels. In the example given above, a person might eat the bear, seal, fish, or even the algae. The polar bear might eat the fish (or person) as well. When a species has but a single organism on which it feeds, its survival absolutely depends on the persistence of its food supply. If Eskimos were to overfish drastically, the numbers of seals and polar bears would also decline because of lack of food. Clearly, those species using many different organisms as food have a better chance of surviving temporary declines or even elimination of one of their food sources.

For this reason, the tremendous number of species in the tropics with their many possible trophic interactions are thought to stabilize the species populations and confer resilience against loss or reduction of a single species.

host plant's use; and (IV) the autolysis pathway of decomposition without microbial action. Humid tropical forests differ from temperate ecosystems in the greater significance of pathways I and III in nutrient recycling.

Two major food chains are also shown in the figure. The one labeled (1) is dependent on large arthropods, especially grasshoppers, katydids, crickets, and ants that graze on the fallen leaves and fragment them to the extent that microbial decomposition may take place. The macroarthropod grazers are food sources for arthropod predators, especially spiders, centipedes, beetles, and ants. The food chain labeled (2) is based on the fungi that grow

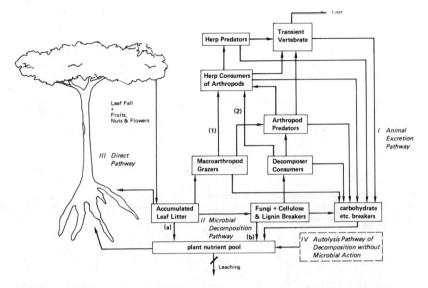

FIGURE 2-9 Schematic portrayal of the role of leaf-litter organisms in a tropical forest community. "Herp" refers to the amphibian and reptile components of this assemblage.

on the leaf remains left by the arthropod grazers. Decomposer consumers, especially orbatid mites and springtails, feed on the fungi, and, together with earthworms, millepedes, cockroaches, and termites, consume much of the remaining leaf detritus. Like the macroarthropod grazers, these animals are eaten by an array of arthropod predators. The leaf-litter, herpetofaunal predators, primarily frogs, lizards, and some small snakes, feed on all trophic levels of prey organisms: macroarthropod grazers, decomposer consumers, detrital consumers, and arthropod predators. The secondary level of herpetofaunal predators feeds on the lower level of herpetofaunal consumers. Transient vertebrate predators (large snakes, birds, and mammals) harvest some energy from the ecosystem as well.

REFERENCES

Andriesse, J. P. 1974. Tropical lowland peats of Southeast Asia. Communication No. 63. Royal Tropical Institute, Amsterdam. 63 p.

Aubert, G. 1965. Classification des sols ultilisée par la section les pédalogues francais. FAO World Soil Resources Reports 32:78–94.

Baldwin, M., C. E. Kellogg, and J. Thorpe. 1938. Soil classification. Pages 979–1000 *in* Soils and men. Yearbook of Agriculture, U.S. Department of Agriculture. U.S. Government Printing Office, Washington, D.C.

Brown, S., A. E. Lugo, and B. Liegel. 1980. The role of tropical forests in the world carbon cycle. U.S. Department of Energy, CONF-800350, UG11. 156 p.

Buol, S. W., and P. A. Sanchez. 1978. Rainy tropical climates: physical, potential, present and improved farming systems. Trans. 11th Congr. Int. Soc. Soil Sci. (Edmonton) 2:292–312.

Cline, M. G., A. S. Ayres, W. Crosby, P. F. Philipp, R. Elliott, O. C. Magistad, J. C. Ripperton, E. Y. Hosaka, M. Takahashi, G. D. Sherman, and C. K. Wentworth. 1955. Soil survey of the Territory of Hawaii. Soil Science Series 1939-25. U.S. Department of Agriculture, Washington, D.C.

Costa de Lemos, R. 1968. Main tropical soils of Brazil. FAO World Soil Resources Reports 32:95–106.

Dent, F. J. 1980. Major production systems and soil-related qualities in humid tropical Asia. Pages 79–106 in Priorities for alleviating soil-related constraints to food production in the tropics. International Rice Research Institute, Los Baños, Philippines.

Dudal, R. 1980. Soil-related constraints to agricultural development in the tropics. Pages 23–37 in Priorities for alleviating soil-related constraints to food production in the tropics. International Rice Research Institute, Los Baños, Philippines.

FAO (Food and Agriculture Organization). 1975. Soil map of the world. Vol. IV, South America. UNESCO, Paris.

FAO (Food and Agriculture Organization). 1977. Soil map of the world. Vol. V, Africa. UNESCO, Paris.

FAO (Food and Agriculture Organization). 1978. Soil map of the world. Vol. VI, South Asia, and Vol. IX, Southeast Asia. UNESCO, Paris.

Greenland, D. J., and R. Lal, eds. 1977. Soil conservation and management in the humid tropics. Wiley, New York. 283 p.

Holdridge, L. S. 1967. Life zone ecology. Tropical Science Center, San José, Costa Rica. 206 p.

IRRI (International Rice Research Institute). 1980. Research priorities. Pages 451–457 in Priorities for alleviating soil-related constraints to food production in the tropics. International Rice Research Institute, Los Baños, Philippines.

IUCN (International Union for the Conservation of Nature and Natural Resources). 1975a. The use of ecological guidelines for development in the American humid tropics. IUCN Publ. New Series No. 31, IUCN, Morges, Switzerland. 249 p.

IUCN (International Union for the Conservation of Nature and Natural Resources). 1975b. The use of ecological guidelines for development in tropical forest areas of Southeast Asia. IUCN Publ. New Series No. 32, IUCN, Morges, Switzerland. 185 p.

Janzen, D. H. 1981. A primer of Costa Rican field biology. Museo Nacional de Costa Rica, San José.

Klinge, H. 1965. Podzol soils in the Amazon Basin. J. Soil Sci. 16:95–103.

Klinge, H. 1975. Root mass estimation in lowland tropical rain-forests of central Amazonia, Brazil. III. Nutrients in fine roots from giant humus Podzols. Trop. Ecol. 16:28–39.

Klinge, H., W. A. Rodriques, E. Brunig, and E. J. Fittkau. 1975. Biomass and structure in a central Amazonian rain forest. Pages 115–122 in F. B. Golley and E. Medina, eds. Tropical ecological systems. Springer-Verlag, New York.

Lal, R. 1975. Soil erosion problems on an Alfisol of western Nigeria and their control. Monograph No. 1, International Institute of Tropical Agriculture, Ibadan, Nigeria. 159 p.

Moorman, F. R., and D. J. Greenland. 1980. Major production systems and soil-related qualities in humid tropical Africa. Pages 55–78 in Priorities for alleviating soil-related constraints to food production in the tropics. International Rice Research Institute, Los Baños, Philippines.

Moorman, F. R., and A. Van Wambeke. 1978. The soils of the lowland rainy tropical climates, their inherent limitations for food production and related climatic restraints. Trans. 11th Congr. Int. Soc. Soil Sci. (Edmonton) 2:272-291.

Nieuwolt, S. 1977. Tropical climatology: an introduction to the climates of the low latitudes. Wiley Interscience, New York.

NRC (National Research Council). 1980a. Conversion of tropical moist forests. National Academy of Sciences, Washington, D.C. 205 p.

NRC (National Research Council). 1980b. Research priorities in tropical biology. National Academy of Sciences, Washington, D.C. 116 p.

Persson, R. 1974. World forest resources. Review of world's forest resources in the early 1970's. Department of Forest Survey, Royal College of Forestry, Stockholm.

Projecto RADAM-Brasil. 1972-1978. Levantamento de Regiao Amazonica. Vols. 1-12. Ministerio das Minas e Energia, Departmento Nacional da Producao Mineral, Rio de Janeiro, Brasil.

Sanchez, P. A. 1976. Properties and management of soils in the tropics. Wiley, New York.

Sanchez, P. A. 1979. Soil fertility and conservation considerations for agroforestry systems in the humid tropics of Latin America. Pages 79-124 *in* H. O. Mongi and P. A. Huxley, eds. Soils research in agroforestry. International Council for Research on Agro-Forestry, ICRAF 001e, Nairobi, Kenya.

Sanchez, P. A., and S. W. Buol. 1975. Soils of the tropics and the world food crisis. Science 188:598-603.

Sanchez, P. A., and T. T. Cochrane. 1980. Soil constraints in relation to major farming systems in tropical America. Pages 107-139 *in* Priorities for alleviating soil-related constraints to food production in the tropics. International Rice Research Institute, Los Baños, Philippines.

Soil Survey Staff. 1975. Soil taxonomy. A basic system of soil classification for making and interpreting soil surveys. Handbook 436. U.S. Department of Agriculture, Washington, D.C.

Sombroek. W. G. 1979. Soils of the Amazon region. International Soils Museum, Wageningen, Netherlands. Unpublished paper. 15 p.

Soulé, M., and B. Wilcox, eds. 1980. Conservation biology: an evolutionary-ecological perspective. Sinauer Associates, Sunderland, Mass. 395 p.

Stark, N. 1978. Man, tropical forests and the biological life of a soil. Biotropica 10:1-10.

UNESCO. 1978. Tropical forest ecosystems. A state-of-knowledge report prepared by UNESCO/UNEP/FAO. Natural Resources Research XIV. Paris. 683 p.

SUGGESTED READING

Odum, H. T., and R. F. Pigeon, eds. 1970. A tropical rain forest. A study of irradiation and ecology at El Verde, Puerto Rico. 3 vols. U.S. Atomic Energy Commission, Office of Information Services, Oak Ridge, Tenn.

Richards, P. W. 1952. The tropical rain forest: an ecological study. Cambridge University Press, Cambridge, U.K. 450 p.

Walter, H. 1971. Ecology of tropical and subtropical vegetation. Van Nostrand Reinhold Company, New York. 539 p.

Whitmore, T. C. 1975. Tropical rainforests of the Far East. Clarendon Press, Oxford, England. 278 p.

Yanney Ewusie, J. 1980. Elements of tropical ecology. Heinemann, London. 205. p.

3
Evaluation of Renewable Natural Resources

The first step in incorporating ecological viewpoints into development planning is to evaluate the quality and quantity of renewable natural resources—goods and services—that will receive the impact of such actions as are taken. Of prime concern are the interactive relations of project development, resource utilization and conservation, and subsequent effects on other ecosystems. A basic knowledge of the kinds of organisms in the affected ecosystem and of their resiliency or sensitivity under conditions of change is essential.

Two principal kinds of resource surveys are needed: biological inventories and ecological baseline studies. The former, as the term suggests, document the kinds and approximate numbers of organisms that occur in a given area. Clearly, in most areas of the humid tropics, essentially complete inventories are impossible because of the extreme diversity of the flora and fauna and the relatively small amount of effort devoted to their study in the past. Nevertheless, a useful inventory can be devoted to tree species and major understory plants, large vertebrate animals, and birds, plus a quantitative sampling of invertebrate groups using various trapping techniques. If a substantial area is involved, analysis of vegetational distribution and animal co-occurrences must be undertaken as well. Typical data to be obtained are discussed below.

Ecological baseline studies provide environmental data relating to conditions at a particular site or along sample lines across a larger area. These data make it possible to assess the organization of the ecosystem, determine its most significant abiotic and biotic components, and evaluate the effects of perturbation upon them. Since the baseline data are established prior to the initiation of a project, they may be used in the planning process and also to monitor changes as the project develops.

RENEWABLE-NATURAL-RESOURCE SURVEYS

The diversity of tropical organisms can only be estimated, because they are so very numerous and relatively poorly known, but certain inferences are possible.

In the roughly three centuries during which people have been attempting to classify and catalog organisms, names have been assigned to about 1.5 million different kinds. About two-thirds of them occur in temperate regions and about one-third, or 500,000 of the named species, in tropical regions. When these numbers are examined as regards relatively well-known groups—birds, mammals, or butterflies—there are about twice as many species of organisms in the tropics as in temperate regions. A very rough estimate suggests, then, that the total number of species of plants, animals, and microorganisms in temperate regions is about 1.5 million and in the tropics about 3 million. In other words, perhaps one out of six tropical organisms has been accorded some measure of scientific attention.

As recently reported by the National Research Council (1980a), even such relatively conspicuous and economically important groups of organisms as freshwater fishes or higher plants are, in many cases, very poorly known. For example, it is estimated that about a third of all the kinds of land plants in the world, perhaps amounting to some 80,000 species, occur in Latin America. Of these, perhaps one-eighth have yet to be classified and are completely unknown to science. Similarly, of the roughly 5,000 species of freshwater fishes that are estimated to occur in tropical South America, it is estimated that about 40% have not yet been discovered and named (Böhlke *et al.*, 1978). In view of the fact that active development of the forest and fisheries resources of Latin America is contemplated, this lack of knowledge must be taken with the utmost seriousness.

Many groups of less conspicuous organisms are even more poorly known. For example, nematodes comprise at least several hundred thousand kinds worldwide, of which fewer than 15,000 have been cataloged. Many are parasites of plants and animals of economic importance. Yet there is only a handful of specialists capable of dealing with the systematics of nematodes. The fungi, another economically important group of organisms, cause tens of billions of dollars of damage annually (Day, 1977). Despite this, it is at present virtually impossible to prepare regional catalogs for any area, because there are none in the tropics for which the fungi are even relatively well known.

RELEVANCE OF SURVEYS

There are at least four main reasons why more knowledge about the plants, animals, and microorganisms that occur in tropical ecosystems is highly desirable.

Scientific Curiosity

The interactions between green plants and the organisms that depend on them are of interest for their own sake as well as for economic reasons. The human race has long subscribed to the principle that it is important to know about the earth's plants, animals, and microorganisms and that unpredictable benefits may well derive from them. Most educated people would agree that such knowledge is valuable for its own sake and justifies continued study.

Derivation of Useful Products

Worldwide, the human race has used only about 5,000 kinds of plants, or about 2% of the total available, as food. We currently use, on a major scale, only a few dozen (see Chapter 4). In addition, some 25% of the prescriptions written in the United States contain drugs ultimately derived from organisms (NRC, 1978). The annual cost of these prescriptions approximates $3 billion (Farnsworth and Morris, 1976).

As many as one out of eight kinds of plants in Latin America alone may be unknown to science, and very little is known about most of the remainder. Then, too, there is in Southeast Asia a whole array of cultivated and semicultivated plants used as food, many on a local basis, a number of which could become important elsewhere if they were adequately studied and disseminated.

The forests of Southeast Asia were the source of the cultivated bananas that resulted from hybridization of two or three native species and eventually produced a whole array of cultivars. Many other wild and partly cultivated fruits, such as carambola (*Averrhoa*), sugarpalm (*Arenga pinnata*), mangosteen (*Garcinia*), and species of genera such as *Nephelium, Lansium, Sandoricum,* and *Diospyros,* are common in the forests of this area but have never been used widely. Also, wild populations of domesticated crops such as the taros (*Alocasia* and *Calocasia*), cloves (*Eugenia aromatica*), nutmeg (*Myristica fragrans*), and cinnamon (*Cinamomum*) are found here. Many other plants—sources of food, medicines, agricultural implements, natural dyes, fibers, fish poisons, insecticides, perfumes, and tannins—have been noted in the literature on Southeast Asia. In almost every case, they merit further study.

The recent discovery of a wild, perennial, diploid relative of corn, *Zea diploperennis*, in the Sierra de Manantlán, Jalisco, Mexico (Iltis *et al* , 1979) is indicative of what we have yet to learn about germplasm, even that of species closely related to major cultivated crops. The importance of maintaining comprehensive collections of different crop germplasms has been stressed by many. The resistance of the newly discovered relative of corn to the seven most common viral diseases of corn in the United States shows the value of seeking additional genetic material. A recent publication on underexploited tropical plants with promising economic value (NRC, 1975) cites many examples of plants that are not now in cultivation, but which could be utilized to advantage.

Many concerned people (Myers, 1979; Soulé and Wilcox, 1980; Ehrlich and Ehrlich, 1981; Frankel and Soulé, 1981) are convinced that an increased knowledge of the world's biota would be of great economic advantage. But, they can be used only if they are studied, cataloged, and understood.

Role in Normal Functioning of Ecosystems

To understand the functioning of tropical ecosystems, it is necessary to understand the nature and functioning of their principal components. Pimentel *et al.* (1980) summarized the role of these components in ecosystems as follows:

Natural biota, the nonmanipulative or uncultivated organisms, perform many essential functions for agriculture, forestry, and other segments of human society, such as preventing the accumulation of wastes; cleaning water and soil of pollutants; recycling vital chemical elements within the ecosystem, including biotic nitrogen as fertilizer; buffering air pollutants and moderating climatic change; conserving soil and water; serving as sources of certain medicines, pigments, and species; preserving genetic material for agriculture; and supply food via the harvest of fish and other wildlife. In addition to these important ecosystem functions, the natural biota are of great aesthetic value to society.

The intricacies of tropical ecosystems and the importance of understanding individual organisms to effective manipulation of ecosystems have been stressed in several recent reports (Farnworth and Golley, 1974; NRC, 1980a). In spite of the limited numbers of biologists able to work effectively with the classification of tropical ecosystems, such knowledge about them as can be obtained is important.

New Insights for Managed Ecosystems

In the past, people have generally regarded renewable natural resources as something to be used or consumed but not intensively managed. Such exploitation required little information, especially where such single products as forest trees were extracted. But this is a singularly poor way to approach the array of potentially renewable natural resources found in the humid tropics.

Recent studies by Michael Goulding, in the Brazilian Amazon, concerning fish that move out onto and feed in seasonally flooded areas have received much attention (Maugh, 1981; Webster, 1981). The possibility of farming, cultivating, or enhancing native populations of fish, turtles, and other vertebrates has also been emphasized (Morán, 1981). Yet if 40% of the freshwater fish fauna of South America are, as postulated, totally unknown (NRC, 1980a), consider the difficulties of building a productive system. The more critical the information we have available, the better opportunity there is for putting together systems that are capable of producing on a sustained basis (Grainger, 1981). The creation of large lakes and impoundments, drainages, and other alterations in freshwater systems in the tropics, which may well drastically affect the native fish population, virtually obligates us to an early effort to study these fish populations while they are still in a relatively unmodified state. Sporadic efforts made thus far will not produce the comprehensive knowledge upon which a sound system of managing these populations can ultimately be based.

PRACTICAL SOLUTIONS

To gain the information about biological diversity that is indispensable to improve the human condition in tropical countries, we must greatly accelerate our efforts by undertaking inventories of renewable natural resources in areas under development and by training local scientists to carry out such activities.

Inventory and Screening

Hard choices must be made as to the most important kinds of information to be obtained (NRC, 1980a). Priority ought to be given to groups of organisms of known or potential economic importance, including flowering plants, certain key vertebrates, fungi, nematodes, and certain groups of insects. For them, a countrywide or regional study, conducted rapidly in a pragmatic fashion, would be a desirable precursor to development projects, or the study should be conducted concurrently with it. Every country should have a national biological survey that would give it ready access to information about the distribution of economically important and ecologically indicative organisms. The implementation of such surveys is clearly a logical, worthwhile activity that deserves support by foreign-assistance funds.

The surveys would provide useful matrixes for ordering the information gained from the kind of short-range studies we advocate in connection with development projects.

Groups of organisms of potential economic importance ought to be screened rapidly for promising characteristics. For example, inventories should be made of groups of plants that have edible fruits or unique leaf chemistry, and the prospects for cultivating them, either directly or preceded by genetic improvement, should be evaluated promptly. Surveys should also be made of other groups of plants of potential importance as sources of drugs, insecticides, or other products. The materials should be evaluated and plants found to have the highest value cultivated and ultimately put into production.

Examples of the kinds of data needed in surveys of this type are presented in the following checklist. It would be advantageous to computerize such a data base in view of its dimension and complexity.

INVENTORY OF ORGANISMS: A MANAGER'S CHECKLIST

A. Inventory objectives: Gather information about a unit of habitat on which to base rational choices about use of natural resources contained in it. (Ffolliott, 1978)
   1. Multiple-use evaluation: Gather information that provides a basis for estimating present and future natural-resource products and uses.
   2. Estimate of benefits and costs: Gather information associated with implementation of management practices.
   3. Suitability determination: Information in the inventory should enable a decision-maker to determine suitability for any proposed end use or management practice.
B. Levels of activity (States, 1978)
   1. Literature review
   2. Researcher interviews
   3. Field observations and sampling strategies
   4. Integration with land-use planning or other aspects of development project
C. Plants
   1. Species composition and diversity; number of individuals and density; presence or absence, frequency, and distribution; relative importance and dominance (Chambers, 1980; Myers and Shelton, 1980)
   2. Vegetational aspects, such as area occupancy and cover; successional stage
   3. Sampling strategies: These strategies should account for variation in vegetation from place to place and specify acceptable level of precision.
   4. Screening of species for primary or secondary products: Special labs or local industries should be responsible for this activity.

D. Fauna (States, 1978)
   1. Abundance of species: Categorize as very common, common, rare, irreguar, present.
   2. Occurrence of species: Categorize as resident (found year round), seasonal, or unknown; specify where it breeds, if possible.
   3. Habitat and species status: On basis of changes anticipated, categorize as unaffected, benefited, or adversely affected.
   4. Habitat requirements: If enough information on species is available, categorize changes in habitat observed and predicted, and compare natural versus man-made environments.

Chambers (1980) listed several shortcut methods for gathering information on renewable natural resources for several types of development projects. Development planners, as nonspecialists in survey methodology, can take advantage of the expertise that exists throughout the world for various groups of organisms. The experts could assist them in design and implementation of appropriate inventories. Several recent works serve as examples (Hurlbert, 1977; Sims, 1980; Geesink et al., 1981). Also, special computer-linked documentation services are now available both nationally and internationally (CAB Abstracts, TROPAG, WATER LIT, AGRICOLA, AGRIS with FAO, and so on). Access to such facilities is sorely needed by users in tropical countries. All these efforts should be integrated within a reasonable renewable natural resources information model (Figure 3-1).

These activities—inventories of selected groups of organisms on a regional basis, and specific screening of groups of organisms with useful characteristics at a more intense level—should be accelerated in areas about to be altered by such major changes as large-scale water impoundments, extensive clearing associated with roadbuilding, and the development of intensive agriculture. The areas involved should first be sampled systematically, and the private or public interests engaging in development should provide the funds therefor. Not to do so is to lose, perhaps permanently, the opportunity to gain knowledge leading to better modes of development.

Enhancement of Local Capabilities

Only the scientists living in the countries where development is taking place have a long-term capability of making significant and sustained contributions to an understanding of the diversity of the organisms found in those countries (Budowski, 1975). Only they are able to make effective use of this information directly in influencing private or governmental action. Such scientists should be encouraged to study abroad, when appropriate, and to take advantage of foreign collections and libraries.

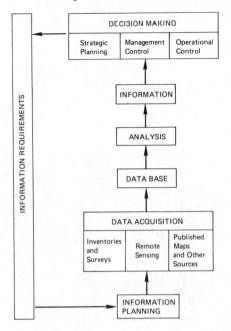

FIGURE 3-1   Renewable-natural-resources information model. From Gregory (1978).

The most significant contribution that the institutions of the temperate countries can make will be in building institutions capable of dealing with these problems on their own terms. According to Revelle (1980),

[I]f the developing countries are to control their own destinies, they must build scientific and technical establishments that can create and use technology based on their own comparative advantages. These enterprises are likely to be pale shadows of those in the developed countries unless they can leapfrog over the past into the science and technology of the future.... [I]n the production of foods and fibers, for example, agricultural technology based on land, water, and energy resources should be replaced by biologically based technologies, with emphasis on plant and animal genetics, increased photosynthetic efficiency, and protection against competing organisms. Equally obvious is the need for better biological technologies in preserving food, improving human health and nutrition, lowering human mortality, and controlling human fertility.

Weiss (1979) has contributed additional insights by stating,

[T]he fact that the technology which seems suited to a local situation is not used is a symptom of a deep problem. In the language of experimental science, technology is a probe which reveals issues that might otherwise have escaped capacity of individual institutions. But it is essential that the international structure does not swamp the fragile national institutions that it is supposed to serve.

He goes on to argue that basic research on a modest scale is a good investment for developing countries and that it ought ideally to be organized around local problems. Weiss demonstrates that there are many areas on which technology and the scientific enterprise of developing countries could profitably be focused in a way that would contribute immediately to their welfare.

The Role of Reserve Natural Areas

In considering natural preserves, selective attention should be given to ecosystems or regions that are being disrupted rapidly and permanently (NRC, 1980a,b). It is estimated (e.g., by Barney, 1980) that 15%–20% of all species on earth could become extinct within the next 20 years, mainly through loss of wild habitats in the tropics. A like percentage of the remaining species, or even more, could become extinct during the next century. To the extent possible, representative samples of tropical ecosystems should be set aside as focal points for detailed scientific studies because they retain certain options for the future. As a National Research Council (NRC, 1978) report phrases it, "The preservation of habitats is not only the most convenient means of maintaining gene pools of many species of unknown value; it is the only means of maintaining the germplasm of unknown organisms." In those ecological zones for which available development technology is conspicuously inadequate, development should be discouraged, perhaps by creation of reserves, so that development could be undertaken more rationally when adequate technology becomes available.

It can be assumed that the nature of research relating to energy and food production is about to change substantially. As Peter Ashton (Harvard University, personal communication, 1980) has pointed out, most of our research in the past has been based on the assumption that energy sources for mechanized farming, for fertilizers, for pesticides, and for hormone-mediated growth would remain abundant and cheap. We are now entering a situation where food crops are needed that remain productive, probably at the cost of higher labor intensiveness, and at lower energy demand. Novel and alternative sources of renewable energy and food must be sought and developed. Much could be done by encouraging the exchange of available crops between different tropical areas (see Chapter 5), an exchange that has been relatively limited in the past.

Integration of Renewable-Natural-Resource Surveys and Development Projects

The principal roles of renewable natural resource surveys in development projects are:

- to estimate the diversity and abundance of species, particularly mammals, birds, amphibians, reptiles, higher plants, freshwater fishes, and perhaps certain groups of insects, on the development site with special reference to rare and endangered forms
- to provide an opportunity during the early phases of site selection, survey, and preparation for intensive biological sampling of areas that will be substantially modified

Estimating species diversity and relative abundances of the more obvious components of the biota at a given site is difficult and arduous. Clearly, the most effective method is to employ a group of host nation naturalists to assemble preliminary species lists. Usually the local naturalists have some idea as to the status of rare and endangered species at the site. In most situations, preparation of a definitive list of species in a short time is probably beyond the abilities of any team of scientists, since many forms will be new to science and many groups do not have available specialists to assist with identifications.

In this phase, data must therefore concentrate on the occurrence and distribution of rare, endangered, hunted, trapped, and threatened animals, especially mammals and birds. As for plants, prime attention must be given to forest trees, which provide much of the structure and organization to the ecosystem. Estimates as to diversity and abundance of insect species are important and can best be made by light traps, ground traps, and sweep samples. When appropriate, a sampling of freshwater fish should be made to determine those that are rare or endangered, those normally used as food, or those threatened by environmental modification.

A development project can also contribute substantially to the inventory process if, as a built-in feature of site survey, selection, preparation, and modification, opportunities are provided for sampling the organisms of the area. In this manner, substantial new data can be accumulated on tropical species in areas where major changes are occurring.

ECOLOGICAL BASELINE STUDIES

The concept of ecological baseline studies derives from the principle that an organized quantitative review of any proposed development project is a necessary part of any planning process. The baseline study attempts to record key environmental factors in selected areas so that ecological parameters and concerns may be integrated with the design of the project at the beginning. In addition, ideally, subsequent ecological sampling at the baseline sample sites can provide information on project-induced changes in the environment that may aid in ameliorating subsequent difficulties and in providing guidance for action in future projects. For these reasons, it is most effective to utilize paired or comparable baseline analyses, one within the area of proposed development and a second in an adjacent area of similar environment that will not be affected.

Although the key environmental factors that require sampling and analysis at any terrestrial site are similar, humid tropical situations may require a much greater expenditure of effort than in temperate regions or less humid tropical areas. It is therefore important to focus on a series of indicator factors that show strong correlations with other features that cannot be measured or fully evaluated within the usual time frame and fiscal resources available for preproject evaluation. The peculiarities of humid tropical situations and the pressures for undertaking a particular development project require special attention to a minimum of key environmental indicators with strong predictive value. (See, in this connection, Appendix E.)

SUMMARY

Baseline studies and surveys of organisms and ecosystems are integral components of development projects, especially large-scale ones. Tropical organisms are very poorly known, only about one in six (500,000 out of an estimated 3 million) having been assigned names. Many species of plants, animals, and microorganisms make up the complex ecosystems of the humid tropics. An understanding of their individual properties and the ways in which they interact is of fundamental importance because of the need to improve utilization of individual species for particular purposes and to find ways in which the properties of the individual organisms affect the capacity of the ecosystem for change. National and regional surveys, particularly of species of known or presumed economic importance, should be set up to provide a framework or context into which data or questions from individual projects could be arrayed for efficient handling and maximum information content. These surveys, as well as the information developed in connection with individual projects, should be computerized. Such efforts should form an integral part of foreign assistance programs because of their general interest, economic importance, and potential in institution building.

REFERENCES

Barney, G. O. 1980. The global 2000 report to the President. A report prepared by the Council on Environmental Quality and Department of State. Vol. II, The technical report. U.S. Government Printing Office, Washington, D.C.

Böhlke, J. E., S. H. Weitzman, and N. A. Menezes. 1978. Estado atual da sistematica dos peixes de agua doce do America do Sul. Acta Amazonica 8(4):657-677.

Budowski, G. 1975. Scientific imperialism. Unasylva 27:24-30.

Chambers, R. 1980. Shortcut methods in information gathering for rural development projects. Paper presented at World Bank Agricultural Sector Symposium, January 1980. World Bank, Washington, D.C.

Day, P. R., ed. 1977. The genetic basis of epidemics in agriculture. New York Academy of Sciences, New York.

Ehrlich, P., and A. Ehrlich. 1981. Extinction: the cause and consequences of the disappearance of species. Random House, New York. 305 p.

Farnworth, E., and F. B. Golley, eds. 1974. Fragile ecosystems. Springer-Verlag, Berlin, Heidelberg, and New York. 258 p.

Farnsworth, N. R., and R. W. Morris. 1976. Higher plants: the sleeping giant of drug development. Am. J. Pharm. 148:46-52.

Ffolliott, P. F. 1978. A multifunctional inventory approach to multiple use analysis. Pages 395-402 *in* Integrated inventories of renewable natural resources. Proceedings of a workshop, Tucson, Arizona, January 1978. Gen. Tech. Rept. RM-55. U.S. Forest Service, Rocky Mountain Forest and Range Experiment Station.

Frankel, O., and M. Soulé. 1981. Conservation and evolution. Cambridge University Press, Cambridge. 327 p.

Geesink, P., A. J. M. Leeuwenberg, C. E. Ridsdale, and J. F. Veldkamp. 1981. Thonner's analytical key to the families of flowering plants. Vol. 5, Leiden Botanical Series. Leiden University Press, The Hague. 229 p.

Grainger, A. 1981. Rainforest survival tied to ecosystem research. World Wood (April 1981): 26-27.

Gregory, R. P. 1978. Integrated inventories in the Tennessee Valley region. Pages 412-419 *in* Integrated inventories of renewable natural resources. Proceedings of a workshop, Tucson, Arizona, January 1978. Gen. Tech. Rept. RM-55. U.S. Forest Service, Rocky Mountain Forest and Range Experiment Station.

Hurlbert, S. H., ed. 1977. Biota acuática de Sudamerica austral, siendo una recopilación de bibliografías taxónmicas referentes a la fauna y flora de aquas continentales del Sur de Sudamerica. San Diego State University, San Diego. 342 p.

Iltis, H. H., J. F. Doebley, R. Guzman M., and B. Pazy. 1979. *Zea diploperennis* (Gramineae): a new teosinte from Mexico. Science 203:186-188.

Maugh, T. H. 1981. A fish in the bush is worth . . . Science 211:1151.

Morán, E. F. 1981. Developing the Amazon. Indiana University Press, Bloomington. 292 p.

Myers, L. W., and L. R. Shelton. 1980. Survey methods for ecosystem management. John Wiley & Sons, New York. 403 p.

Myers, N. 1979. The sinking ark. Pergamon Press, New York. 307 p.

NRC (National Research Council). 1975. Underexploited tropical plants with promising economic value. National Academy of Sciences, Washington, D.C. 189 p.

NRC (National Research Council). 1978. Conservation of germplasm resources: an imperative. National Academy of Sciences, Washington, D.C. 118 p.

NRC (National Research Council). 1980a. Research priorities in tropical biology. National Academy of Sciences, Washington, D.C. 116 p.

NRC (National Research Council). 1980b. Conversion of tropical moist forests. National Academy of Sciences, Washington, D.C. 205 p.

Pimentel, D., E. Garnick, A. Berkowitz, S. Jacobson, S. Napolitano, P. Blank, S. Valdes-Cogliano, B. Vinzant, E. Hudes, and S. Littman. 1980. Environmental quality and natural biota. BioScience 30(11):750-755.

Revelle, R. 1980. Energy dilemma in Asia: the needs for research and development. Science 209:164-174.

Sims, W. R., ed. 1980. Animal identification. A reference guide. 3 vols. British Museum, London, and John Wiley & Sons, New York.

Soulé, M., and B. Wilcox, eds. 1980. Conservation biology: an evolutionary-ecological perspective. Sinauer Associates, Sunderland, Massachusetts. 395 p.

States, J. G. 1978. A practical approach to biological inventories for ecological baseline studies. Pages 447-453 in Integrated inventories of renewable natural resources. Proceedings of a workshop, Tucson, Arizona, January 1978. Gen. Tech. Rept. RM-55. U.S. Forest Service, Rocky Mountain Forest and Range Experiment Station.

Webster, B. 1981. Fish-forest interdependence found. The New York Times (Science Times), July 15.

Weiss, C., Jr. 1979. Mobilizing technology for developing countries. Science and Public Policy (October 1979):359-371.

4

Germplasm and Conservation of Genetic Resources

Germplasm represents the genetic potential of living organisms. Diversified germplasm allows organisms to adapt to changing environmental conditions. No individual of any one species, however, contains all the genetic diversity for that species. The genetic potential of a population is referred to as the gene pool.

Now that genetic engineering offers new potential for economic betterment, the mandate to maximize our options by maintaining the genetic resource base is clear (Figure 4-1). Germplasm is used to improve economically important plants and animals through selective breeding (OTA, 1981). The potential of genetic resources for tropical countries appears great, but more attention must be paid by concerned agencies to the preservation of germplasm on an international scale, especially in the tropics (AAAS, 1981).

With reasonable attention to maintenance, a given gene pool should last indefinitely, but genes can be maintained only in living systems. There are four devices for conserving genetic diversity:

- viable seed stored at low temperatures and humidities
- *ex situ* clonal repositories
- *in situ* populations in natural preserves
- *in vitro* cell lines

The sequence of generations is easily broken by such factors as human interventions and natural disasters that result in habitat destruction. Once

77

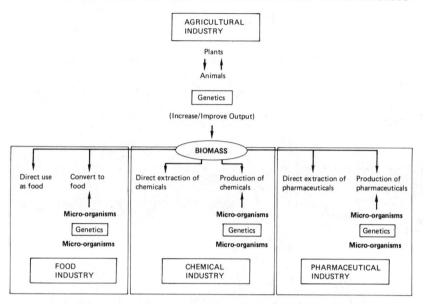

FIGURE 4-1   Applications of genetics. From OTA (1981).

lost, there is no way to recapture germplasm: extinction is forever. The banking of genes, unlike the banking of other resources, requires the foresight to maintain this living chain (Wilkes, 1977a).

Historically, human beings have used only about 5,000 plant species for food and fiber. At present, only about 150 species are used extensively; 3 species supply over half of all human energy requirements (Wilkes, 1981). (See Figure 4-2 and Table 4-1.) These few species are efficient in terms of space, water, and labor; flavorful; reasonably nutritious; and easily transported and marketed (Mangelsdorf, 1966). They stand between humans and starvation and should be the focus of attention regarding world germplasm conservation.

Each of the world's basic food plants originated in or (after being introduced) underwent a rapid evolution in a relatively confined geographic region. These regions overlap for a number of crops, but nine major and three minor centers in Asia, Africa, and the Americas (North, Central, South) have been identified as accounting for most of the genetic diversity in cultivated plants (Figure 4-3; Table 4-2). Often spoken of as Vavilov Centers, after the noted Russian plant breeder and geneticist, these valuable reservoirs of crop plant germplasm are rapidly disappearing because of extensive modification of habitats and the extension of industrialized agriculture.

CONCERN FOR GERMPLASM

The very existence of the Vavilov Centers of diversity in the tropics is being threatened today by rapidly expanding human populations, increased demand for agricultural land, destruction of natural vegetation, and worldwide changes in agricultural technology. Cultivated plants have not always existed as genetically uniform populations growing in monocultures on carefully tended field plots. In the past, agriculture met human demands for increased food by habitat rearrangement (see Chapter 6) and by breeding for high production and genetic uniformity. Because environments are constantly changing as insect pests or plant diseases threaten, or as climate changes in the longer term (Jackson, 1977), agriculture must rely on the continued input of genetic diversity. As for crops indigenous to the humid tropics (Table 4-2), opportunities for continued input of diversity are dwindling because the wild plants from which the domesticated plants were derived are threatened by the forces mentioned above. The varieties,

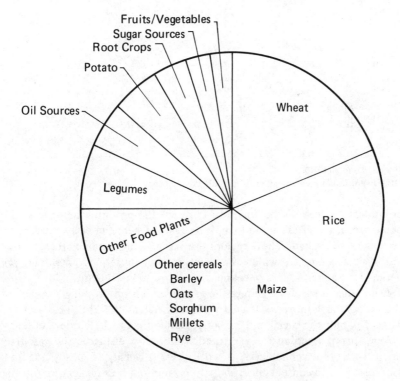

FIGURE 4-2 Human calorie sources from plants.

TABLE 4-1   Major Global Crop Harvest (First 25 Crops by Weight)

	Production[a] (millions of metric tons)	Approx. Water (%)	Protein (%)	World Calories (%)	World Protein (%)[b]
Wheat	360	10	12.1	21.1	27.9
Rice	320	10	6.1	20.3	12.5
Maize	300	10	8.2	18.8	15.7
Potato	300	75	1.4	3.3	2.7
Barley	170	10	8.7	10.4	9.5
Sweet potato	130	70	1.2	2.1	1.0
Cassava	100	70	0.5	1.5	0.3
Sorghum	50	10	7.0	2.9	2.5
Millet	45	10	8.9	2.6	2.6
Grape	60	75	0.5	0.6	0.2
Soybean	60	10	30.8	4.3	11.8
Oats	50	10	12.9	3.4	4.1
Sugar cane	50	70	0	0.6	0
Banana	35	70	0.7	0.4	0.2
Tomato	35	90	1.0	0.1	0.2
Sugar beet	30	70	0	0.4	0
Rye	30	10	10.9	1.8	2.1
Orange	30	80	0.7	0.2	0.1
Coconut	30	50	3.2	1.8	0.6
Apple	20	80	0.1	0.2	0
Yams	20	70	1.6	0.3	0.2
Peanut	20	10	23.0	2.0	2.9
Watermelon	20	95	0.2	0	0
Cabbage	15	90	1.0	0.1	0.1
Onion	15	90	1.2	0.1	0.1

[a]Baseline is FAO (1976).
[b]It is assumed that these are all consumed directly by people.

or cultivars, closest to the ancestral form are the primitive land races still being grown in certain humid tropical regions where the crops have been very long established. These regions are the genetic resource areas, or living bank accounts, to which the plant breeder must turn for additional germplasm, a step that is becoming more and more difficult.

Over large areas of the tropics the genetic uniformity of a few varieties is displacing the hundreds of local varieties (Wilkes, 1977b). This process raises a paradox in social and economic development: the product of technology (plant breeding for yield and uniformity) displaces the resource upon which the technology is based (genetic diversity of locally adapted land races). As a consequence, short-term solutions become long-term irreversible liabilities.

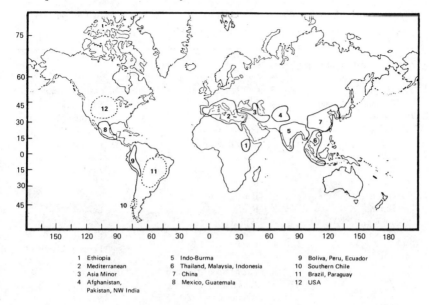

1 Ethiopia
2 Mediterranean
3 Asia Minor
4 Afghanistan, Pakistan, NW India
5 Indo-Burma
6 Thailand, Malaysia, Indonesia
7 China
8 Mexico, Guatemala
9 Boliva, Peru, Ecuador
10 Southern Chile
11 Brazil, Paraguay
12 USA

FIGURE 4-3   Centers of origin and variability of cultivated plants. After Vavilov (1935).

CONSERVATION OF GENETIC RESOURCES

Practical Solutions

Management Options

Genetic resources can be divided into four major groupings, in terms of decreasing intensity of management (Frankel and Hawkes, 1975; Frankel and Soulé, 1981):

- cultivated plants and domesticated animals
- wild relatives of domesticated plants and animals
- wild species used directly by people
- wild species of no current use to people

Cultivated plants include such tropical crops as plantains, yams, taro, cassava, sugar cane, cowpeas, and peanuts, which account for approximately 15% of the calories consumed by people worldwide and for more than 50% of the calories consumed by people in the tropics. Domesticated tropical animals include various breeds of cattle and buffalo, swine, and fowl.

Wild relatives of domesticates hold great genetic potential. For example,

TABLE 4-2   Vavilov Centers of Origin of Some Cultivated Crops (Asterisks Mark Crops Originating in the Humid Tropics)

Centers in Africa and Asia

1. *Ethiopia*
   *Banana (endemic)
   Barley
   Castor bean
   *Coffee
   Flax
   Khat
   *Okra
   Onion
   Sesame
   Sorghum
   Wheat

2. *Mediterranean*
   Asparagus
   Beets
   Cabbage
   Carob
   Chicory
   Hops
   Lettuce
   Oats
   Olive
   Parsnip
   Rhubarb
   Wheat

3. *Asia Minor*
   Alfalfa
   Almond (wild)
   Apricot (secondary)
   Barley
   Beets (secondary)
   Cabbage
   Cherry
   Date palm
   Carrots
   Fig
   Flax
   Grapes

3. *Asia Minor* (cont.)
   Lentils
   Oats
   Onions (secondary)
   Opium poppy
   Pea
   Pear
   Pistachio
   Pomegranate
   Rye
   Wheat

4. *Central Asia (Afghanistan, Pakistan, NW India)*
   Almond
   Apple (wild)
   Apricot
   Broad bean
   Cantaloupe
   Carrots
   Chickpea
   Cotton (*G. herbaceum*)
   Flax
   Grapes (*V. vinifera*)
   Hemp
   Lentils
   Mustard
   Onion
   Pea
   Pear (wild)
   Sesame
   Spinach
   Turnips
   Wheat

5. *India, Burma*
   Amaranths
   *Betel nut
   *Betel pepper

5. *India, Burma* (cont.)
   Chickpea
   Cotton (*G. arboreum*)
   *Cowpea
   Cucumber
   *Eggplant
   *Hemp
   *Jute
   Lemon
   Millets
   *Citrus
   *Pepper (black)
   *Rice
   *Sugar cane (wild)
   *Taro
   *Yam

6. *Thailand, Malaysia, Indonesia*
   *Banana
   *Betel palm
   *Breadfruit
   *Coconut
   *Ginger
   *Citrus
   *Sugar cane (wild)
   *Tung
   *Yam

7. *China*
   Adzuki bean
   Apricot
   Buckwheat
   Chinese cabbage
   *Cowpea (secondary)
   Kaoliang (sorghum)
   Millets
   Oats (naked)
   *Orange (secondary)

TABLE 4-2 *(Continued)*

7. *China* (cont.)
   *Paper mulberry   *Soybean
   Peach   *Sugar cane (endemic)
   Radish   *Tea
   Rhubarb

Centers in the Americas

8. *Mexico, Guatemala*	9. *Peru, Ecuador, Bolivia*	10. *Southern Chile*
Amaranths	Bean (*P. vulgaris*)	Potato
Bean (*P. Vulgaris*)	Bean (*P. lunatus*)	Strawberry
Bean *(P.*	*Cacao	(Chilean)
multiflorus)	Corn (secondary)	
Bean (*P. lunatus*)	Cotton (*G.*	
Bean (*P.*	*barbadense*)	11. *Brazil, Paraguay*
acutifolius)	*Edible roots or	*Brazil nut
Corn	tubers such as	*Cacao
*Cacao	oca, ullucu,	(secondary)
*Cashew	arracacha	*Cashew
Cotton (*G.*	Guava	*Cassava
hirsutum)	*Papaya	Mate
*Guava	Pepper (*Capsicum* spp.)	*Para rubber
*Papaya	Potato (many species)	*Peanut
Pepper (*capsicum* spp.)	*Quinine	*Pineapple
*Sapodilla	Quinoa	
Sisal	Squash (*C. maxima*)	12. *United States*
Squash	Tobacco (*N. tabacum*)	Sunflower
*Sweet potato	Tomato	Blueberry
Tobacco (*N. rustica*)		

a recent improvement in resistance of peanuts to leafspot has been of enormous economic benefit (Wilkes, 1981). This needed resistance was found in wild forms (such as *Arachis monticola, A. batizoçoi,* and *A. vilosa*) from the tropical forest of Amazonia and has an annual value estimated by the International Crops Research Institute for Semi-Arid Tropics (ICRISAT) at $500 million (U.S.). In another instance, two species of wild green tomatoes, *Lycopersicon chmielewskii* and *L. parviflorum,* discovered in an isolated area of the highlands of Peru in the early 1960's, have contributed genes for marked increase in fruit pigmentation and soluble-solids content worth nearly $5 million (U.S.) per year to the tomato-processing industry (Iltis, 1981). Similar large-scale benefits of wild-relative germplasm could be documented for the tropical crops of

TABLE 4-3   Priorities for Further Germplasm Collections for Food Plants of the Humid Tropics (First Two Groups) as Listed by the International Board for Plant Genetic Resources [a,b]

Priority Groups	Americas	Africa	Asia	Pacific
First	Maize	Finger millet	Finger millet	Breadfruit
	Phaseolus beans	Starchy banana and plantains	Coconut	Sugar cane
	Tree fruits and nuts	Rice (*O. glaberrima*)	Sugar cane	Yam
	Vegetables	Coffee	Maize	Taro
	Cassava	Tree fruits and nuts	Starchy banana and plantains	Coconut
	Sweet potato	Vegetables	Rice	Starchy banana and plantains
		Cassava	Tree fruits and nuts	
		Sweet potato	Vegetables	
			Sweet potato	
Second	Peanut	Cowpen	Peanut	
	South American oil palms	Bananas	Chickpea	
	Cocoa	Bambara groundnut	*Vigna* spp.	
			Winged bean	
			Bananas	
			Cassava	
			Soybean	

[a] IBPGR (1981).
[b] Three additional priority groups (third, fourth, fifth) are listed by IBPGR.

rubber, coconuts, and oil palm (Frankel and Soulé, 1981) and for tropical forage species (CIAT, 1980).

Wild species used by people include a much larger array than is commonly recognized (Wetterberg *et al.,* 1976; De Vos, 1977; Wetterberg, 1980): Brazil nuts, freshwater fishes and prawns, mushrooms, timber, medicinal plants, and many others. There are obvious commercial outlets for bird plumage and reptile skins, primates for biomedical research, and numerous extracts used in medicine.

Biome or habitat conservation of species not currently known to be useful (Prescott-Allen, 1981) is perhaps the most important in the long run. This is also the most difficult for the nonecologist to appreciate (CEQ, 1980; Soulé and Wilcox, 1980). The most obvious place to discover new crops is to look in new places. Although it is doubtful that any new major crop plant will be found in Europe or North America, it is entirely likely that one or more might be found in the humid tropical forests.

Support from Ongoing Efforts

One of the simplest and most cost-effective ways to assist humid tropical countries in preservation of genetic resources is to support the ongoing efforts of major international institutions, especially the International Board for Plant Genetic Resources (IBPGR) and the International Union for the Conservation of Nature and Natural Resources (IUCN), by expanding their activities in pertinent areas.

The IBPGR is an autonomous, international, scientific organization operating under the aegis of the Consultative Group on International Agricultural Research (CGIAR). The IBPGR was established in 1974 and its executive secretariat is provided by the Food and Agriculture Organization of the United Nations. The basic function of the IBPGR is to promote an international network of genetic resources centers to further the collection, conservation, documentation, evaluation, and use of plant germplasm. Tables 4-3 and 4-4 and Appendix Tables 7-9 list selected crop species that deserve attention by the development community.

IUCN is an independent, international organization with a membership derived from sovereign states and international and national agencies, whose purpose is to promote the conservation of wildlife species and their habitats. Through its World Conservation Strategy, formulated in 1980 (IUCN, 1980), it hopes to maintain essential natural processes and life-support systems, preserve the genetic diversity essential for protecting and improving cultivated plants and livestock and for scientific and medical purposes, and sustain species and ecosystems that support productive rural communities and major industries.

TABLE 4-4 Crops of Special Importance to the Humid Tropics and Their Priority Groups, as Listed by the International Board for Plant Genetic Research[a]

Crops	Priority
Cereals	
Sorghum	Priority 2 generally; priority 1 in Africa and parts of Southeast Asia
Finger millet	Priority 2 generally; priority 1 in Africa and Asia
Grain amaranth	Priority 3 generally; priority 2 in Andean zone
Rice	Priority 2 generally; priority 1 in areas of India, Indochina, and the Pacific
Maize	Priority 3 generally; priority 1 in northeast Brazil, Venezuela, and the Guyanas
Food legumes	
Phaseolus beans	Priority 1 generally
Groundnut	Priority 2 generally; priority 1 in South Asia, Southeast Asia, and Central America
Soybean	Priority 2 generally; priority 1 in Indonesia and parts of Southeast Asia
Cowpea	Priority 2 generally; priority 1 in South Asia and West Africa
Yardlong bean	Priority 2 generally; priority 1 in Southeast Asia
Winged bean	Priority 2 generally; priority 1 in Pacific and South and Southeast Asia
Grams (*Vigna radiata; V. mungo*)	Priority 2 generally; priority 1 in South and Southeast Asia
Bambara groundnut (*Voandzeia*)	Priority 3 generally; priority 2 in West Africa
Dolichos and *Lablab* species	Priority 4 generally
African yam bean	Priority 4 generally
Root and tuber crops	
Cassava	Priority 1 generally
Sweet potato	Priority 1 generally
Yam	Priority 3 generally; priority 1 in the Pacific
Taro and aroids	Priority 4 generally; priority 1 in the Pacific
Minor South American tuber crops	Priority 4 generally; priority 1 in Andean zone
Minor African tuber crops	Priority 4 generally
Starchy fruits	
Starchy banana and plantain	Priority 2 generally; priority 1 in Pacific, Southeast Asia, and West Africa

TABLE 4-4   *(Continued)*

Crops	Priority
Breadfruit and jackfruit	Priority 3 generally; high priority in South and Southeast Asia; priority 1 in Pacific
Oil crops	
Coconut	Priority 2 generally; priority 1 in Southeast Asia and Pacific
Oilseed brassicas	Priority 2 generally; priority 1 in South Asia
Oil palm	Priority 3 generally; priority 2 in restricted areas of South America
Sugar crops	
Sugar cane	Priority 2 generally; priority 1 in Pacific and South and Southeast Asia
Rubber	
Rubber (*Hevea brasiliensis*)	Priority 2 generally
Beverages	
Coffee	Priority 1 generally
Cacao	Priority 2 generally; priority 1 for Criollo varieties
Tea	Priority 4 generally
Tree fruits and nuts	
Banana	Priority 2 generally; priority 1 in Southeast Asia
Citrus	Priority 2 generally; priority 1 in South and Southeast Asia
Mango	Priority 2 generally; priority 1 in Southeast Asia
Avocado	Priority 3 generally; priority 1 in Central America; priority 2 in Andean zone
Cashew	Priority 3 generally; priority 2 in South Asia
Papaya	Priority 3 generally; priority 2 in Central America and Andean zone
Lansium, durian, and rambutan	Designated for further study generally, priority 1 in Southeast Asia
Annona and *Passiflora*	Designated for further study generally; priority 1 in Andean zone
Vegetables	
Tomato	Priority 1 generally
Leaf amaranths	Priority 2 generally; priority 1 in West Africa and South and Southeast Asia

TABLE 4-4 *(Continued)*

Crops	Priority
Brassicas (*campestris, juncea, oleracea*)	Priority 2 generally; priority 1 in South and Southwest Asia
Cucurbits	Priority 2 generally; priority 1 in Latin America
Eggplant	Priority 2 generally; priority 1 in South and Southeast Asia and West Africa
Okra	Priority 2 generally; priority 1 in the Pacific
Onion	Priority 2 generally
Pepper (Chili)	Priority 2 generally; priority 1 in Latin America and South and Southeast Asia
Radish	Priority 2 generally
Bitter gourd	Priority 3 generally; priority 1 in Southeast Asia
Sokoyokoto (*Celosia argentea*)	Priority 3 generally
Bottle gourd	Priority 4 generally; priority 2 in Latin America
Carrot	Priority 4 generally
Chaya (*Cnidoscolus chayamansa*)	Priority 4 generally
Chayote (*Sechium edule*)	Priority 4 generally; priority 1 in Central America
Cucumber (*Cucumis sativus*)	Priority 4 generally
Fluted pumpkin (*Telfairia*)	Priority 4 generally
Indian or Ceylon spinach (*Basella alba*)	Priority 4 generally
Kangkong (*Ipomoea aquatica*)	Priority 4 generally; priority 1 in Southeast Asia
Lettuce	Priority 4 generally
Muskmelon, cantaloupe	Priority 4 generally
Watermelon	Priority 4 generally
Spinach	Priority 4 generally

*a*IBPGR (1981).

THE ROLE OF SPECIES DIVERSITY IN TROPICAL DEVELOPMENT

Whereas genetic diversity is a measure of the variety of genes in a population, species diversity is a measure of the variety of species in a habitat.

Species diversity in the humid tropics offers many utilitarian benefits, although much yet remains to be discovered (CEQ, 1980). Some examples follow.

The tropical moist forest almost certainly contains many new wild relatives of modern food plants (bananas, peanut, pineapple, cassava, cacao, coffee, rubber, yams, and many oil and fiber palms) that are still unknown. Once discovered, they may be used by plant breeders. During this century genetic materials from the wild have saved several important tropical crops, including bananas, sugar cane, cacao, and coffee.

Species diversity also makes possible wholly new uses for plants. Examples here are the fish poisons—derived from *Derris* spp. (Asian moist tropics) and *Lonchocarpus* spp. (American moist tropics)—which are the basis of many insecticides.

Pharmaceuticals are often chemically complex, and the likelihood of finding plants with complex chemistry is much better in the moist tropics than elsewhere (Moreno Azorero and Schvartzman, 1975; Myers, 1979). Examples include the 3,000 plant species known to possess anticancer properties, 70% of which are from the humid tropical forests (Wilkes, 1981).

Given future needs, genetic resources can be reckoned among society's more valuable raw materials. The fundamental issue, however, is that the greatest genetic diversity is in the humid tropics *now*. Any reduction in the diversity of resources narrows the scope of society's response to new problems and opportunities. To the extent that we cannot be certain what needs may arise in the future, it makes sense to keep options open and take into account the preservation and maintenance of genetic diversity in the humid tropics.

PRIORITY RESEARCH NEEDS

It is not possible to set aside sufficient primary tropical ecosystems to conserve all the genotypes of organisms in these systems. Nothing short of preserving all remaining primary humid tropical ecosystems could stop the extinction of species, estimated to be occurring at the rate of one to three per day (CEQ, 1980). Most of the genotypes could not receive full attention for decades. Indeed, careful scientific study of certain systems and components of special interest, over a long period, may be warranted even at the expense of ignoring other systems entirely.

Support for biological research must be so oriented that the information of greatest benefit, both in terms of conserving the ecosystems and in terms of prospective human values, receives due priority. Furthermore, the results of such research must be put to use promptly.

Relevant topics for ecological research that could well be supported by development agencies are listed below in order of decreasing priority:

1. The biological basis for sustainable land-use systems that preserve and utilize germplasm resources

- integrated, multipurpose forest management system
- diversified crop, pasture, and agroforestry systems
- supplementary collection and storage of germplasm

2. Comparative data on and predicted biological values of different primary ecosystems as criteria in ranking them for preservation

- synthesis of existing knowledge as a basis for classifying remaining ecosystems in terms of the relative urgency of their conservation
- further assessment of diversity, fragility, and rarity as parameters for ecosystem conservation priorities
- identification and location of genotypes or genotypic groups especially worthy of study as a basis for improved conservation priorities

3. The role of human intervention with regard to the germplasm resources of primary ecosystems

- relative vulnerability of various ecosystem components to various degrees of intervention, from hunting and gathering, through selective timber extraction, to burning, cultivation, and pasturing
- the significance of land-use patterns as a factor in the survival of the germplasm resources of primary ecosystems—size, shape, and proximity of modified areas
- secondary ecosystems as a fallback source of germplasm

4. Genetic diversity as an environmental imperative

- diversity as a source of stability of ecosystems and of site productivity
- diversity as a prerequisite for the conservation of germplasm
- diversity as a source of human knowledge and values

SUMMARY

Germplasm represents the genetic potential of living organisms and the raw material for breeding of new varieties of plants, animals, and microorganisms. Genes are the biological information that allows organisms to "unlock" and survive in particular environments. No one individual possesses all the genetic diversity for that species; the total genetic potential or gene pool is contained only in populations. Diversified germplasm allows populations to adapt to changing environmental conditions both spatially and over time. Human activities, such as hunting, gathering, or lumbering, habitat modification, and intensive agriculture all decrease genetic diversity. The genetic diversity of a gene pool is the foundation for biological renewable resources such as agriculture and forestry. At present, only about 150 species of plants and a smaller number of animals stand between the human race and starvation. Germplasm in the humid tropics is a matter of concern for two reasons. First, the source areas of many of these useful animal and plant gene pools are contracting and disappearing; second, the genetic uniformity of a few cultivated plants and domesticated animals is displacing the genetic diversity of hundreds of local varieties. The potential of genetic resources for humid tropical countries appears great, provided the germplasm base is not eroded by inappropriate management. Without greater attention by concerned agencies and institutions to the preservation of germplasm on an international scale, the potential of the gene pools in the tropics will continue to contract.

REFERENCES

Anonymous. 1979. Consulta sobre los recursos fitogenéticos de los países circundantes del Caribe. Plant Genetic Resources Newsletter 39:23. Published by International Board for Plant Genetic Resources, Rome.

AAAS (Ameican Association for the Advancement of Science). 1981. Recommendations of the genetic engineering expert panel, AAAS. American Association for the Advancement of Science, Washington, D.C.

CEQ (Council on Environmental Quality). 1980. Environmental quality—1980. The eleventh annual report of the Council on Environmental Quality, Washington, D.C. 497 p.

CIAT (Centro International de Agricultura Tropical). 1980. Beef program. Annual report for 1979. CIAT, Calí, Colombia.

De Vos, A. 1977. Game as food. Unasylva 29(116):2–12.

FAO (Food and Agriculture Organization). 1976. Production yearbook, 1975. Vol. 29. FAO, Rome.

Frankel, O. H., and G. J. Hawkes, eds. 1975. Crop genetic resources for today and tomorrow. Cambridge University Press, Cambridge. 492 p.

Frankel, O. H., and M. Soulé. 1981. Conservation and evolution. Cambridge University Press, Cambridge. 327 p.

IBPGR (International Board for Plant Genetic Resources). 1981. Revised priorities among crops and regions. International Board for Plant Genetic Resources, Rome. 17 p.

Iltis, H. H. 1981. The National Science Foundation, the Reagan Administration, and wild green tomatoes. Manuscript. 15 p.

IUCN (International Union for the Conservation of Nature and Natural Resources). 1980. World conservation strategy. IUCN, Gland, Switzerland.

Jackson, J. J. 1977. Climate, water and agriculture in the tropics. Longman, New York. 248 p.

Mangelsdorf, P. C. 1966. Genetic potentials for increasing yields of food crops and animals. Pages 66–71 *in* Prospects of the world food supply: a symposium. National Academy of Sciences, Washington, D.C.

Moreno Azorero, R., and B. Schvartzman. 1975. 268 plantas medicinales utilizades para regular la fecundidad en algunas países de Sudamerica. Reproducción 2:163–183.

Myers, N. 1979. The sinking ark. Pergamon Press, New York. 307 p.

NRC (National Research Council). 1980. Research priorities in tropical biology. National Academy Press, Washington, D.C. 116 p.

OTA (Office of Technology Assessment). 1981. Impacts of applied genetics: micro-organisms, plants, and animals. Office of Technology Assessment, Congress of the United States, Washington, D.C. 331 p.

Prescott-Allen, R., and C. Prescott-Allen. 1981. *In situ* conservation of crop genetic resources. A report to the International Board for Plant Genetic Resources from the International Union for the Conservation of Nature and Natural Resources. IUCN, Gland, Switzerland. 145 p.

Soulé, M., and B. A. Wilcox, eds. 1980. Conservation biology: an evolutionary–ecological, perspective. Sinauer Associates, Sunderland, Massachusetts. 395 p.

Vavilov, N. I. 1935. The phytogeographic basis of plant breeding. Pages 13–54 *in* The origin variation, immunity, and breeding of cultivated plants: selected writings of N. I. Vavilov (translated from the Russian by K. Starr Chester). Chron. Bot., vol. 13, 1949/50. Chronica Botanica, Waltham, Massachusetts.

Wetterberg, G. B. 1980. A case study: Brazil's wildlife management and conservation program. Paper presented at international workshop on wildlife management in developing countries, National Forest Institute, Peshawar, Pakistan, November 1980. 23 p.

Wetterberg, G. B., M. Ferreira, W. Luiz dos Santos Brito, and V. Campbell de Araujo. 1976. Amazon fauna preferred as food. FAO Technical Report 6. Brasília, Brasil. 17 p.

Wilkes, H. G. 1977a. The world's crop plant germplasm—an endangered resource. Bull. Atmos. Sci. 33:8–16.

Wilkes. H. G. 1977b. The green revolution. Pages 41–47 *in* D. Lapedes, ed. McGraw-Hill encyclopedia of food, agriculture and nutrition. McGraw Hill Book Co., New York.

Wilkes, H. G. 1981. New and potential crops, or what to anticipate for the future. Paper presented at the annual meeting of the American Association for the Advancement of Science, January 1981, Toronto, Canada.

SUGGESTED READING

Frankel, O. H. 1977. Genetic resources. Pages 332–344 *in* P. R. Day, ed. The genetic basis of epidemics in agriculture. New York Academy of Sciences, New York.

Harlan, J. R. 1977. Sources of genetic defense. Pages 345–356 *in* P. R. Day, ed. The genetic basis of epidemics in agriculture. New York Academy of Sciences, New York.

Harlan, J. R., and K. T. Slacks. 1980. Germplasm resources and needs. Pages 253–273 *in* F. G. Maxwell and P. R. Jennings, eds. Breeding plants resistant to insects. John Wiley & Sons, New York.

Knott, D. R., and J. Dvorak. 1976. Alien germplasm as a source of resistance to disease. Annu. Rev. Phytopathol. 14:211–235.

Leppik, E. E. 1970. Gene centers of plants as sources of disease resistance. Annu. Rev. Phytopathol. 8:323–344.

NRC (National Research Council). 1978. Conservation of germplasm resources: an imperative. National Academy of Sciences, Washington, D.C. 118 p.

Sprague, G. F. 1980. Germplasm resources of plants: their preservation and use. Annu. Rev. Phytopathol. 18:147–165.

Zeven, A. C., and P. M. Zhukovsky. 1975. Dictionary of cultivated plants and their centres of diversity. Centre for Agricultural Publishing and Documentation, Wageningen, Netherlands, 219 p.

5

Agriculture in the
Humid Tropics

Half of the world's population is engaged in agriculture, the vast majority in the tropics and subtropics. Their agricultural practices are highly diverse, ranging from peasant and tenant small plots (shifting cultivation through to wet rice culture) to plantation export crops (Grigg, 1969, 1974; Duckham and Masefield, 1970; Manshard, 1974; Ruthenberg, 1976). In this chapter, evolutionary and ecological concepts relevant to tropical agricultural development are summarized (Tosi and Voertman, 1964; Bowonder, 1980; Dickinson, 1981).

From an ecological perspective, farming entails a rearrangement of the ecosystem, usually leading to increased productivity of useful materials. Its origins can be traced back at least 8,000 years (Helbaek, 1959; MacNeish, 1964; Ucko and Dimbleby, 1969). There were at least five, and probably more, independent centers of origin of farming systems (Ames, 1939; Vavilov, 1950; Zeuner, 1963; Sauer, 1965; Chang, 1970; Harlan, 1971). Most agriculture involves clearing of land and the establishment of such less mature ecosystems as annual crops (Anderson, 1952; Smith, 1974). Productivity depends on modification of the environment (e.g., soil preparation, irrigation, and weeding) and on genetic changes that accompany domestication of animals and plants (Parodi, 1938; Sauer, 1952; Epstein, 1955; Schwanitz, 1966).

AGRICULTURE AS REARRANGEMENT
OF THE ECOSYSTEM

Any farming system shortens and simplifies a food chain. The crucial question is: How much modification can the ecosystem tolerate and still retain its capacity for sustained production? Any agricultural activity, to be successful, should meet the following criteria:

• The system must be productive (caloric yields must be greater than human energy expended in tending the crop) and economically profitable.
• Subsistence crops or food purchased in the market must be nutritious, although balanced nutrition on the table is sometimes as much a function of actions taken in the kitchen as of the plants grown in the field.
• Yields must be relatively stable year in and year out; a cropping system must therefore be such as not to build up disease epidemics and insect plagues, or deplete the soil, or lower the water table, or erode the land excessively (Wilkes, 1977a,b).

The first criterion is easiest to measure and is the most frequently taken as the mark of success; it is basically the same for tropical as for temperate agriculture. Annual production is used as the measure rather than the longer-term turnover time necessary for regaining fertility in shifting agriculture.

Nutritional adequacy, in many parts of the tropics, is difficult to assess at the present time, because knowledge of dietary interactions, food fermentations, and complementary foods for many truly tropical diets is inadequate (Getahum, 1974; Majer, 1976; Hesseltine and Wang, 1980). Most schemes to improve the diets of tropical peoples have stressed such yield-responsive grasses as rice, wheat, and corn, and not other crops such as beans, taro, plantains, cassava, sweet potatoes, yams, winged bean, pigeon peas, and coconuts, which latter group have responded more slowly to efforts at yield improvement. In fact, the tropics contain many less known crops that have not been examined in any systematic way (Appendix Table 9; Parlerm, 1967; Kay, 1979; Gottlieb, 1981). They are less known not because they are inherently inferior crops, but because they are essentially unfamiliar to many agricultural research institutions.

Yield stability is probably the most difficult to measure because we know so little about these issues in tropical environments (Janzen, 1973; Horn, 1974; Richards, 1977).

PRODUCTIVITY OF TROPICAL AGRICULTURAL SYSTEMS

Shifting Cultivation

Shifting agriculture is the one farming system indigenous to the humid tropics of Africa, Asia, and Latin America.

ECOLOGICAL CONCEPT

Yield

Yield refers to the rate at which an ecosystem produces useful products. Yield is usually a fraction of the ecosystem's net primary productivity. One objective of management is to maximize yields by channeling as much net production to the product in question as is possible. Thus a forester may be interested in wood yield, a farmer in the yield of potatoes, a fisherman in the yield of fish. Managers use a variety of terms to refer to different aspects of yield. Each term denotes how it is calculated and how the system is managed to obtain such a yield. Examples are:

Sustained yield: yield that can be maintained over long periods without significant reduction in rate of production
Maximum sustainable yield: a term used in fisheries biology, or other population management sciences, to describe the maximum harvest possible in populations of fish, or other wildlife, or trees, that are subjected to management; such yield is calculated from mathematical models of population growth phenomena
Optimal yield: yield calculations that take into account social, ecological, and economic factors

The yield of an ecosystem is closely related to its primary productivity and this, in turn, to the carrying capacity of the environment. Thus, it is important to consider these two factors when making yield calculations or when projecting yield. Excessive harvesting may lead to exhaustion of the resource. Examples of this resource decline are abundant in fisheries, in avian populations, and in selected tree species.

Ideally, resources are managed for optimal yield according to the following guidelines:

• estimates of the maximum productivity of the ecosystem through estimates of primary productivity rates
• analyses of the food chains, or life support systems, leading to the resource in question in order to provide estimates of potential energy transfers from primary producers to target species
• analyses of all factors acting on the managed species, including the physical, chemical, and human factors that affect productivity
• analyses of social and economic pressures on the ecosystem
• energy analyses for each yield-producing activity

Although now largely confined to the tropics of the Americas, Asia, and Africa, historically it has also been known in Europe and North America. Each region has its unique elements; in general, they follow the pattern of use here described. The following list indicates the diversity of these systems:

Asia

ladang (Indonesia, Malaysia)
jumah, humah (Java)
ray (Vietnam)
tam-ray, rai (Thailand)
hay (Laos)
kaingin (Philippines)
chena (Sri Lanka)
karen (Japan, Korea, Taiwan)
bewar, dhya, dullee, dippa,
    erka, jhum, kumri, penda,
    pothu, podu (India)

Latin America

milpa (Mexico, Central America)
ichali (Guadaloupe)
coamile (Mexico)
roca (Brazil)
conuco (Venezuela, Dominican
    Republic)
chacra (Peru, Bolivia, Ecuador)

Africa

masole (Zaire)
tavy (Madagascar)
chitimene, citimene (Rhodesia,
    Tanzania, Zaire)
proko (Ghana)
bush fallow (West Africa)

More than 240 million people living at or near the subsistence level practice shifting agriculture. They cultivate small patches of cleared land in tropical forests, which are for the most part located on the poorer soils (UNESCO, 1978a). Fields are cut out of secondary (usually) or primary forests leaving only the largest trees standing. Felled vegetation is burned at the onset of the rains, and the crops (seed and root) are planted with a minimum of soil preparation. After one or two harvests, the plot is abandoned, or a third cropping may take place before the site is allowed to regenerate a vegetative cover (FAO, 1957). There are three reasons for shifting the field plots: deceased soil fertility, weed buildup, or pest outbreak.

Although the yearly plots of shifting agriculturists are small (1–2 hectares), the total land tied up in shifting cultivation is enormous because of the lengthy fallow period. It is estimated that shifting cultivators in the tropics tie up twice the area (33 million km^2) used by temperate continuous cropping systems (Manshard, 1974).

Under biologically stable conditions, a shifting agriculture site may not be reutilized for up to 70 years, but under increased pressure of limited land and increasing populations fallow periods have decreased to generally unacceptable levels, averaging perhaps less than 5 years (Bartlett, 1956; Corner, 1960; Brown, 1971). These shorter cycles do not allow enough forest regeneration to restore soil fertility levels adequate for sustained agricultural productivity (Figure 5-1). Stripped of their vegetative cover, the soils of these short-fallow fields are often highly erodible, particularly immediately after abandonment (Cook, 1921; Whittlesey, 1937; Conklin, 1961; Clarke, 1966; Spencer, 1966; Walter, 1971).

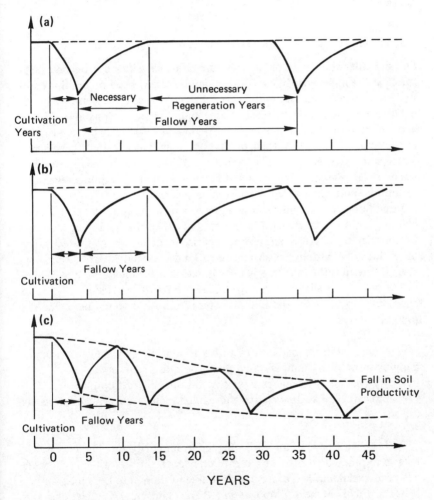

FIGURE 5-1 The relation between length of fallow and soil productivity in shifting cultivation. From Ruthenberg (1976).

Shifting agriculturalists of the tropics have traditionally been hunters, eating a wide variety of animals (snakes, monkeys, large rodents, birds, insects, and fish). Many shifting cultivators still hunt and fish for part of their protein requirement, and in point of fact the secondary forest created by shifting cultivation is often more productive of wild animal resources than is the primary forest. The animals that shifting cultivators husband are usually pigs, goats, tropical sheep, chickens, and ducks; they are scavengers of rough food (root, peels, stems, insects) not used by the household.

Constraints to Shifting Cultivation

Shifting cultivation is stable at low population densities but becomes unstable at the higher densities. As more land is used, weed populations and weed seed pools increase, and forest barriers to pest movement are eliminated. The population increase in the moist tropics is pushing shifting agriculture toward land shortage. Only now are we achieving alternative agricultural systems other than plantation crops that will allow permanent agriculture (Greenland, 1975; Sanchez, 1977; UNESCO, 1978a,b; Harwood, 1979). Research on sustained farming systems as viable alternatives to shifting cultivation should receive high priority.

In addition to the biological components of a productive tropical agriculture, a number of social dimensions that affect the quality of life must be considered. There is a sense of security in doing things the way they have always been done (slash-and-burn land clearing, interplanting, terracing), because the outcome is known and new technologies, new economies, and new social orders introduce uncertainties. Historically, most agricultural policies for the humid tropics from the colonial period to the present consisted of:

- reorganization of agriculture with the aim of increasing its productivity by introducing temperate crops to the moist tropics
- construction of a transport system and opening of forests
- application of technology to the exploitation of natural resources as exports

Such policies have emphasized higher productivity but not necessarily long-term productivity. To attain this latter goal, there is still considerable need for research aimed especially at problems unique to the moist tropics (Chang, 1968; Gómez-Pompa et al., 1972; Janzen, 1973; Nations and Nigh, 1980).

Clearly, although shifting agriculture is tedious, heavy work, indiscriminate mechanization (see Chapter 7) does not appear to be the route to sustained productivity.

Cultivated Land as an Ecosystem

In subsistence agriculture, the individual cultivator (family), the land that is cultivated, and the immediate surrounding area constitute the unit of management. Therefore, it should be viewed as both a human-oriented habitat reconstruction and an economic unit of production (Harris, 1969; Higgs and Jarman, 1969; Blum, 1971; UNESCO, 1978a). Although this unit is goal-oriented, decision-making can be extremely complex, involving not only economic but social or political factors. Ultimately, management decisions tend to seek either prestige or family survival (Hernandez-X, 1970). The preference of most cultivators is to manage toward a steady state, but their trial-and-error means of adapting traditional agricultural practices in a gradually changing environment is inadequate to deal with the rapid environmental change brought about by increasing population and externally created market pressures. The customary response has been to shorten the fallow period, to increase purchased inputs, to move toward a monoculture and to create the most favorable conditions for growth. Shifting cultivation adaptations, on the other hand, involve site assessment (soil, slope, amount of weed growth), the genotype of the crops, the organization of the cropping sequence (mixed cropping, sequential planting, and next year's rotation), and the concept of how long to fallow the land. These management systems maximize resources but are not elastic enough to accommodate increasing population. In subtropical (dry savannas) and high elevations in the tropics, the gradual intensification of land use has culminated in permanent cultivation. The general trend from shifting agriculture to permanent land use is usually accompanied by a number of changes, such as the following:

- from long-fallow to short-fallow systems
- from short-fallow systems to permanent land use
- from low-intensity labor crops to high-intensity labor crops
- from natural grazing to cultivated fodder
- from rain-fed farming to irrigated farming
- from planting of perennial crops to annuals or plantation crops
- from multiple cropping to single crop
- from the natural regeneration of soil fertility by fallow to intensive systems of manuring and fertilizing

- from hoe-cultivation to animal traction or tractors
- from traditional production methods to increasingly high-technology methods involving an increasing volume of purchased inputs

But in the humid tropics, except for systems that mimic the forest ecosystems such as tree plantations, shelter wood systems (tree canopy), and in some places wet rice, it is extremely difficult to find systems without such external inputs as fertilizer that are more productive of labor and soil than the low-density shifting cultivation of the past. Shifting agriculture will not support a high density of people (neither the Mayan cities nor Angkor Wat were long-lasting) that characterized the cereal-based agriculture that developed in Meso-America (maize, beans, squash), the Near East (wheat, barley, peas), and China (rice, soybeans, vegetables) (Dobby, 1955; Watters, 1960; Dumond, 1961; Dunn, 1975).

HUMID TROPICAL AGRICULTURE AS VEGECULTURE/POLYCULTURE

Historically, humid tropical agriculture has been more vegeculture than cereal-based. Unique crops originated in both the New and Old Worlds (Safford, 1905; Merrill, 1941; Barrau, 1958; Bennett, 1961; Chang, 1970). The earliest farming system in Southeast Asia was tropical vegeculture based on such root and tuber crops as yams and taro, tree crops such as coconut and banana, and wild fruits and leaves. Vegetable propagation and streamside fishing (hunting with fish poisons) expanded to the south and east through Malaysia, where breadfruit and sago palm were added. Today, this cultivation can still be seen in its furthest extension into Melanesia and Polynesia. Rice cultivation came after vegeculture and had spread into southern China, east into India, and southward into the Malaysian archipelago by 3,000 B.C.; it had not spread into Melanesia or Polynesia by 1650.

In the Americas, vegeculture developed with cassava, sweet potatoes, arrowroot, and peanuts and moved up the eastern slopes of the Andes to give rise to a whole new set of plants: oca, ulluco, anu, arracacha, and ultimately the potato. These crops and others diffused quickly throughout the tropics of the Old World, introduced first by the Portugese and then the Spanish (Sauer, 1950; Dressler, 1953; Heiser, 1965; Cutler, 1968).

In Southeast Asia, vegeculture almost certainly preceded seed (rice) agriculture. This is less certain for the Americas (maize) and is in some doubt for tropical Africa south of the Sahara. In West Africa, vegeculture with indigenous yams and the oil palm has long been practiced along the margin between tropical forest and the savanna (UNESCO, 1978b). A second and entirely different agriculture has developed around millet and sorghum, probably independently, in Ethiopia and the Sudan. The intensity of agricultural practices in tropical Africa does not match that of the Americas or Southeast Asia, and until 2,000 years ago little penetration of the humid tropical zone had taken place. Substantial penetration did not take place until the nineteenth century with the introduction of steel tools and the diffusion of Asian and American crops (cassava especially, because of the pest resistance of bitter manihot) (Greenway, 1944; Irvine, 1949; Davies, 1960; Miracle, 1964; Payne, 1964; Morgan, 1968; Seddon, 1968; NRC, 1974).

The progression of agricultural practices from shifting cultivation to short rotation, to mixed farming, to the specialization of continuous cropping has supported an expanded population. Today wet rice supports the highest densities of people in the humid tropics, especially in the Far East. It is currently being adopted in humid tropical Africa, where previously bananas, cassava, maize, and yams were grown on a long-fallow rotation basis (Manshard, 1974). Unlike some other crops of the moist tropics, wet rice is tolerant of a wide range of soil and other environmental conditions if supplied with sufficient water. A unique aspect of standing water is that it acts as a mimic of the natural vegetation cover in that the soil is protected from high temperatures, rain does not result in erosion, and the puddling of water restricts vertical movement of nutrients (Sanchez, 1973). The growth of such N-fixing crops as *Azolla* spp. and blue-green algae before rice planting and of confined fish after planting adds nutrients to the soil.

ANIMAL PRODUCTS

Wild, feral, and domestic pigs, chickens, ducks, cattle, water buffalo, goats, and tropical sheep are the mainstay of the meat and fowl available for people in the humid tropics. A variety of animals (sometimes dubbed "bushmeat") are available to hunters in the less populated areas (Ajayi, 1971; Heymans and Maurice, 1973; Asibey, 1976; Wetterberg *et al.*, 1976). These include monkeys, reptiles, birds, and amphibians. Insects are also considered delicacies in certain areas and make a small contribution to the diet of local people. In most areas of the humid tropics, aquatic animals, including crayfish, crocodiles, and caimans (or alligators), are also important elements of the diet (see Chapter 8).

Although considerable attention is given to the development of new plant species for food and fiber, animals (other than cattle) as sources of protein are frequently overlooked in development enterprises (De Vos, 1977). Traditional thinking centers on species that have been domesticated for millenia. Some redirection of activities should be devoted to domestication of

Number of humid (or dry) months	10–12 (0–2)	9–10 (2–3)	7–9 (3–5)	3½–6 (6–8½)	2–3½ (8½–10)	1 (11)	0 (12)
Mean annual precipitation in mm	Mainly > 2000 mm	Mainly > 1500 mm	Mainly > 1000 mm	750 – 1000 mm	> 400 mm	Under 400 mm	
Schematic graph of annual rainfall	Axim 2103 mm	Tafo 1658 mm	Tamale 1081 mm	Kano 846 mm	400 mm	200 mm	
Examples:	Rubber, Tropical timbers	Oil palm, Cocoa, Coffee	Yams	Cotton, Millet, Ground-nuts	Ground-nuts		
Typical economically useful plants							
Simplified transect sketch							
Plant-geography terms (Manshard, 1960)	Wet evergreen forest (rain forest)	Partly deciduous seasonally green wet forest (monsoon forest)	Wet savanna (with galleried and riparian forest)	Dry savanna	Thorn-bush savanna	Semi-desert	Desert

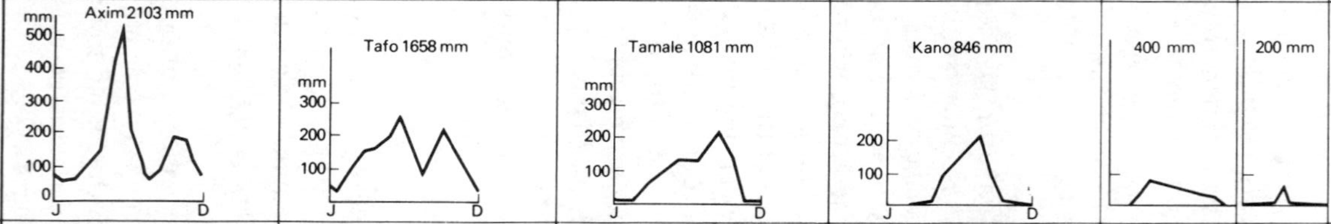

FIGURE 5-2 Schematic summary of tropical vegetation formations and major crops that have become associated with them. After Manshard (1974).

species that may be potentially more efficient at converting vegetation to animal protein than cattle are (Den Hartog and De Vos, 1973) and to development of game cropping for efficient harvesting of animal protein from wild vertebrate populations (Ojasti and Medina Padilla, 1972). Modest efforts are under way in Costa Rica to domesticate the paca (*Cuniculus paca*), but the potential for other species should be explored (T. Yuill, University of Wisconsin, personal communication).

EXPORT CROPS

Generally, export crops have been plantation crops. The most valuable, which can be grown only in the tropics, include coffee, cacao, coconuts, bananas, rubber, oil palm, and spices (especially cloves, nutmeg, and cardomon cinnamon); such fiber crops as jute and manila hemp; and such nut crops as cashews. Others that can be grown in the subtropics include tea, cotton, sugar cane, pineapple, tobacco, peanuts, and some oil seeds such as tung. All these have been the basis of plantation culture in the humid tropics and have a long history of use there, but their importance as items of trade arose during the period of European expansion (Burkhill, 1938; Wickizer, 1958; Purseglove, 1963). Figure 5-2 shows those climatic regions where selected export crops are best grown. In many regions of the humid tropics, plantation tree crops have evolved as the most economically useful crops (Manshard, 1974).

Plantation crops, historically, have been associated with low population densities, cheap labor, and large capital outlay, e.g., bananas in Central America, sugar in the West Indies, rubber in Malaya. Today, many of these crops are produced by small landholders: cacao in Ghana, bananas in Ecuador, coffee in Colombia. In all, about 5% of the world's cropland is in plantation crops in the moist tropics (Ruthenberg, 1976).

Many of the poorer people in the humid tropics look to these crops as cash crops and as their key to economic well being. Unfortunately, export crops are both capital-intensive and require finely tuned husbandry skills (Khan, 1961). The fluctuating pricing structure for these crops on the world market, in general, works against the small producer. The traditional plantation crops are tree crops (rubber, coconuts, oil palm, cacao, coffee, and spices) and herbaceous perennials treated as trees (bananas, manila hemp, and black pepper). The longer growth cycle of perennials introduces new aspects to agricultural management. In the case of most plantation crops, there is a lengthy period before the first harvest, following that is a period of maximum yield (up to 100 years in the case of coconuts), then a decline in productivity. The period of economic dependency before a cash crop can be harvested requires either that the crop be a secondary crop if on a family landholding (cacao in West Africa), or that a large corporation finance the operation (coffee fincas in Guatemala). The decision to increase holdings must be made years before the crop starts to bear, and even after it bears the producer is subject to price fluctuations because short-term changing of crops is not possible. The crop usually requires considerable attention: pruning and picking of coffee, tapping of rubber, stripping and drying of cinnamon bark. Capital investment for processing is often needed (the more quickly and uniformly many plantation crops are processed, the more desirable the product), as well as good transport and communication systems between producer and buyer. Many of these tree plantations mimic the natural vegetation (the extreme case is coconuts, which may be the climax natural cover), providing continuous ground cover and a protective overstory. Because most plantation crops end up in either Europe, Japan, the United States, or Canada, they are, for many decision-makers, the crops that typify the tropics.

LINKAGES BETWEEN TROPICAL AND TEMPERATE ZONES

The productivities of Temperate-Zone and tropical agriculture were essentially comparable before the age of discovery and circumnavigation, with its subsequent diffusion of major crops, livestock, and farming techniques (Grigg, 1969). Today, tropical agriculture, with the exception of certain plantation crops and wet rice, is less productive than Temperate-Zone agriculture in terms of unit area per person engaged in farming. The economic developments of the last hundred years that have accompanied industrialization, urbanization, and commercialization in the temperate zone, characterized by modern transportation networks, farming technologies, and improvements in plant breeding, have revolutionized its agriculture. Five factors stand out:

- use of fertilizer for more intensive cropping
- use of monocultures that require elaborate and expensive pest and disease management systems
- accurate timing of planting, irrigation, and harvest
- institutional support such as credit, pricing systems, and transportation to market
- mechanization and energy-intensive technologies such as grain drying and refrigerated transport

In many instances, when these technologies are transferred to the humid tropics results have not been very impressive (Grigg, 1969, 1974; IRRI, 1972; Janzen, 1973; Pimentel et al., 1973; Pimentel and Pimentel, 1979).

In the agriculture of Europe and North America, the agrarian evolution stretched over centuries (Brothwell and Brothwell, 1969; Struever, 1971; Renfrew, 1973). Two major stages were apparent: the medieval three-field rotation system (White, 1970) and energy-intensive field production (Arnon, 1963). Today, a similar transformation is rapidly taking place in the humid tropics, with but little time for the type of trial-and-error experimentation that occurred in the Temperate Zone. In an attempt to exploit local resources and feed an expanding population, the tropics are employing many direct technology transfers: herbicides, pesticides, mechanization, and fertilizers.

Fundamental differences between temperate and tropical agriculture should be carefully scrutinized before development projects attempt simple transfer of technology (Table 5-1). Alternatives that produce more stable and productive systems should be sought. The most stable agricultures are those that mimic the natural vegetative cover. The change from grasslands to wheatfields, or from deciduous forest with a 5-month

TABLE 5-1   Contrast Between Temperate-Zone and Humid Tropical Agriculture

Conditions and Practices	Temperate-Zone Agriculture	Humid Tropical Agriculture
Controlling factors	Mostly physical	Mostly biological
Growing season	3–8 months	12 months
Dieback, frost, aridity	Common	None
Deforestation (land clearing)	Customary	Partial
Bare soil present	Common	Ideally none
Changes in water relationships	Common	Common
Nutrient cycle	Open	Partly open
Annuals and perennials	Quick annuals (3 months)	Perennials and annuals (more than 5 months)
Dominant crops	Seed	Vegetative, root, and seed
Year-to-year fluctuation in production	Wide variance	Little variance
Labor factor in productivity	Machine-intensive	Hand-labor-intensive
Planting density	High	Low
Field structure	Monoculture	Polyculture
Diversity of genotypes	Low	High
Competitors	Few	Many
Storage of products	Long-term	Short-term (fungi and pests abundant)
Individual biomass	Low	High
Food chains	Short	Long, complex
Cropping pattern	No stratification of fields	Multicropping

growing season to cornfields in the Temperate Zone, may be less extreme than most of the high-technology agricultures that are transferred to the tropics.

NUTRITION IN THE HUMID TROPICS

Currently there is a rapid movement away from the millenia-long situation, wherein the cultivators ate the crops they cultivated. Each of the major centers where agricultural systems have evolved has domesticated plant resources rich in proteins. These proteins are to be found either in storage organs such as fruits and seeds or in the actively growing tissues such as the leaves of vegetables (Herklots, 1972).

The shift to crops for sale is lowering the nutritional quality of crops grown in many parts of the tropics (Lappe and Collins, 1979). The result of this trend has been a decrease in production of many legume crops (20–35% protein) and leafy vegetables and their replacement in the human diet by cereals (7–14% protein) that are responsive to abundant fertilizer and water (Wilkes, 1977b).

For adequate human nutrition, it is necessary to strike a balance between proteins and calories. Many tropical agricultures and household cooking styles evolved to maximize the available protein sources. This natural selection promoted the cultivation of complementary protein plants such as maize (deficient in lysine and methionine) and beans (deficient in cystine) in Meso-America and of wheat (deficient in lysine and typtophan) and curded milk in the Near East and South Asia. In addition, it promoted the development of cooking styles that maximize the amount of digestible protein in the final product, such as refried beans and quick-fried vegetables. And it led to development of fermented or partly digested plant products, such as beers from sorghum in Africa and soybean curds in the Far East, and the supplementation of cultivated carbohydrate-rich root crops with trace nutrients from wild-collected pot herbs for gruels, sauces, and soups. At present we know less about the mechanisms that promote nutrient adequacy and balance in these indigenous tropical agricultures than we know about those mechanisms for most Temperate-Zone crops (Gopalan *et al.*, 1978).

STABILITY OF TROPICAL AGRICULTURAL SYSTEMS

For the human race, most of the caloric margin between survival and starvation consists of rice, wheat, maize, sorghum, barley, potatoes, sugar cane, sugar beet, cassava, bananas, coconuts, peanuts, common beans, and soybeans. The worldwide human diet is even more specialized than

ECOLOGICAL CONCEPT

CARRYING CAPACITY AND POPULATION GROWTH

Carrying capacity is an ecologic attribute of the environment. It refers to the number of individuals of a given species that can be stably sustained by that environment. That a population will stabilize within its environmental constraints has been demonstrated in laboratory experiments with microorganisms.

Such microorganism populations behave in the following fashion:

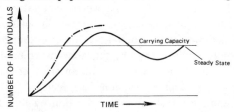

The solid line depicts a population that has stabilized with its environment at a number of individuals defined as the *carrying capacity* for that organism in the environment. At steady state, the number of new individuals entering the population by birth or immigration is exactly compensated by the number of individuals dying or emigrating. Steady state is established because:

• Birth rates decline (in accord with the rate at which new food enters the environment) as largely unexploited initial reserves of foodstuffs are used up.

• Death rates increase as a large population accumulates toxic wastes that are insufficiently removed from the environment.

Usually a period of population fluctuation is required for establishment of steady state because of time-lag in the adjustment responses of birth and death rates to environmental changes induced by the population. If the time-lags are sufficiently long (as in the dash–dot line in the above figure), a population may so overshoot carrying capacity that all individuals receive too little food and too many wastes accumulate, resulting in drastic population decline.

Populations of organisms in nature do not always conform to the stereotypical behavior of laboratory organisms. However, a sufficient number of animal populations have been observed in nature to confirm this model as reasonable. Departures from theoretical population behavior occur because natural environments are far more complex than laboratory situations. Organisms in nature experience greater time-lags in birth- and death-rate adjustments to their environment.

this implies. Over 60% of the human caloric intake from plants is attributed to the cereals; rice alone accounts for half the daily calorie requirements of half the world's population, i.e., one-quarter of total human caloric intake.

In general, this extreme dependence on a small number of plants has come about since the industrial revolution and has accelerated rapidly with the application of modern technology since the 1950's. Not only did our dependence on a decreasing number of basic food plants increase, but emphasis shifted from crops-to-eat to crops-to-sell. The Green Revolution of the late 1960's speeded this process throughout the tropics. Today, many minor food plants that were once nutritionally important locally no longer exist in native tropical agriculture. Acreage in legume crops has decreased as cereal acreage increased. Diet is being influenced more by the labor/yield economic equation than by the labor/nutritional-balance equation. The full implications of this loss in protein and nutritional balance in tropical agriculture are just now becoming appreciated.

If efforts to eliminate hunger and malnutrition by the end of this century are taken seriously, food production must increase at least threefold, in view of the current maldistribution of food supplies and projected population increases (Wilkes, 1977a,b). To reach this goal, there is strong incentive to promote agricultural technology in the tropics without really knowing or assessing adequately the system that the technology replaces.

Except for the Chinese system of relay planting and alternate growth strategies, systems are just now being developed as alternatives to continuous cultivation in the moist tropics. There is good potential in using diverse crops and improved germplasm (of crops other than rice) to develop several new farming systems that mimic natural ecosystems (Barton, 1960; Budel, 1966; Dalrymple, 1971; Leakey and Wills, 1977; Sanchez, 1977; Okigbo, 1980).

Continuous cropping by systems of intercropping, companion planting, and relay planting are possible because of the continuous growth conditions through 12 months of the year. Such systems would more closely mimic the original vegetation. Mixed cropping also protects the soil from both erosion and baking by the sun. Polycultures ensure against crop failure, because the effects of environmental variables and various hazards are spread out over several different crops and the likelihood of collapse is decreased (Browning, 1975). In sequential cropping (serial planting), the harvest is spread over a prolonged period, and both early- and late-maturing varieties can be used to further reduce the risk of failure in any particular crop. Also, many root and vegetative crops are best stored in the ground or field until used, which achieves an economy of labor, although it exposes the soil at critical times. Since the field is under

ECOLOGICAL CONCEPT

CARRYING CAPACITY AND HUMANS

The density of people and their standard of living are functions of the carrying capacity of the environment (see CARRYING CAPACITY AND POPULATION GROWTH, page 107). Using knowledge and technology, people are able to raise the natural carrying capacity of the environment by supplementing local ecosystems through the importation of energy and resources. These subsidies make possible the support of a larger human population and higher standards of living than would be achieved with the local natural environment alone. However, it should be realized that:

• The higher carrying capacity will be sustained only as long as a steady supply of energy and resources is available to maintain it.
• The geographic region that gains in carrying capacity does so at the expense of a carrying capacity loss in other regions from where resources and energy are exported.
• With any lowering in the availability of energy or resources, carrying capacity will decrease in proportion.
• If the local natural-resource base is for any reason degraded during the period of carrying capacity expansion, natural carrying capacity will be lower after the external subsidies are withdrawn.

constant management, minor crops used only for sauces or as greens (and possibly medicinal herbs) can be harvested continuously and used fresh. Such intensive labor in the field can optimize the harvest by taking it at full maturity, facilitating assessment of the genetic potential of each clone for replanting, keeping the soil litter low and decreasing the buildup of pest populations, and staggering the planting time of the next crop. If many root crops are used, they can exploit different levels of the soil; intercropped legumes can do the same and in addition supply nitrogen to the companion crop (NRC, 1979). A pictorial representation of a polycultural system is presented in Figure 5-3.

Polyculture in humid tropical agriculture is in a sense a microreproduction of the natural plant cover of the region (Brookhaven National Laboratory, 1969; May, 1973). One such integrated element is dispersed horticultural plantings (Terra, 1954; Rasmussen, 1960; Jong *et al.,* 1973; Soemarwoto *et al.,* 1975). Single specimens of a particular variety of a seasonal fruit-bearing tree are often planted around house sites to serve as indicators for other widely dispersed trees of the same variety in the regenerating forest on old shifting-cultivation sites, which still belong to the fam-

FIGURE 5-3 Hypothetic polycultural agroecosystem. From *The Evolution of Economic Society: An Introduction to Economics*, by Martin Gerhard Giesbrecht. W. H. Freeman and Company. Copyright © 1972.

ily that planted them, however long ago. The large number of exceptional and underexploited fruits in both Southeast Asia and the American tropics attest to lack of attention (Dodds, 1963). Tropical fruits are a neglected resource. Many of the New World fruits have not diffused to the Old World, and the lesser fruits (other than citrus and bananas) of Southeast Asia are not found in the Americas.

The potential for research with tropical legumes is substantial (Barton, 1960). They are the most important daily protein source in many tropical countries. About 75% of the world's food legumes are grown and consumed in tropical countries (Ruthenberg, 1976). The other major plant protein source in many of these diets is local leafy vegetables, mostly cultivated (Grubben, 1977; Martin and Ruberté, 1979). Stream fishing and hunting were, and in many areas still are, important animal protein sources.

Because 75% of the world's lesser crops are grown and consumed in tropical countries, the industrial nations have tended to ignore them both as nutrition sources and as germplasm resources for the future (Wulf and Maleeve, 1969; NRC, 1975).

With the exception of the chicken, pig, and water buffalo, the major animal domesticates have originated in the arid grasslands or grassland/forest zones, primarily in the Near East. The mix of wet rice and fish is of long standing in the humid tropics, but other mixes of cropping and livestock (coconuts and cattle, for instance) are of recent origin. Considerable research is possible with animal-and-crop mixes. Export cattle production in the moist tropics is of considerable economic importance in the New World and marginally so in Asia and Africa (Phillips, 1961; Zeuner, 1963).

PRIORITIES FOR AGRICULTURAL DEVELOPMENT

Improving the Plants of the Humid Tropics

The plant-breeding arsenals for Temperate-Zone plants and tropical plants are very different. The migration of European peoples around the world spread temperate crop varieties to diverse habitats far from where they originated. The only migrations of tropical peoples were as cheap laborers, not free farmers: Africans to the Americas (sugar cane and cotton), Tamils to Ceylon (tea) and Malaya (to tap rubber). No substantial exchange of tropical crops (plantation crops excepted) has taken place since the early introductions of the Portuguese and Spanish. Despite the potential of tropical American plants for the Old World (avocados for one), and Old World plants for the New, there is no systematic exchange or experimentation with acclimatization (CIMMYT Review, 1980).

Until very recently, the payoff from plant breeding of tropical crops (except for rice and some plantation crops) has been small. The agricultural stations needed to test the acclimatization of crops and to carry out variety trials are very sparse. Promising candidates for intensive-breeding experiments include: tropical yams (Africa, Asia, the Americas); pigeon peas, cowpeas, and other legumes; tropical palms (oil palm excepted); crops designed specifically for companion planting (legume and root crops) and plantings that improve tropical soils; Asian and New World minor fruit trees and *N*-fixing crops for wet rice cultivation. More complete lists are found in Appendix Tables 7-9 (see also Hutchinson, 1958; IBPGR, 1981).

The humid tropics have neither the agricultural schools nor the extension field station systems that characterize the Temperate Zone. Because most tropical countries cannot maintain large independent programs, emphasis should be placed on a freer and more abundant interchange of research information and materials.

RESEARCH NEEDS

Agricultural research in the humid tropics should recognize the variety of habitats (Chapter 2) and species available for cultivation (Appendix Tables 7-9), the increasing human population, and the shrinking proportion of people engaged in agriculture. Increasing population will, in the future, require greater surpluses of food, particularly for transport to ever-growing urban areas.

For West Africa, Albrecht and Vallaeys (1977) have outlined major gaps in research that the Committee feels are appropriate to other regions. In general terms, increased effort in the following areas is required:

• exchange of research information and techniques
• application of successful research to other areas
• interdisciplinary problem-solving in government and research institutions

In specific terms, the following areas deserve high priority:

• research to raise fertility levels, particularly on the acid infertile soils, in a cost-effective manner in order to encourage orderly transition from shifting to more permanent agriculture
• crop improvement through plant breeding and selection of cultivars

that offer potential for transfer throughout the humid tropics (Appendix Tables 7–9 list many of these species and varieties.)

• protection of the germplasm of potential crop species and varieties through the establishment of facilities for maintenance thereof

• research on agroecosystems and farming systems in addition to single-crop species

• development of methods to address malnutrition through qualitative screening of plant materials for total protein, specific essential-amino-acid, and micronutrient content

AGRICULTURE AND CONSERVATION

The incorporation of conservation objectives must be included in future agricultural planning for the tropics. Clearly, the demographic increases and technological progress of people in the tropics are restructuring natural ecosystems. The establishment of shifting-agriculture zones around national parks and reserve natural areas will serve as buffer zones and preserve shifting cultivation as a system. Properly designed, these areas have potential for attracting tourists.

Given present trends, the tropics will probably be the most altered regions of the globe in the twenty-first century. Without attention to conservation, the result may be irreversible erosion of genetic resources of the region, a decrease in the resilience of the existing systems, and diminution of the public-service function of vast tracts of tropical forest (Walter, 1971; Arasu, 1975; Whitmore, 1975; Brazier *et al.*, 1976; Kemp *et al.*, 1976; Sommer, 1976; Opler *et al.*, 1977; Wilkes, 1977b; Marshall, 1978; Soulé and Wilcox, 1980; Prescott-Allen and Prescott-Allen, 1981).

SUMMARY

Half the world's population is engaged in agriculture, mostly in the tropics and subtropics. Their agricultural practices are very diverse; some are traditional and some modern. From an ecological viewpoint, all these farming systems represent rearrangements of the ecosystem, usually leading to increased productivity of useful materials. Most agriculture involves the clearing of land and the establishment of a less mature ecosystem. Productivity usually derives from modification of the environment (e.g., soil preparation, irrigation, and weeding) and on genetic changes that accompany the domestication of animals and plants.

Farming systems restructure a food chain by shortening and simplifying it. The crucial ecological question is: How much modification can the ecosystem tolerate and still retain its capacity for sustained production?

ECOLOGICAL CONCEPT

TERMS USED IN TROPICAL AGRICULTURE

Farm System: A farm system is a collection of distinct functional units, such as crop, livestock, processing, investment, and marketing activities, that interact because of joint inputs they receive from the environment, deliver their outputs to the environment, and have the common objective of satisfying the farmer's (decision-maker's) aims. The definition of the borders of the system depends on circumstances. Often it includes not only the farm (economic enterprise), but also the household (in farm-and-household systems).

Rotational System: Time-bound use of land.

Continuous cropping: One crop planting following soon after harvest, without seasonal fallowing. Continuous cropping may be achieved by sequential cropping or relay-planting techniques.

Multiple cropping: The growing of more than one annual crop on the same land in one year (Harwood, 1979). Multiple cropping has the following subclasses: sequential cropping; ratooning; intercropping, including relay planting.

Crop Mixtures: Any type of crop combination grown at a given time.

Double-cropping: Two crops are grown per year on one field, one after the other.

Intercropping: The growth of two or more crops in different but proximate, usually alternate, rows.

Interplanting: Seeding or planting a crop into a growing stand.

Mixed cropping: Two or more crops are grown simultaneously in the same field at the same time.

Relay planting: A maturing annual or biennial crop is interplanted with seedlings or seeds of the following crop. Relay planting is a subclass of intercropping, so long as both are on the same field.

Sequential cropping: One crop is planted after the other without in-between fallowing. Sequential cropping may take the form of double-cropping or triple-cropping.

Special Cropping Patterns

Monoculture: 1. (agronomic definition): A sole stand of one crop is repeatedly followed by the same crop. 2. (economic definition): Only one crop is grown on the farm.

Wet rice: Rice grown with artificial irrigation (water led to the field or water impounded in the paddy field) and deep-water rice.

At the present time, our fund of knowledge is such that this question cannot be fully answered in many areas, but with good management skills and appropriate technology it is possible to achieve sustainable production for the current population of the humid tropics. If current patterns continue, however, there is risk of progressive deterioration as the human population in the moist tropics increases. Nations with limited capital are the ones that can least afford to underutilize or overutilize the products and services offered by natural and managed ecosystems. Accelerated research is needed to develop alternative farming systems to replace short-fallow shifting cultivation. Research on sustained farming systems as a viable alternative should receive high priority. It should be possible, in the humid tropics, to develop new farming systems that use diverse crops and improved germplasm, especially for some of the neglected resources such as tropical fruits, the palms, some of the leafy vegetables, and combinations of animals and plants.

REFERENCES

Ajayi, S. S. 1971. Wildlife as a source of protein in Nigeria: some priorities for development. The Nigerian Field 36(3):115-127.

Albrecht, H. R., and G. Vallaeys. 1977. Research strategies. Pages 1-5 *in* C. L. Leakey and J. B. Wills, eds. Food crops of the lowland tropics. Oxford University Press, London.

Ames, D. 1939. Economic annuals and human cultures. Botanical Museum, Harvard University, Cambridge, Massachusetts.

Anderson, E. 1952. Plants, man and life. Little Brown and Company, Boston.

Arasu, N.T. 1975. Conservation and utilization of genetic resources in agricultural research in Malaysia. Pages 241-246 *in* J. T. Williams, C. Lamoureaux, and Wulijarni-Soetjipto, eds. Plant genetic resources in Southeast Asia. National Biological Institute, Bogor, Indonesia.

Arnon, I. 1963. The transition from primitive to intensive agriculture in a Mediterranean environment. World Crops 15:126-134.

Asibey, E. O. A. 1976. The effects of land use patterns on future supply of bushmeat in Africa south of the Sahara. Working party on wildlife management and national parks, Fifth Session. FO:AFC/WL:76/6/4. FAO, Rome. 9 p. Mimeographed.

Barrau, J. 1958. Subsistence agriculture in Melanesia. Bull. 2189. Bernice P. Bishop Museum, Honolulu.

Bartlett, H. H. 1956. Fire, primitive agriculture and grazing in the tropics. Pages 692-720 *in* W. L. Thomas, ed. Man's role in changing the face of the earth. University of Chicago Press, Chicago.

Barton, D. W. 1968. Horticultural germplasm: its exploration and preservation. Hortic. Sci. 3:241-243.

Barton, T. F. 1960. Growing rice in Thailand. J. Geogr. 37:12-29.

Bennett, D. C. 1961. The basic food crops of Java and Madura. Econ. Geogr. 37:12-29.

Blum, J. 1971. The European village as a community: origins and functions. Agric. Hist. 45:157-178.

Bowonder, B. 1980. Environmental management and the Third World. Science and Public Policy (June):185-198.

Brazier, J. D., J. F. Hughes, and C. B. Tabb. 1976. Exploitation of natural tropical forest resources and the need for genetic and ecological conservation. *In* J. Burley and B. T. Styles, eds. Tropical forest trees: variation, breeding and conservation, Academic Press, London.

Brookhaven National Laboratory. 1969. Diversity and stability in ecological systems. Brookhaven National Laboratory, Upton, New York. 264 p.

Brothwell, D., and P. Brothwell. 1969. Food in antiquity: a survey of the diet of early peoples. Thames and Hudson, London. 239 p.

Brown, L. H. 1971. The biology of pastoral man as a factor in conservation. Biol. Conserv. 3:93–100.

Browning, J. A. 1975. Relevance of knowledge about natural ecosystems to development of pest management programs for agro-ecosystems. Proc. Am. Phytopathol. Soc. 1:191–199.

Budel, J. 1966. Deltas—a basis of culture and civilization. *In* Scientific problems of the humid tropical zone deltas and their implications. Proceedings of a symposium, Dacca, March 1964. UNESCO, Paris. 422 p.

Burkhill, I. H. 1935. A dictionary of the economic products of the Malay Peninsula. 2 vols. Horticultural Books, Stuart, Florida.

Chang, J. 1968. The agricultural potential of the humid tropics. Geogr. Rev. 58:333–361.

Chang, K. 1970. The beginning of agriculture in the Far East. Antiquity 44:175–185.

CIMMYT (Centro Internacional de Mejoramiento de Maíz y Trigo) Review. 1980. CIMMYT, México, D. F. 100 p.

Clarke, W. C. 1966. From extensive to intensive cultivation: a succession from New Guinea. Ethnology 5:352–355.

Conklin, H. A. 1961. The study of shifting cultivation. Curr. Anthropol. 2:27–61.

Cook, O. F. 1921. Milpa agriculture, a primitive tropical system. Pages 307–326 *in* Annual Report (1919) of the Smithsonian Institution, Washington, D.C.

Corner, E. J. H. 1960. Botany and prehistory. Pages 38–41 *in* Symposium on the impact of man on humid tropics vegetation. Goroho, Papua New Guinea.

Cutler, H. C. 1968. Origin of agriculture in the Americas. Lat. Am. Res. Rev. 3:3–21.

Dalrymple, D. G. 1971. Survey of multiple cropping in less developed nations. Foreign Economic Development Service, USDA, in cooperation with AID, Washington, D.C. 108 p.

Davies, O. 1960. The neolithic revolution in tropical Africa. Trans. Hist. Soc. Ghana 4:14–20.

Den Hartog, A. P., and A. de Vos. 1973. The use of rodents as food in tropical Africa. FAO Nut. Let. 11(2):1–14.

De Vos, A. 1977. Game as food. Unasylva 29(116):2–12.

Dickinson, J. 1981. Una perspectiva ecologica sobre el desarrollo. Intercienca 6:30–37.

Dobby, E. H. G. 1955. The changing significance of padi-growing in south-east Asia. J. Trop. Geogr. 6:81–88.

Dodds, K. S. 1963. The origins of fruits and vegetables. Span 6:64–67.

Dressler, R. L. 1953. The pre-Columbian cultivated plants of Mexico. Bot. Mus. Leafl., Harv. Univ. 16:115–163.

Duckham, A. N., and G. B. Masefield. 1970. Farming systems of the world. Praeger, New York. 524 p.

Dumond, D. E. 1961. Swidden agriculture and the rise of Maya civilization. Southwest. J. Anthropol. 17:301–316.

Dunn, F. L. 1975. Rainforest collectors and trades: a study of resource utilization in modern and ancient Malaya. R. Asiat. Soc. Malay Br. Monogr. 5.

Epstein, H. 1955. Domestication features in animals as functions of human societies. Agric. Hist. 29:137–146.

FAO (Food and Agriculture Organization). 1957. Shifting cultivation. Trop. Agric. 34: 159–164.

Getahum, A. 1974. The role of wild plants in the native diet of Ethiopia. Agro-Ecosystems 1:45–56.

Gómez-Pompa, A., C. Vazquez-Yanes, and S. Guevara. 1972. The tropical rain forest: a non-renewable resource. Science 117:762–765.

Giesbrecht, M. G. 1972. The evolution of economic society. W. H. Freeman, San Francisco. 353 p.

Gopalan, C., B. V. Rama Sastri, and S. C. Belasubramanian. 1978. Nutritive value of Indian foods. National Institute of Nutrition, Hyderabad, India. 204 p.

Gottlieb, O. R. 1981. New and underutilized plants in the Americas: solutions to problems of inventory through systematics. Interscienca 6:22–29.

Greenland, D. J. 1975. Bringing the Green Revolution to the shifting cultivator. Science 190:841–844.

Greenway, P. J. 1944. Origins of some East African food plants. East Afr. Agric. J. 10:34–39, 115–119, 177–180, 251–266, and 11:56–63.

Grigg, D. B. 1969. The agricultural regions of the world: review and reflections. Econ. Geogr. 45:95–132.

Grigg, D. C. 1974. The agricultural systems of the world. Cambridge University Press, Cambridge, England. 359 p.

Grubben, G. J. H. 1977. Tropical vegetables and their genetic resources. In H. D. Tindall and J. T. Williams, eds. AGPE:IBPGR 77/23. International Board of Plant Genetic Resources, Rome.

Harlan, J. R. 1971. Agricultural origins: centers and noncenters. Science 174:468–474.

Harris, D. R. 1969. Agricultural systems, ecosystems and the origin of agriculture. Pages 3–16 in P. Ucko and G. Dimbleby, eds. The domestication and exploitation of plants and animals. Duckworth, London.

Harwood, R. R. 1979. Small farm development. Understanding and improving farming systems in the humid tropics. Westview Press, Boulder, Colorado. 160 p.

Heiser, C. B., Jr. 1965. Cultivated plants and cultural diffusion in nuclear America. Am. Anthropol. 67:930–947.

Helbaek, H. 1959. Domestication of food plants in the Old World. Science 130:365–372.

Herklots, G. A. C. 1972. Vegetables in Southeast Asia. Hafner Press, Hong Kong. 525 p.

Hernandez-X, E. 1970. Exploración ethnobotánica y su metodolgía. Escuela Nacional de Agricultura, México, D. F. 69 p.

Hesseltine, C. W., and W. Wang. 1980. The importance of traditional fermented foods. Bio-Science 30:402–404.

Heymans, J. C., and J. S. Maurice. 1973. Introduction à l'exploitation de la faune comme ressource alimentaire en République du Zaire. Forum Univ. 2:6–12.

Higgs, E. S., and M. R. Jarman. 1969. The origins of agriculture: a reconsideration. Antiquity 43:30–40.

Horn, H. A. 1974. The ecology of secondary succession. Ann. Rev. Ecol. Syst. 5:25–37.

Hutchinson, J. B. 1958. Genetics and plant improvement of tropical crops: an inaugural lecture. Cambridge University, Cambridge, England. 31 p.

IBPGR (International Board for Plant Genetic Resources). 1981. Annual Report, 1980. Rome. 107 p.

IRRI (International Rice Research Institute). 1972. Rice, science & man. Papers presented at the 10th anniversary celebration of the IRRI. IRRI, Los Baños, Philippines. 163 p.

Irvine, F. R. 1949. Indigenous food plants of West Africa. Econ. Bot. 3:436–444.

Janzen, D. H. 1973. Tropical agroecosystems. Science 182:1212-1219.

Jong, K., B. C. Stone, and E. Soepadmo. 1973. Malaysian tropical forest: an underexploited genetic reservoir of edible-fruit tree species. Pages 113-121 in Proceedings of the Symposium on Biological Resources and National Development. Malaya Naturalist Society, University of Malaya, Kuala Lumpur.

Kay, D. E. 1979. Food legumes. TPI Crop and Product Digest No. 3, Tropical Products Institute, London, 435 p.

Kemp, R. H., L. Roche, and R. I. Williams. 1976. Current activities and problems in the exploration and conservation of tropical forest gene resources. In J. Burley and B. T. Styles, eds. Tropical forest trees: variation, breeding, and conservation. Academic Press, London.

Khan, M. H. 1961. The rise and decline of cash crops in Java. Indones. Geogr. J. 1:47-55.

Lappe, F. M., and J. Collins. 1979. Exploding the hunger myths. Institute for Food and Development Policy, San Francisco, California. 30 p.

Leakey, C. L. A., and J. B. Wills, eds. 1977. Food crops of the lowland tropics. Oxford University Press, London. 345 p.

MacNeish, R. S. 1964. Ancient mesoamerican civilization. Science 143:531-545.

MacNeish, R. S. 1965. The origins of American agriculture. Antiquity 39:87-94.

Majer, J. D. 1976. The maintenance of the ant mosaic in Ghana cocoa farms. J. Appl. Ecol. 13:123-144.

Manshard, W. 1974. Tropical agriculture. Longman, London. 226 p.

Marshall, A. G. 1978. Man and nature in Malaysia: attitudes to wildlife and conservation. Pages 23-33 in P. A. Scott, ed. Nature and man in Southeast Asia. School of Oriental and African Studies, London.

Martin, F. W., and R. M. Ruberté. 1979. Edible leaves of the tropics. Agricultural Research, Southern Region, Science and Educational Administration, USDA, New Orleans. 235 p.

May, R. M. 1973. Stability and complexity in model ecosystems. Princeton University Press, New Jersey. 265 p.

Merrill, E. D. 1941. Man's influence on the vegetation of Polynesia with special reference to introduced species. Proc. 6th Pac. Sci. Congr. 4:629-639.

Miracle, M. P. 1964. Traditional agricultural methods in the Congo basin. Food Research Institute, Steinford, F. R. Germany.

Morgan, W. T. W. 1968. The role of temperate crops in the Kenya highlands. Acta Geogr. 20:273-278.

Nations, J., and R. Nigh. 1980. Tropical rainforests. Bull. Atmos. Sci. 36:12-19.

NRC (National Research Council). 1974. African agricultural research capabilities. National Academy of Sciences, Washington, D.C. 221 p.

NRC (National Research Council). 1975. Underexploited tropical plants with promising economic value. National Academy of Sciences, Washington, D.C. 189 p.

NRC (National Research Council). 1979. Tropical legumes: resources for the future. National Academy of Sciences, Washington, D.C. 337 p.

Ojasti, J., and G. Medina Padilla. 1972. The management of capybara in Venezuela. Pages 268-277 in Transactions of the 37th North American Wildlife and Natural Resources Conference. Wildlife Management Institute, Washington, D.C.

Okigbo, B. N. 1980. Development of multiple-use management for tropical forests through research in Africa. Pages 26-37 in Research on multiple use of forest resources. IVFRO/MAB Conference, Flagstaff, Arizona. Gen. Tech. Rept. WO-25. U.S. Forest Service, Washington, D.C.

Oplor, P. A., H. G. Bakor, and G. W. Frankie. 1977. Recovery of tropical lowland forest ecosystem. Pages 379–421 *in* J. Cairns and K. Dickson, eds. Recovery and restoration of damaged ecosystems. University Press of Virginia, Charlottesville.

Palerm, A. 1967. Agricultural systems and food patterns. Pages 26–52 *in* M. Nash, ed. Social anthropology handbook of Middle American Indians. Vol. 6. University of Texas Press, Austin.

Parodi, L. 1938. Procesos biológicos de la domesticación vegetal. Rev. Argent. Agron. 5:1–24.

Payne, W. J. A. 1964. The origin of domestic cattle in Africa. Emp. J. Exp. Agric. 32:97–113.

Phillips, R. W. 1961. World distribution of the main types of cattle. J. Hered. 52:207–213.

Pimentel, D., and M. Pimentel. 1979. Food, energy and society. Edward Arnold, London. 165 p.

Pimentel, D., L. E. Hurd, A. C. Bellotti, M. J. Forster, I. N. Oka, O. D. Sholes, and R. J. Whitman. 1973. Food production and the energy crisis. Science 182:443–499.

Prescott-Allen, R., and C. Prescott-Allen. 1981. *In situ* conservation of crop genetic resources. A report to the International Board for Plant Genetic Resources by the International Union for the Conservation of Nature and Natural Resources. IUCN, Gland, Switzerland. 145 p.

Purseglove, J. W. 1963. Some tropical tree crops and their centers of origin. Span 6:126–129.

Rasmussen, T. F. 1960. Population and land utilization in the Assam Valley. J. Trop. Geogr. 14:51–76.

Renfrew, J. M. 1973. Palaeoethnobotany, the prehistoric food plants of the Near East and Europe. Methuen, London. 219 p.

Richards, P. W. 1977. Tropical forest and woodlands: an overview. Agro-Ecosystems 3:225–238.

Ruthenberg, H. 1976. Farming systems in the tropics. Clarendon Press, Oxford. 366 p.

Safford, W. E. 1905. The useful plants of the Island of Guam. Contrib. U.S. Wash. Herb. 9:1–416.

Sanchez, P. A., ed. 1973. A review of soils research in tropical Latin America. N.C. Agr. Exp. Stn. Tech. Bull. 219. 197 p.

Sanchez, P. A. 1977. Alternativas al sistema de agricultura migratoria en america latina. Centro International de Agricultura Tropical, Calí, Colombia. 38 p.

Sanchez, P. A. 1978. Soil fertility and conservation considerations for agroforestry systems in the humid tropics of Latin America. Pages 79–124 *in* H. O. Mongi and P. A. Huxley, eds. Soils research in agroforestry. ICRAF Bulletin 0001E. International Council for Research on Agroforestry, Nairobi, Kenya.

Sauer, C. O. 1950. Cultivated plants of South and Central America. Pages 487–543 *in* J. H. Steward, ed. Handbook of the South American Indians. Vol. 6. Bull. 43. Bureau of American Ethnology, Smithsonian Institution, Washington, D.C.

Sauer, C. O. 1952. Agricultural origins and dispersals. American Geographical Society, New York.

Sauer, C. O. 1965. Cultural factors in plant domestication in the New World. Euphytica 14:301–306.

Schwanitz, F. 1966. The origin of cultivated plants. Harvard University Press, Cambridge, Massachusetts.

Seddon, D. 1968. The origins and development of agriculture in East and South Africa. Curr. Anthropol. 9:489–494.

Smith, R. L. 1974. Ecology and field biology. 2nd ed. Harper and Row, New York. 850 p.

Soemarwoto, O., I. Soemarwoto, E. Karyono, E. M. Soekartadiredja, and A. Ramlan. 1975.

The Javanese home-garden as an integrated agro-ecosystem. Pages 193-197 *in* Science for better environment. Proc. Inst. Congr. on Human Environmenta (HESC), Kyoto, Japan, November 1975. The Asahi Evening News, Tokyo.

Sommer, A. 1976. Attempt at an assessment of the world's tropical forests. Unasylva 28:5-25.

Soulé, M., and B. Wilcox, eds. 1980. Conservation biology: an evolutionary-ecological perspective. Sinauer Associates, Sunderland, Massachusetts. 395 p.

Spencer, J. E. 1966. Shifting cultivation in southeastern Asia. Publ. Geogr. No. 19. University of California, Berkeley.

Struever, S., ed. 1971. Prehistoric agriculture. Natural History Press, Garden City, New York.

Terra, G. J. A. 1954. Mixed-garden horticulture in Java. Malay. J. Trop. Geogr. 4:33-43.

Tosi, J. A., and R. F. Voertman. 1964. Some environmental factors in the economic development of the tropics. Econ. Geogr. 40:189-205.

Ucko, P. J., and G. W. Dimbleby, eds. 1969. The domestication and exploitation of plants and animals. Duckworth, London.

UNESCO. 1978a. Tropical forest ecosystems. A state of knowledge report prepared by UNESCO/UNEP/FAO. Natural Resources Research XIV. UNESCO, Paris. 681 p.

UNESCO. 1978b. Management of natural resources in Africa: traditional strategies and modern decision-making. Man & Biosphere (MAB) Technical Notes 9. UNESCO, Paris. 81 p.

Vavilov, N. I. 1950. The origin, variation, immunity and breeding of cultivated plants. Chron. Bot. 13:1-366.

Walter, H. 1971. Ecology of tropical and subtropical vegetation. Van Nostrand Reinhold Company, New York. 539 p.

Watters, R. F. 1960. The nature of shifting cultivation: a review of recent research. Pac. Viewpoint 1:59-99.

Watters, R. F. 1971. Shifting cultivation in Latin America. FAO Forestry Development Paper No. 17. FAO, Rome.

Wetterberg, G. B., M. Ferreira, W. L. dos Santos Brito, and U. Campbell de Araújo. 1976. Amazon fauna preferred as food. FO:DP/BRA/71/545, Tech. Rep. 6. FAO, Brasilia, Brasil.

White, K. D. 1970. Fallowing crop rotation and crop yields in Roman times. Agric. Hist. 44:281-290.

Whitmore, T. C. 1975. Tropical rain forests of the far east. Oxford University Press, Oxford, England. 296 p.

Whittlesey, D. 1937. Fixation of shifting cultivation. Econ. Geogr. 13:139-154.

Wickizer, V. D. 1958. Plantation crops in tropical agriculture. Trop. Agric. (Trinidad) 35:171-187.

Wilkes, H. G. 1977a. The world's crop plant germplasm—an endangered resource. Bull. Atmos. Sci. 33:8-16.

Wilkes, H. G. 1977b. Native crops and wild food plants. Ecologist 7:312-317.

Wulf, E. W., and O. F. Maleeve. 1969. The world resources of the useful plants. Academy of Sciences of the USSR, Moscow. 563 p.

Zeuner, D. E. 1963. A history of domesticated animals. Harper and Row, New York.

6
Ecological and Management Considerations for Forested Lands

Forests are the main organic system in the biosphere, producing about 65% of terrestrial plant matter (Baumgartner, 1979) and serving many valuable functions (Figure 6-1). Two facts focus attention on forested lands in the humid tropics: the pressure to use intact forest is accelerating deforestation, and the potential of many tropical countries to meet an evergrowing local and global demand for wood and wood products, especially for fuelwood, is significant.

The ecological concerns here highlighted relate to: use of natural forests for timber, use of natural forests for pulp, plantations, small-scale agroforestry, and rehabilitation of degraded land (reforestation). Although this assemblage is not inclusive of all ecological issues, it is representative of major concerns related to the contribution of ecology to forestry development in these regions.

In addition to selected ecological issues, this report addresses several matters of concern to development planners during the planning and pre-operational stages of a forestry project: tree system desired; size of the project; degree of current or past use; time-scale allocation of land use; special sociocultural, abiotic, and biotic constraints; and institutional capabilities.

OPTIONS FOR DEVELOPMENT OF FOREST SYSTEMS

Development options in the forestry sector are primarily determined by: type of forest system present or desired, size-scale of the project, and pre-

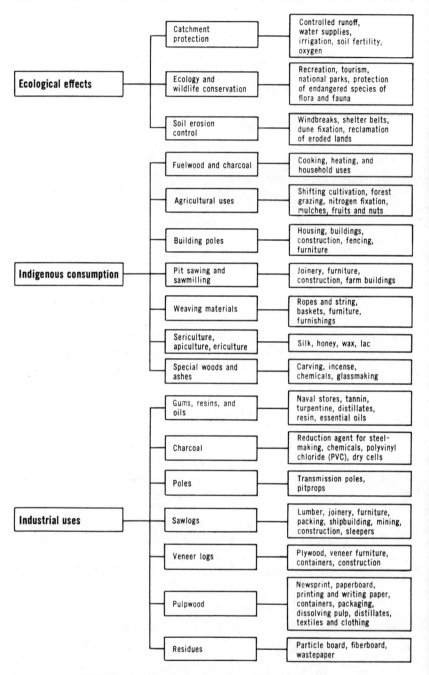

FIGURE 6-1   The role of forests. From World Bank (1978).

operational site conditions. Forest systems are arrayed along a continuum from relatively simple monocultural systems involving a single species, through mixed, several-species stands, to complex, highly diverse polycultural primary (virgin) or secondary (cut over at least once, but in various stages of succession) humid tropical forests. Issues that arise when small- and large-scale areas are under consideration affect the degree to which ecological guidance can assist developers in selecting sites and projects that have a good chance of succeeding. For example, personnel familiar with large-scale industrial operations may find it difficult to make the transition to small-scale, village-level enterprises. Limits may be placed on the availability of options by preexisting site conditions. For example, the extremes of quality of potential sites are intact forest as against degraded lands, where natural forest regeneration does not occur. The use and restoration possibilities available at each extreme are:

Use of intact forest

- protection of ecosystems for maximizing nature's services
- increased production of usable wood by naturally regenerating the present stand with a better one
- increased production of usable wood by enrichment planting without elimination of the present stand
- increased production of usable wood by conversion to plantations
- harvest of such other natural products as nuts, medicinal plants, or wildlife

Restoration of degraded land

- monospecific or mixed-species plantations, possibly including exotics
- small-scale agroforestry

Forestry development options are unique in that they neither necessitate nor presume a cleared landscape as a starting point. Land clearing may disrupt natural systems of energy, mineral-nutrient, and soil and water functioning, thereby requiring external subsidies, for example, of fertilizer or energy to maintain productivity. Complete forest conversion to a fruit or sap tree plantation is a land use more compatible with internally sustained yield-producing systems than is broad-scale conversion to herbaceous crops in an agronomic context. In some cases, reforestation of degraded lands after long-term agricultural or pastoral use is extremely difficult but is possible with such subsidies.

The Committee proposes that development planners consider four items at the preoperational stage of a forestry project:

• *Time scale*   The time scale for forestry planning requires special attention by nonforesters. Tree stands require continuous management, often for longer than the life of any individual tree or project, and are subject to changes in a host of environmental and economic aspects (UNESCO, 1978). For example, a long lead time is required for production, harvest, and regeneration in some types of natural forest management. Markets can change, infrastructures to handle management concerns can deteriorate under conditions of political turmoil, and increasing population pressures can erode away the land base that is so vital to large-scale forestry operations. Given such time-related factors, determining what is practical to implement and ensure a modest degree of success deserves high priority.

• *Special constraints to development*   Several considerations constrain the use of forested lands. In one group are certain sociocultural factors, including economic feasibility; access to available technology; existence of the necessary infrastructure to plan, evaluate, and implement management objectives; such land-use conflicts as colonization programs for agricultural development, need for watershed maintenance for hydropower production, and requirements for natural parks and reserves. In another group are abiotic and biotic factors related to soil parameters (such as fertility, topography and erosion hazards, and hydromorphic state), to the availability of suitably adapted tree species, and to the need to preserve adequate reservoirs of genetic diversity (Goodland *et al.*, 1978).

• *Allocation of land use*   The best potential use of forest lands should be systematically determined according to some suitable decision matrix. One such is shown in Figure 6-2. In addition to the variables identified in this diagram, selection of suitable project sites is contingent upon soil properties outlined in Chapters 2 and 7. Areas with fertile soils, such as Fluvents (nonfloodable, alluvial soils) and the high-base-status soils (such as Alfisols, Mollisols, and Vertisols), should receive high priority for intensive production of annuals and perennials with high nutrient requirements. Part of these areas should be left as natural reserves in order to maintain genetic diversity.

It is suggested that forestry projects in the humid tropics concentrate on the acid-infertile soils, such as Oxisols and Ultisols, using natural forests or species adapted to the soil constraints. For example, *Pinus caribea* is adapted to sandy Ultisols; *Gmelina arborea* appears to be best adapted to loamy and clayey Ultisols and Oxisols. In areas with extreme soil constraints (see Chapter 7), where removal of the natural vegetation for agri-

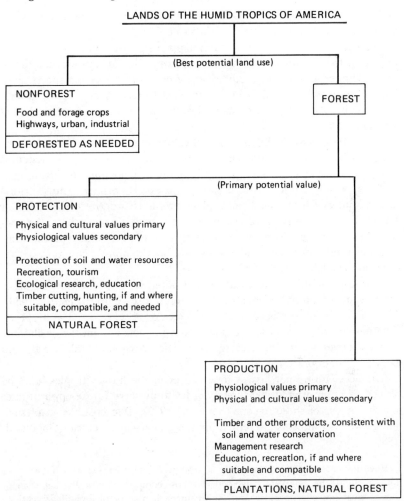

FIGURE 6-2 Sequential allocation of land uses. From Wadsworth (1975). (Reproduced by permission of the author and the International Union for Conservation of Nature and Natural Resources.)

culture or establishment of a tree plantation would cause severe soil erosion, development projects would incur a high risk of failure. Examples are the deep white sandy soils such as Spodosols or Psamments, which are so infertile that even the native forest is unique and adapted to those areas. Nutritional requirements and erosion hazards in such soils are so high that it is inadvisable to recommend any use other than maintenance of the natural forest cover. Other hazard soils include those with steep slopes and located on shallow bedrock (see Chapter 2).

The success or failure of forest development projects depends to a great extent on the formulation of a management policy for appropriate multiple- or limited-purpose (sometimes single-purpose) use of the spectrum of biotic resources harbored in humid tropical forests. A productive natural resource base can be maintained through a balanced consideration of several factors.

Short- and long-term environmental values should be used to determine the potential uses of forests (Figure 6-2). Some form of multiuse system is desirable in order to preserve as many options as possible for future generations: wood (roundwood, fuelwood, firewood); primary (nuts, fruits) and secondary (drugs, medicinal) plant products; wildlife preservation or harvesting; and reservoirs of tree genetic diversity, among others. An adequate inventory is necessary to make this evaluation; one type that emphasizes total biotic potential is presented in Chapter 3. Numerous other types are available (FAO, 1973c; UNESCO, 1978).

Land-use capability classification and other methods are now available for the identification of constraints to forest use (Qureshi *et al.*, 1980). Emphasis should be placed on the presence or absence of an appropriate data base on which to base decisions about projects and on the availability of alternatives in an engineering, economic, environmental, social, and political framework (Arnold, 1971).

The accelerating net loss of forest cover in the humid tropics must be slowed by appropriated measures in order to preserve future opportunities for the people of these regions (Sommer, 1976). One possible set of such mitigative measures is presented in the following checklist (Goodland, 1980).

Environmental reconnaissance/site selection: Tribal areas, special habitats, or refugia should be completely avoided; low-cost component covering a few man-weeks must precede appraisal and be an integral part of project identification/preparation.

Ecosystem inventory: Provides an opportunity to salvage or collect any significant organisms or conduct other ecological studies before the forest tract is destroyed.

Methods of clearing: Ranked by degree of environmental damage, from worst (e.g., heavy equipment) to least (e.g., chainsaw-plus-winch); early project documents should specify the type of acceptable clearing methods.

Buffer zone establishment: Goal is preservation of protective forest strips along watercourses, on slopes and around reservoirs in all irrigation headwaters; dimensions of tract should be commensurate with slope, and other factors; such tracts should be specified in project identification documents and compliance should be monitored.

Optimal use of cut forest: One example would be broadening the spectrum of species harvested, thus reducing the area to be exploited in order to obtain the same volume of wood; promotion of less commercially valuable species would be part of this parcel.

Reforestation component: This is a significant and effective component of any deforestation project, but one that requires technical competence and local support infrastructure.

Compensatory preserve: The establishment of forest preserves comparable or commensurate with the tract removed helps compensate for the loss of forest cover and species extinctions; augments a country's national park system; can be sited adjacent or elsewhere.

• *Institutional Factors* Institutional factors can either improve or complicate project planning. Their proper consideration is necessary for the long-term functioning of forestry field projects. Special institutional needs that should be identified include: knowledge about land ownership and tenure; status or effectiveness of local administrations; land use and forest policies (World Bank, 1978); such socioeconomic factors as the quantification of externalities (Lugo and Brinson, 1978; see Chapter 1 of this report); appropriate technology issues such as sustainable sources of energy and commodities (Goodland et al., 1978); and development of technological capacity (Weiss et al., 1980).

One goal of development of forest resources could be the integration of sociocultural needs with practical land-use development enterprises at the local and regional levels (Brünig, 1979). Systems analysis offers some possibilities for achieving compatibility of information about integrative models of the natural and cultural systems involved (Holling, 1978). The role of such organizations as the Food and Agriculture Organization, the International Union of Forest Research Organizations, and the International Council for Research on Agroforestry, which serve as consulting agencies and clearinghouses for information on forestry matters, could be expanded to include better cooperation at the bilateral, as well as the multilateral, level of development assistance.

NATURAL FORESTS MANAGED FOR TIMBER

Two successful sustained-yield management schemes have been used for production of saw and veneer logs in the lowland humid tropics: the Malayan Uniform System (MUS) and the Tropical Shelterwood System (TSS). The MUS was applied to Malesian forests that are atypical of lowland tropical forests in having several dominant species of the single family Dipterocarpaceae. Many members of this family have uniformly high roundwood quality. Because this family of trees produces copious wind-dispersed

ECOLOGICAL CONCEPT

ECOLOGICAL SELECTION OF TIMBER SPECIES

Ecological criteria for selection of species to be used as timber for saw wood and veneer logs should be better developed and applied in addition to the usual criteria of wood quality, tree volume, and bole straightness. The objective of these criteria is selection of species that can be managed for enrichment by natural regeneration and are compatible with practical and economical harvest. The criteria might include:

• Ecological amplitude—Does the species occur in a broad range of habitats?
• Stand volume—Is the species relatively abundant within a habitat?
• Seed production—Are numerous seeds produced for an extended period?
• Germination—Does a high percentage of seeds germinate, or are germination requirements restrictive?
• Seedling survival—Can seedlings persist for several months before release by canopy opening?
• Growth rate—Is wood production rapid?
• Mutualistic associates—Does the species extensively employ mycorrhizal fungi that help prevent mineral loss from the stand, or nitrogen-fixing bacteria?

Pentaclethra macroloba (Mimosaceae), a Costa Rican humid forest dominant and potentially an economically important timber species with rot resistance and a moderately heavy dark red wood, exhibits some of the characteristics. *Pentaclethra macroloba* has a broad ecological amplitude achieving about 20% of stand abundance on residual volcanic soils in northeastern Costa Rica. It fruits annually, releasing tens of thousands of 3-cm (diameter) flattened seeds in July–August. They are eaten by parrots and rodents, but are well protected by a high alkaloid content so that many survive. Germination is rapid, a high percentage of seeds germinating, so that *P. macroloba* seedlings carpet the forest floor. These seedlings persist under a closed canopy for perhaps 6 months on their seed reserves alone, but do not grow. In forest light-gap areas (trees that die or are blown down create open patches in the tropical forest), this species supports extensive nitrogen-fixing bacterial nodules and grows rapidly. More research on this species and others with similar characteristics might greatly improve the potential for management of tropical forests.

seeds at about the same time of the year, removal of adults of unwanted species before seeding serves to release a cohort of desired seedlings from canopy suppression. The TSS is an extrapolation of the MUS to forests lacking a family with the characteristics of Malesian dipterocarps, but nonetheless with several abundant, desirable timber species of the family Meliaceae. Harvest of desired species is highly selective, leaving adequate mature individuals to seed areas from which timber is removed.

Selection of appropriate silvicultural methods is complex for a number of reasons. In general, the existing management systems that maintain dense forest in a nearly natural state, such as the TSS and MUS and other similar systems, have had limited success except in the Dipterocarp forests of Southeast Asia (Catinot, 1974). The inconsistency of applicability is due to unpredictable natural regeneration; floristic composition; long time required for production, harvest, and regeneration; increasing population pressure eroding the land base needed for proper management, particularly for the TSS; and inability to predict production levels of species, classes of timber, or total marketable wood (King, 1972).

Spears (1980) concluded from a detailed examination of 10 tropical forestry projects that two major management alternatives exist for saw and veneer logs. One is to promote natural regeneration and assume that, with the second round of forest cutting, secondary species will command a higher value than at present. The other is to establish tree plantations to relieve pressures on intact forest and to supply rising domestic demand for forest products. A difficulty inherent in utilizing natural regeneration is that even after careful selective logging, regeneration of the preferred harvest species may be inadequate for subsequent harvests. And unless there is a sufficiently large cohort of seedlings at the time of timber harvest, there will be little or no regeneration. For humid tropical lowland forests, with the exception of Malesian Dipterocarp forests, such a cohort of seedlings is unlikely.

The seed of most humid lowland tree species have no dormant period (Garrad, 1955). Unless canopy opening is rapid and occurs immediately prior to seed release, sufficient stocking of seedlings is unlikely (Hartshorn, 1978). Except for certain species, such as *Carapa guianensis* (Meliaceae), that produce moderate numbers of large seeds that give rise to shade-tolerant, persistent seedlings, species that recruit abundantly (often light-requiring species) tend to have limited survival capacity (1 or 2 months).

Foresters, cognizant of this fact 50 years ago, established minimum girth requirements, but these have failed to ensure adequate regeneration. Data from tropical forests on age-specific recruitment and mortality for a given species may shed light on this problem, but few are available. Hartshorn (1975) accumulated information to model mathematically the population dynamics of *Pentaclethra macroloba* (Mimosaceae). He found that removal of individuals in the immediately prereproductive classes had the greatest effect in slowing the population growth rate. Thus a minimum girth requirement for *P. macroloba* would not preclude removal of trees large enough to contribute to continuance of the population. Nor will leaving only reproductive individuals ensure persistence of the population. Management of *P. macroloba* might most likely succeed if immediately prereproductive individuals and some reproductive individuals are left standing. The timber volume of only a few tropical trees will economically allow the bypassing of many individuals. In the absence of desirable dominants such as *P. macroloba* or *Shorea* spp. (a Dipterocarp), management for enrichment by a single species may be impossible. Knowledge of the population dynamics of dominant species suggests how these species might be appropriately managed.

One further problem with selective logging based on a mininum girth requirement is that the juvenile stages left uncut may not be in optimal conditions for rapidly reaching the forest canopy. In Central American lowland humid forests, many species seem to demand light for growth, tending to regenerate only in the canopy light-gaps created by falling trees (Hartshorn, 1978). Indeed, some species may be specialized to favor portions of these gaps, perhaps taking advantage of the exposed mineral soil of tip-up mounds created at the root ends of uprooted trees. Moreover, it has been suggested that offspring are not likely to be located near parent trees because (1) high levels of seed predation occur where seeds are most abundant nearest a parent tree and (2) host-specific herbivores have the best chance of locating seedlings in high density (Janzen, 1970). In general, seeds fall most abundantly nearest the parent (Smythe, 1970), although the relative proportions vary with the dispersal mechanism in question. Thus, even if juveniles could escape mortality caused by harvesting adults, they are unlikely to be located in the canopy light-gap created by parent removal. Management for the coordinated increase of several species complementary in their ecological requirements, or seed release, might achieve sustained yields. Management for enrichment involving several complementary species might foster provisions of environmental requirements needed for optimizing rates of regrowth and could be successful in suppressing "trash tree" competitors.

NATURAL FORESTS MANAGED FOR PULPWOOD

Management of natural forests in the humid tropics for pulpwood is another option intermediate between management of natural forests for timber and management of monocultures for pulpwood, firewood, or such forest products as cacao or oils. Usage of the many species found in these forests is now technologically possible (Kyrklund, 1978; Laundrie, 1978;

Phillips *et al.*, 1978). Retention of polyspecific stands in both the harvest-able and regenerating phases may mitigate the potential pest hazards of monocultures (Newman, 1980) and preserve the multitude of genetic resources available in such forests (Mazuera, 1979; Ladrach, 1981). Fostering adequate natural regeneration, reducing mineral removal, maintaining watershed integrity, and disturbing delicate soil biota functions are ecological concerns in these practices. The ability to use most species is not insurance against abuse by overcutting. As this technology is new, it should be applied cautiously.

Methods of clearing the forest and removing wood can be crucial concerns in clear-cutting for pulpwood in humid areas. As in agriculture on Ultisols and Oxisols, mechanical harvesting by bulldozers and other heavy equipment on heavy clay soils may lead to severe soil compaction and in some cases is simply impractical because of the soggy nature of the soils. Compaction can greatly retard establishment of seedlings. Quick reestab-lishment of a vegetative cover is important for mineral retention and to prevent erosion. It appears that the best way to ensure quick regeneration is to leave the soil surface and litter layer as undisturbed as possible (Figure 6-3). Manual cutting with chain saws and wood removal by over-head cable systems have worked well in some areas (Ladrach, 1981). Cutting should also be coordinated with fruiting periods to ensure that adequate numbers of seeds or seedlings are on the ground. These will sprout or grow rapidly as the forest canopy is opened by cutting. They will also take up minerals released from the litter as decomposition is accelerated by raised soil temperature due to exposure to the sun. Minerals may also be retained in logged sites by debarking and cutting logs to the desired length *in situ*. Adequate stocking can be promoted by cutting relatively small patches in a mosaic pattern so that reproductive individuals are left near freshly cut sites (Ewel and Conde, 1978). If mineral supplementation is needed, it can be provided by sowing a nitrogen-fixing crop as cover.

Such practices as those mentioned above (with the exception of the last-mentioned) have been used successfully in sustained pulpwood production in an extremely wet site in Colombia (Ladrach, 1981). In the undistrubed forest, average total height was 20 m and average wood volume was 159 m^3 per ha; the forest, regenerated after clearout, grew to nearly 18 m and achieved a volume of 115 m^3 per ha. Projections are that within 30 years after clear-cutting, the naturally regenerated forest should have compo-sition and stature very similar to those of the primary forest.

TREE PLANTATIONS AND MONOCULTURES

Monocultures are cultivated expanses of single species, but their ecologi-cal evaluation may apply equally well to combinations of a few species. As

TABLE 6-1 Comparison of Current Annual Rural Reforestation Programs in Selected Countries with the Approximate Size of Program Needed to Meet Domestic Fuelwood Requirements to the Year 2000[a]

	Current Annual Reforestation Program (thousands of ha)	Approximate Annual Program Needed to Meet Domestic Fuelwood Requirements to the Year 2000[b] (thousands of ha)	Total Planting Target Needed by the Year 2000 to Meet Domestic Requirements (millions of ha)	Multiplication of Present Annual Rate of Planting Needed to Meet Domestic Requirements in the Year 2000
Burundi	1.5	5.4	0.11	3.6
Ecuador	2.0	13.0	0.26	6.5
India	20.0	250.0	5.00	12.5
Malawi	2.5	13.0	0.26	5.2
Nigeria	10.0	100.0	2.00	10.0
Peru	5.0	20.0	0.40	4.0
Rwanda	1.5	13.0	0.26	8.6
Sierra Leone	0.5	2.5	0.05	5.0
Thailand	10.0	75.0	1.50	7.5
Tanzania	2.5	20.0	0.40	8.0

[a]Data from World Bank (1978).
[b]Based on the assumption that between one-third and half of total rural energy requirements could be met by using forms of energy other than wood, such as biogas plants or solar cookers, and by introducing greater end-use efficiency.

FIGURE 6-3 View of humid forest in Buenaventura, Colombia, after clear-cutting. Because cable logging is used, the ground is undisturbed, and a good seed source is ready to germinate when full sunlight enters after cutting. (Courtesy, W. E. Ladrach)

the number of interplanted species increases, both the pest hazard and the harvest and management advantages associated with monocultures may be expected to diminish proportionally. The lowland tropical monocultures here discussed are restricted to trees for fruits, saps, charcoal, pulpwood, and timber.

Plantations are attractive development projects if assessed by conventional economic criteria (Spears, 1980), but are frequently limited by shortages of seed or seedlings and by lack of technical expertise (UNESCO, 1978). Demand and plantation-reforestation activities in selected countries in the humid tropics indicate that rates of plantation establishment will be dramatically increased in the coming decades (Table 6-1). Appropriate cultivation practices are well established for a variety of conditions. Management and harvest are simpler than in polycultures. The attractiveness of plantations increases when modest effort is made to quantify the value of tree crops from which only fruits or sap is harvested, or the benefits derived from preventing massive soil erosion. Because fruit or

ECOLOGICAL CONCEPT

Mycorrhizae

Mycorrhizae (literally, "fungus-roots") are the mineral- and water-absorbing organs of most vascular plants. In nature, the roots of most higher plants are intimately associated with beneficial fungi. Filaments (hyphae) of the fungi penetrate the root, transferring materials to it. They also extend many centimeters away from the root into the surrounding soil. Mycorrhizal fungi are far more efficient at extracting minerals from soil than are uninfected plant roots, which depend on root hairs. For example, they can absorb phosphorus (frequently an important limiting factor to plant growth) from lower concentrations than those accessible to uninfected plant roots. Thus they offer special promise for sustaining plant growth on phosphorus-immobilizing Oxisols and Ultisols, the most common soil type in the humid tropics.

Two types of mycorrhizae are of major economic importance: (1) ectomycorrhizae, formed in the tropics by pines, some dipterocarps, legumes, and eucalypts; and (2) vesicular–arbuscular (VA) mycorrhizae, formed by most forest tree species and almost all crops, including coffee, sugar cane, tea, citrus, oil palm, date palm, cocoa, coconut, avocado, and the Brazilian rubber tree.

It has been demonstrated repeatedly that both ectomycorrhizae and VA mycorrhizae markedly stimulate host plant growth. At the existing levels of fertility of most tropical soils, many trees may neither grow nor survive without mycorrhizae. Therefore, ensuring adequate mycorrhizal infection in plantations and production forests is imperative. A word of caution is needed: Fertilization of herbaceous crops and some trees, as a substitute for mycorrhizae, can lead to difficulties. One is that continuous mineral supplementation may be more expensive than management to ensure maintenance of adequate populations of mycorrhizal fungi. Another is that fertilization may lead to requirement for increasing additions, because it causes suppression of mycorrhiza formation, and may thereby reduce mycorrhizal populations. Although mycorrhizae are unlikely to produce yields equal to those produced by fertilization, they are often more cost-effective in the long term. They are the cornerstone of mineral conservation by natural tropical forests.

Innoculation of tropical pine plantations with ectomycorrhizal fungi is regularly practiced. Because pines are not native to most areas of the lowland humid tropics, their mycorrhizal fungi must be imported before pines can be established. Nurse or mother trees are commonly used to inoculate nursery seedlings, and commercial inoculum of at least one ectomycorrhizal fungus species may soon be available.

A major concern for VA mycorrhizae is that enough inoculum will be available in the soil. Modification of ecosystems may markedly lower the chances of natural inoculation by reducing the fungal population below effective levels. At present, these fungi cannot be grown in pure culture, and no methods are available for large-scale inoculation. Research on the potential of VA mycorrhizae to promote sustainable agriculture, agrosilviculture, and plantation system and research on ways of maintaining beneficial infection levels in such systems should receive high priority.

sap plantations take time to establish, the long-term economic stability of plantations producing export crops subject to world market fluctuations should be considered. For example, cooking oil from palms is a good choice for export production because it is an essential household item. Fuelwood, a local necessity, can be a by-product of a higher-value tree product such as pigeon pea (*Cajanus cajan*) (NRC, 1980a).

The ecological concerns for plantation monocultures are four: (1) mineral decline, because minerals are exported in the tree products and leached from soil; (2) pest buildup and outbreaks; (3) the contribution of plant breeding and germplasm; and (4) the use of exotics as against endemics.

MINERAL DECLINE

Plantations are usually fertilized, unless located on such naturally fertile soils such as Fluvents, because minerals are exported in their products (although less so than with grains or cattle pastures). Although such export may be minor for fruit and sap crops, it is usually significant enough to require some maintenance fertilization. Experience with Brazil nut plantations indicated that increasing fertilization is required (Schubart and Salati, 1980). Even when tree crops maintain natural mineral cycling through the activities of mycorrhizal fungi, some leaching losses from soil can be expected, because root biomass and soil volume exploitation are lower in plantations than in natural forest ecosystems. The soil requirements of perennial crops are very important in this context. For example, rubber, oil palm, coffee (in the highlands), and many palm species are well adapted to Oxisol–Ultisol regions (Sanchez and Salinas, 1981). Many other species are not adapted to Oxisols and Ultisols without heavy fertilization and liming. For example, *Theobroma cacao* does better on Alfisols; *Leucaena leucocephala* does poorly on Oxisols and Ultisols.

Pulpwood ranks reasonably low in nutrient export potential, because pulp that is locally produced contains little more than cellulose. Debarking and sawing *in situ* provides an ecological and economic return, because nutrient-rich production residues are returned to the soils of plantations. It is also beneficial to return ash from fuelwood that is consumed locally because of the economics of transport of fertilizers at great distances from the source. Wood ash is usually rich in phosphorus, a needed plant element. Ash, however, lacks nitrogen, suggesting that selection of atmospheric nitrogen-fixing species, such as legumes, for fuelwood may be appropriate (NRC, 1980a).

The chief uncertainty about fuelwood species at present is the extent to which they utilize and subsequently deplete soil nutrients, especially phosphorus. If slash, tops, and bark are left *in situ,* a large proportion of minerals will be retained, but although concentrations of minerals in wood are usually very low, the tremendous volumes of wood produced in these plantation systems may create a nutrient export problem. Experience with *Gmelina arborea* at Jari, Brazil, indicates that, before the second harvest at year 12, no level of fertilization increased production enough to repay the cost of fertilizing (Toenniessen, 1980). Phosphorus supplementation may be avoidable for some time, because the leaf litter of *G. arborea* is slightly basic and may mobilize phosphorus, as does liming (application of calcium oxide to the soil to reduce its acidity). Nevertheless, soil P will be ultimately depleted if there is no fertilization. The question is: How much fertilization will be necessary and when should it take place?

Also, there is no need for investigation of the mycorrhizal status of *G. arborea* and similar species that are probably facultatively mycotrophic, growing without supporting mycorrhizal fungi when in soils of moderate fertility (Janos, 1980a). If such species can be encouraged to sustain mycorrhizae as fertility declines and if mycorrhizal fungi have persisted in plantation sites or may in some as yet unknown manner be reintroduced (perhaps from forest sources), the anticipated increased need to fertilize fuel and pulpwood plantations in amortization of mineral export may be stabilized at economically viable levels.

The *taungya* system of intercropping vegetables while plantation saplings are being established is desirable for three reasons: profit from crops partly amortizes costs of establishment, intercropping controls weeds, and roots of crop plants that are dependent on mycorrhizal fungi may maintain a reservoir of the fungi for infection of saplings (Janos, 1980b). These fungi, released from the dying roots of harvested trees, can succumb quickly if not supported by suitable living plant roots. Many naturally occurring early pioneer weed species will not support the fungi (Janos, 1980a), but data from tree reestablishment in an overgrazed pasture in Costa Rica suggest that even when seedlings are preinoculated with mycorrhizal fungi, repeated infection from the soil is necessary for best establishment and growth.

PEST OUTBREAKS

Although such species as teak in India and Indonesia and *Eucalyptus* in Brazil (for charcoal for iron smelting) have gone for decades without pest outbreaks, this hazard is the most obvious and inescapable threat to monocultures in the lowland humid tropics (UNESCO, 1978). Natural tree monocultures or tracts with only a few species occur on unusual sites, either with high nutrient input but osmotic and oxygen stress (e.g., mangrove forests) or on extremely oligotrophic sites (e.g., forests on white sands or swamps) of low productivity and large investment by the plant in antiherbivore chemistry. Nevertheless, the race with pests is at best a gamble. Research is needed to learn why certain species manage to avoid difficulty for long periods.

Strong (1974) has shown that the number of species of pests on tropical monocultural plantations increases in direct proportion with the length of time the crop is grown at a site. Pests can build up so rapidly and become so difficult to control that they can cause massive translocations of plantations. For example, losses from Panama wilt (*Fusarium oxysporum*) led plantation owners to shift the culture of bananas from the Caribbean to the Pacific side of Central America and losses from South American leaf blight (*Microcyclus ulei*) to a shift of rubber production from Brazil to Asia.

Prospects for pest control in monocultures are dim in the long run because control requires escalating inputs, especially in the humid tropics where conditions are suitable for pest growth the year-round. Fungi and insect pests can complete many generations in a short time, and they have a high potential for overcoming chemical control measures by evolutionary adaptation. Biological control by introducing sterile forms of the pest species is a useful control measure in that it hinders the pest's ability to overcome it, although it may not be economically feasible in low-yielding systems. It requires the identification, many times by pure chance, of a sterile mutant that is also capable of spreading rapidly through the pest population.

PLANT BREEDING AND GERMPLASM

Plant breeding for resistance to pests may be an effective strategy in the long run because it requires only minimal external inputs and because the work can be done largely by technicians (Hawkes, 1977). It is difficult to accomplish with perennials, however, because resistance may last a shorter time than the useful life of the host plant. Tissue culture techniques show promise in speeding breeding of perennials. The need to breed resistant varieties never ceases whenever the evolutionary race with pests is entered. Breeding requires the preservation of an adequate sampling of the genetic variation present in a species (see Chapter 4). This leaves no alternative but preservation of the forests where the germplasm banks of plantation species are found. Although germplasm seed banks can be of great importance, we are unable to maintain viable seeds of many tropical trees. Induced mutagenesis is extremely inefficient in discovering useful variation, because most mutations are lethal or at least detrimental, and their scope is limited by the diversity present in the treated genome. It requires few individuals to preserve all the variation in a randomly mating population, but most natural populations do not in fact mate at random. Distinct genotypes can be expected from the multitudes of subpopulations into which species are divided. If all, or most, are sampled, this variation can be preserved in a single plantation for the life of the sampled individuals or for their subsequent clones. If only offspring can be retained, attrition of alleles will occur at any single "gene bank" site. For short-lived species, it is not sufficient to attempt to preserve genotypes. We must preserve the selective pressures that gave rise to them as well. It is most efficient to let natural selection maintain variation, using natural ecosystems as biological filters for vigorous and resistant individuals. As selected species become more abundant in native forests managed for enrichment, their resistance might thus keep abreast of pest attack. To assure the genetic resources needed to respond to pest outbreaks, tropical monocultural plantations should be linked through legal or regulatory requirements to preserved areas or managed forests that are as large as or larger than the plantations.

EXOTICS VERSUS ENDEMICS

Although endemic species may have natural pest resistance that can be enhanced by breeding, exotic species may escape pests for some time because they are novel thereto. To maximize this possibility, exotics known for their antiherbivore chemistry and with no closely related species native in the area in which they are to be grown should be selected. This method requires that these tree species be viewed ecologically, that is, according to such factors as life-history peculiarities and constraints to growth and reproduction.

Exotics exert a selective pressure on pests, a pressure made all the more intensive if there are related local plant species that are removed. Janzen (1977) suggests preserving native mahoganies (*Cedrela* spp. and *Swietenia* spp.) in Central America to minimize selection pressures on shoot borers to overcome the resistance of imported *Toona* species. Nevertheless, this will not prevent the ultimate spread of a pest that overcomes *Toona*'s resistance.

An additional concern with the introduction of exotics, especially pines and eucalypts, is the alteration of the indigenous soil mycorrhizal flora. Ectomycorrhizal species planted where native plants have vesicular–arbuscular mycorrhizae exculsively may be ineffective competitors with native weeds that have VA mycorrhizae. If VA mycorrhizal weed species are suppressed, limiting options for wasteland rehabilitation, these beneficial fungi may die out, should sudden devastating pest outbreaks preclude continuation of plantations of ectomycorrhizal species.

SMALL-SCALE AGROFORESTRY SYSTEMS

Agroforestry systems are sustainable land management systems that increase the yield of the land by combining the production of crops (usually tree crops) and forest plants and animals, simultaneously or sequentially, on the same unit of land (Douglas, 1973; King and Chandler, 1978; ICRAF, 1979; Bishop, 1980). In using marginal lands, agroforestry systems in the humid tropics are best located on the same soils where forestry projects are found: the Oxisols and Ultisols. A tree canopy in such areas is advantageous to sound soil management (see Chapter 7).

Several generalizations are possible:

• Agroforestry is highly site-specific, and the potential for transferability of technology should be explored systematically.

• It is a form of multiple-use management and an alternative land use for local people (Okigbo, 1980).

• If viewed as an agroecosystem, it should be framed in terms of ecological insights, technical extension, agricultural planning, and special social (infrastructure, benefits) and economic (markets and product processing) aspects that contribute to rural development (Budowski, 1980; Spears, 1980).

• It is not necessarily restricted to the tropics (Stover, 1979); hence more knowledge from other environments is potentially available.

• Yield advantages are obtained from intercropping; however, the mechanisms that account for this are little known (Vandermeer, 1981).

• It can be a form of minimal-energy-input agriculture, if the proper mix of species is obtained (Felker and Bandurski, 1979) and soil management constraints are kept in perspective (Okigbo and Lal, 1979).

• It can alleviate pressures on intact forests in the humid tropics by providing more stable incomes to rural inhabitants, many of whom practice various forms of shifting cultivation (Budowski, 1980).

• The literature on agroforestry practices and projects is rapidly growing, indicating an interest and need for future consideration of this system.

The Committee believes that the chief ecological concern is for the formulation of a theory that sets down design criteria for agroforestry systems. Such a theory is necessary to supplement the current inefficient empirical-descriptive approach to agroforestry systems design, which has little generalizability among sites. Several ecological principles are involved, perhaps singly or combination, in agroforestry systems:

• Interference production (Vandermeer, 1981): Two or more crop species may give greater yields than an equivalent area planted to a single crop.
• Weed control (Morales *et al.,* 1949): Competition for essential elements, sunlight, space, and water is minimized by removal of unproductive (to the farmer) individual plants or species.
• Avoidance of pests (Litsinger and Moody, 1976): Plant pest populations are kept in check by scattering the crop in space and time, by trap cropping (diverting a pest from the main crop by planting an equally desirable one in an adjacent location), or applying biological or chemical control agents in some integrated fashion.
• Compensation or mutualism (Aiyer, 1949; Rathke and Hegstrom, 1975): Subtle interactions between species reciprocate beneficially, thereby enhancing production; for example, nitrogen-fixing plants benefit their associates.

For most, if not all, agroforestry systems, it is not known precisely (even though many of these systems work well in practice) how competition is minimized or why multiple-cropping systems are more productive, in some cases, than monocultures. Traditional answers suggest the proper use of legumes and of deep- versus shallow-rooted trees, and identification of species that have complementary life-support needs. Development agencies can assist efforts to identify appropriate design criteria for agroforestry systems by supporting model subsistence farms and their research components. At the same time, it is of the utmost importance to identify and record indigenous agroforestry practices that are the result of long evolution.

REFORESTATION AND REHABILITATION OF DEGRADED LANDS

DEFINITION AND EXAMPLES

Degraded lands are ecologically impoverished areas that exhibit disruption of natural cycles of soils or waters, or are areas where economic productivity has been abandoned. For example, the conversion of forest to permanent *Imperata cylindrica* grassland or shrub savanna and the loss of soil due to insufficient or inappropriate vegetation cover has led to difficulty in many parts of the world (Watters, 1971; Denevan, 1975; UNESCO, 1978; Posner and McPherson, 1981). It may be difficult, if not impossible, to restore the productivity of such lands (Catinot, 1974; Nwoboshi, 1975).

A DEVELOPMENT ALTERNATIVE

Restoration of degraded landscapes is a development option that is preferable to forest clearing. It is best accomplished by return to woody vegetation, when possible. For example, an afforestation project in Madagascar demonstrated drastically different levels of erosion for *Eucalyptus* plantation versus field crops: 0.025 t/ha/yr to 59 t/ha/yr (Bailly et al., 1967). But in many instances it may be expensive in the short term, and technologies essential for its accomplishment may be uncertain. It is preferable, however, because it deflects development from primary forest and may provide employment for many people besides producing much-needed wood (Eckholm, 1979). However, shifting cultivators may have to be given employment in plantations if fuelwood poaching is not to become devastating. Rehabilitation options, in the absence of forest seed sources, include

---

ECOLOGICAL CONCEPT

COMPETITORS OR COMPANIONS?

Ecologists tend to view assemblages of plant species as competitors, each reducing the growth of the others by utilizing some of the available light, water, and minerals. Yet agroforestry and mixed-cropping are based on the fundamental assumption that the species grown together will outproduce an equivalent area planted to them singly. This apparent contradiction is resolved when the degree to which species interfere with one another is quantified. The characteristics that allow species to coexist in nature are the same ones that contribute to polyculture yields. Although polyculture species do interfere with one another, they do so weakly. This may be because their mineral requirements are complementary, their root systems are at different depths in the soil and do not overlap, and their light requirements are met by their mutual shade; there may be many other reasons. A priority research need is to identify them. Understanding this will contribute to formulation of general principles for the design of polycultural intercrop or agroforest systems.

small-scale polyculture agroforestry, intensive vegeculture (see Chapter 5), or fuelwood plots in which legumes or other fast-growing trees are established. All of these require some form of inputs in order to ensure their sustainability (Vine, 1953, 1968; Sioli, 1973). In many cases, establishment of such options may be economically and technologically difficult (e.g., Mikola, 1969).

The components of a reforestation program are summarized in the following list. Sources for the list are: Weber, 1977; Conway, 1979; NRC, 1980a; and C. Gallegos, International Paper Company, personal communication, 1981.

• land-use planning: Integration with other land uses by appropriate institutions to ensure wood supply enhancement
• identification of soil types, distribution and constraints to use: Erosion hazard; depth of soil; physical and chemical limitations; need for fertilization; degree of present compaction
• factors such as climate, topography, and issues unique to the site of the proposed project
• species selection: Adaptations for moist sites required
• tree improvement through selective breeding
• special project design aids: Regeneration techniques; propagation, seeding, and planting techniques; nursery planning and management; use and prevention of fire; shelterbelt/windbreak establishment; species identification keys; species life history information; local climatic data
• identification of human factors: Community involvement; local technical/cultural knowledge available; perceptions of need and use; local value systems; present methods of wood procurement; local technologies for wood and wood products; consumption patterns; infrastructure to regulate use of wood; education needs

ECOLOGICAL CONSTRAINTS

The central ecological question is how to develop a system that mimics the restorative functions of natural plant successions by judicious choice of species (NRC, 1979a, 1980a; Budowski, 1980) and of inorganic or organic soil supplements. Methane digestion products and sludges may be useful supplements on small-scale individual farms (NRC, 1977, 1979b). A further problem of weed control, or reduction of competition from unwanted species, complicates the economic feasibility of long-term maintenance of such restorative systems (Kadambi, 1958; FAO, 1974c; UNESCO, 1978).

Regeneration of degraded lands dominated by *Imperata cylindrica* and other coarse grasses depends to a great extent on soil properties and management. Technology has been developed in Indonesia to transform alang-alang land into productive crop areas. This technology includes burning the grass, grazing it heavily after early regrowth, plowing with two passes of a disk harrow, liming, fertilizing, and planting such annual crops as rice and cassava. Apparently, *Imperata* spp. is unable to compete with crops at high fertility levels. Such technology is adaptable only on soils with gentle topography where mechanization is possible; no technology is currently available for reclaiming such lands on steep slopes.

Schemes for rehabilitating degraded landscapes face a major obstacle. Rehabilitation is highly likely to require resolution of a largely unrecognized microbial problem. Janos (1980b) has shown why vesicular–arbuscular mycorrhizal fungi are probably lacking in these areas, a suggestion that has been confirmed by research in overgrazed pastures and aluminum mining areas in Costa Rica (D. Janos, 1981, University of Miami, personal communication). At present, there is no technical know-how suitable for large-scale production of vesicular–arbuscular mycorrhizal inoculum. But if forest source areas are available, it may be possible to transfer the necessary fungi from them.

Although wasteland rehabilitation may appear uneconomical when evaluated on conventional grounds, the value of the environmental services provided by forests may make it worthwhile to deflect development to degraded lands. Because roads in part contribute to overexploitation, they will likely already be in place; therefore, the major cost they represent in establishing a rural infrastructure will be averted. Forest preservation, however, must be an integral part of such a scheme in order to serve as a source area for seeds and mycorrhizal fungi.

PRIORITIES FOR REFORESTATION PROJECTS

The priorities to be considered in reforestation projects in the humid tropics are biotic factors, abiotic factors, sustained yields, and species available for use.

Biotic Factors

How can utilization of the existing forest be achieved? Under tropical conditions, there can be hundreds of tree species growing in each hectare of forest (particularly in Latin America), and relatively few of these trees have been sufficiently tested and developed to facilitate selling their wood products on the open market. The nonusable trees must be removed before reforestation with desirable species can take place, and this can be very expensive if too many residual trees are left on the ground.

Control of weed competition is essential. As many as three or four weedings per year are needed during the first 2 or 3 years if successful plantations are to be developed.

Insect defoliators (leaf-cutting ants and others) can be serious, and special measures must be taken to control these pests, especially during the first years of plantation establishment.

Abiotic Factors

Maintenance of soil nutrient balance and management of organic matter are crucial. Most of the nutrients available in tropical ecosystems are tied up in the aboveground vegetation; some are available in the upper 3–5 cm of surface soil. Practices to reduce nutrient losses and increase organic matter in the soil (e.g., prompt reforestation of cutover areas, planting of nitrogen-fixing cover crops, and fertilization) must be made a part of management. Soil compaction can be severe on the highly weathered, high-clay content soils characteristic of the humid tropics, especially where harvesting, site preparation, planting, etc., are mechanized. To avoid this, most organizations revert to increased use of manual labor. However, manual labor can be prohibitively expensive when the costs of training and housing workers, and of workers' benefits, are taken into consideration. High rainfall and insolation can lead to excessive erosion and leaching of unprotected soils. Therefore, a policy of cutting only areas that can be reforested within a year, and planting exposed, cutover soils as quickly as possible, should be followed.

Sustained Yields

The sustained-yield question is frustrating, even in temperate regions, and much less information is available for the tropics. The key to sustained yield is the maintenance of soil fertility, which can be achieved in the tropics with good soil management.

Species Available for Use

There are comparatively few tree species (either conifers or hardwoods) that can be used successfully in tropical plantations, but there are undoubtedly many native and exotic species that could be tested and developed for this purpose. One difficulty lies in the fact that very little is known about the indigenous tropical species and that many of the potentially valuable exotic species have not been adequately tested. In addition, many of the gene pools in the native forest are being eradicated by shifting agriculture, fuelwood cutters, clearing for grazing, and uncontrolled logging. Concrete measures must be taken to preserve parts of the native forest in an undisturbed state. Genetic material should be collected from desirable species, and individuals within those species, to prevent this loss. The North Carolina State Central America and Mexico Coniferous Resources Cooperative (CAMCORE) exemplifies one such effort.

SUMMARY

Forests are the natural vegetation of much of the lowland humid tropics. Although tropical forests are highly productive biologically, their complexity often hinders their development for economic productivity. The essential concern in the development of forested lands is how to derive the greatest total benefits for man from these lands while retaining their natural productivity. Benefits to be gained include not only food, fuel, and fiber products, but also environmental services such as erosion control, catchment protection, and climate control. The ecologist/developer seeks stable production systems that require minimal mineral, weed-control, and pest-control supplements during the long periods needed for forest projects.

The options for industrial wood production range from management of natural forest for harvest of selected species to complete conversion to plantations of one or a few species. The latter option is viable for production of fruits or other nonwood plant products. The primary ecological concerns in managing natural forest for enrichment bear upon selection of appropriate sites and species in view of soil and tree demographic constraints. If natural forest is to be clear-cut (as for pulpwood), avoidance of mineral loss and fostering adequate regeneration take on major importance.

Plantations can be highly productive, especially of wood, because in their youth they mimic early successional stages characterized by reduced competition and rapid growth. Plantations will require mineral supplements for sustained production, however, to replace the minerals contained in removed products and those lost because of the disruption of natural retention. Fostering mineral retention by manipulation of mycorrhizae and inclusion of cover or companion crops deserves priority in plantation development.

Pest control is an additional priority in plantations or forests highly enriched in single species. Judicious choice of endemics, exotics, or a combination can mitigate pest damage, but forest germplasm and reserves of biological control agents are the critical components of ecologically sound plantation development.

Overall, the forest development manager needs much more information on the dynamics of forests, plantations, and populations of species for design of appropriate silvicultural methods. A forest policy that mitigates deforestation by treating forest as a renewable natural resource instead of a potential timber "strip mine" is urgently required.

Small-scale commercial production may be achieved in an ecologically sound manner by using agroforestry systems. Although labor-intensive, these systems are very productive and show promise for mineral retention and weed and pest control. At present, however, no general theory exists for their design. Integrative research is needed to transcend the current empirical, site-specific approach to agroforestry system development. At the same time, existing agroforestry and mixed-cropping practices of indigenous peoples should be studied and documented. Subsistence-level agroforestry may be one option for the rehabilitation of abandoned, degraded lands. Mineral supplementation and weed control are major problems in rehabilitation that may be solved in an economically conservative way by integrated small-farm systems that involve establishment of fertility through the use of organic wastes. Commercial-scale rehabilitation of degraded land by plantation establishment may prove feasible if mineral recycling can be restored through supplementation of mycorrhizal fungi. Loss of these beneficial fungi often contributes to decline in the fertility of tropical lands, although this has been a largely unrecognized issue. If research reveals ways to focus development in deforested lands, pressure to convert natural forest may be alleviated so that it may be better utilized and better retained as a resource for the future.

REFERENCES AND SUGGESTED READING

This list includes about 100 selected references to the literature on forests in the humid tropics. They deal with developmental, ecological, and management aspects of those forests. They are *selected* in the sense that they are believed to have special value to development planners, technicians, and other workers concerned with forests and trees. Some of these references are cited in Chapter 6, but most are not.

The selected references fall into eight categories:

1	biological/ecological considerations	5	institution building
2	industrial plantation tree farming	6	national forest management
3	industrial projects	7	research needs
4	infrastructure and extraction	8	rural development (forestry, reforestation, and agroforestry)

The categories are keyed to the bibliographic list by means of numerals in the left-hand margin. Each numeral refers to one of the numbered categories (above). Thus, if a reader wishes to review references on biological/ecological considerations, they are to be found by noting the numeral 1 in the margin; industrial plantation tree farming is indicated by the numeral 2; and so on.

6   Anonymous. 1973. Planned utilization of the lowland tropical forests. Regional Center for Tropical Biology, Bogor, Indonesia. 263 p.

8   Acker, F. 1981. Saving Nepal's dwindling forests. New Sci. (April 9):92–94.

7   Adisoemarto, S., and E. F. Brunig, eds. 1979. Trans. second international MAB–IUFRO workshop on tropical rainforest ecosystems research, October 1978, Jakarta, Indonesia. Spec. Rep. No. 2. Chair of World Forestry, Hamburg-Reinbeck, F. R. Germany. 295 p.

8   AID (U.S. Agency for International Development). 1979. Environmental and natural resource management in developing countries. A report to Congress. Vol. I. AID/DOS, Washington, D.C. 184 p.

     Aiyer, A. K. 1949. Mixed cropping in India. Indian J. Agric. Sci. 19:439–543.

     Allen, J. C., and E. Shue. 1981. Deforestation and wood fuels in developing countries. Resources For the Future, Washington, D.C. 40 p. Manuscript.

6   Arnold, R. K. 1971. Forest management by alternatives rather than systems. Page 109 *in* Vol. 1 (Abstracts). Records of proceedings of 12th Pacific Science Congress, Canberra.

8   Ay, P. 1979. The rural energy system of Nigeria. Part 2: Firewood and charcoal in the humid tropics—field research in western Nigeria. Draft report prepared for the U.N. University, Tokyo. 71 p.

     Bailly, C., J. De Vergnette, G. Benoit de Coignac, J. Velley, and J. Celton. 1967. Essai de mise en valeu d'une zone des hauts plateaux malgaches (Manankazo) par l'aménagement rationel. Effet de cet aménagement sur les pertes enterre et le ruissellement. Pages 1362–1383 *in* C. R. Coll, ed. Sur la fertilité des sols tropicaux (Tananarive) II.

1   Barney, G. O. 1980. The global 2000 report to the President. Vol. II: The technical report. Council on Environmental Quality and the Department of State, Washington, D.C. 766 p.

     Baumgartner, A. 1979. Climatic variability and forestry. Pages 223–229 *in* World climate conference: extended summaries. World Meteorological Organization, Geneva.

6   Baur, G. N. 1962. The ecological basis of rain forest management. Forestry Commission of New South Wales, Australia. 499 p.

2   Benedict, W. V. 1971. Protecting plantations of long-fibre tree species from loss by insects and diseases. Tech. Rep. No. 4, UNDP/SP Project MAL/12. FAO, Rome. 24 p.

2   Beneveniste, C. 1974. La boucle du cacao, Côte-d'Ivoire. Étude regionale des circuits de transport. ORSTOM, Paris. 221 p.

2   Bennett, R. M. 1974. A forest plantation scheme for the New Herbides. Department of Agriculture, Port Vila. New Hebrides. 16 p.

6   Bethel, J. S. 1971. Problems in relating economic to biological production. Page 110 *in* Vol. 1 (Abstracts). Records of proceedings of 12th Pacific Science Congress, Canberra.

     Bishop, J. P. 1980. Agro-forestry systems for the humid tropics east of the Andes. I. Integrated foodcrop, swine, chicken and fuelwood production. Paper presented at international conference on Amazonian agricultural and land-use development, Calí, Colombia, April 1980.

1   Bouvarel, P. 1975. Report on forest genetic resources. International Board for Plant Genetic Resources, Rome. 17 p. Multigraphed.

1   Bowonder, B. In press. Deforestation in India. Int. J. Environ. Stud.

3   Brazier, J. D. 1975. Defining end use property requirements or a contribution to the more efficient use of tropical forest resources. FAO, Rome. 9 p. Multigraphed.

8   Brokenska, D., and B. Riley. 1978. Forest, foraging, fences and fuel in a marginal area of Kenya. Paper presented at USAID Africa Bureau workshop on firewood, Washington, D.C. 26 p.

8   Brown, N. L. 1980. Renewable energy resources for developing countries. Annu. Rev. Energy 5:389-413.

7   Brown, S., and A. E. Lugo. 1980. Preliminary estimate of the storage of organic carbon in tropical forest ecosystems. Pages 65-117 *in* The role of tropical forests on the world carbon cycle. Report of a symposium, Rio Piedras, Puerto Rico, March 1980. U.S. Department of Energy, Washington, D.C.

7   Brown, S., A. E. Lugo, and B. Liegel. 1980. The role of tropical forests on the world carbon cycle. U.S. Department of Energy, Washington, D.C. 156 p.

7   Brünig, E. F., ed. 1977. Trans. international MAB/IUFRO workshop on tropical rainforest ecosystems research, Hamburg-Reinbeck, May 1977. Spec. Rep. No. 1. Hamburg-Reinbeck, F. R. Germany. 364 p.

Brünig, E. F. 1979. Pages 273-288 *in* Trans. second international MAB/IUFRO workshop on tropical rainforest ecosystems research, October 1978, Jakarta, Indonesia. Spec. Rep. No. 2. Chair of World Forestry, Hamburg-Reinbeck, F. R. Germany.

2   Budowski, G. 1974. Forest plantations and nature conservation. IUCN Bull. 5:25-26.

Budowski, G. 1980. The place of agroforestry in managing tropical forests. Paper presented at international symposium on tropical forests, Yale University, New Haven, Connecticut, April 1980.

1   Burger, D. 1972. Seedlings of some tropical trees and shrubs, mainly of southeast Asia. UNIPUB, New York. 416 p.

6   Catinot, R. 1965. Sylviculture tropicale en forêt dense africaine. Bois For. Trop. 100:9-18.

2   Catinot, R. 1972. Plantation intensive des essences forestières sous les tropiques humides. Environment et principaux problèmes régionaux de recherches. Pages 271-276 *in* Rapport de la conférence FAO pour l'établissement de programmes coopératifs de recherche agronomique entre pays ayant des conditions écologiques semblables en Afrique. Zone guinéene. FAO, Rome. 313 p.

6   Catinot, R. 1974. Le présent et l'avenir des forêts tropicales humides. Bois For. Trop. 154:3-26.

6   Centre Technique Forestier Tropical. 1971. Économic forestière des pays d'Afrique tropicale de l'ouest. Études Scientifiques, numéro spécial, juin 1971. 78 pp.

4   Chauvin, H. 1976. Factors conditioning the systems and costs for opening up and harvesting the tropical moist forests. FO:FDT/76/6(a). FAO, Rome. 17 p.

8   Chidumayo, N. 1979. Household wood fuel and environment in Zambia. Environmental Report No. 1. Natural Resources Department, Lusaka. 9 p.

8   CIDA (Canadian International Development Agency). 1981. CIDA sectoral guidelines: forestry. CIDA, Quebec. 17 p.

8   Conway, F. J. 1979. A study of the fuelwood situation in Haiti. Prepared for USAID Mission to Haiti (AID-521-C-98).

6   Cunia, T. 1974. Forest inventory sampling designs used in countries other than the United States and Canada. Proceedings of workshop on inventory design and analysis. Colorado State University, Fort Collins.

6   Cunia, T. 1976. Statistical advances in methodology for forest inventory. Proceedings of XVI IUFRO world congress, June 1976. International Union of Forestry Research Organizations, Oslo, Norway.

6   Cunia, T. 1978. A short survey of worldwide forest inventory methodology. Pages 114-120 *in* Integrated inventories of renewable natural resources. Proceedings of workshop Tucson, Arizona, January 1978. General Technical Report, RM-55. U.S. Department of Agriculture, Forest Service, Washington, D.C.

6   Cunia, T. 1981. A review of methods of forest inventory. Pages 9-20 *in* J. J. Talbot and W. Swanson, eds. Woodpower: new perspectives in forest usage. Pergamon Press, New York.

1   Darkoh, M. B. K. 1980. Man and desertification in tropical Africa. Inaugural Lecture Series No. 26. University of Dar es Salaam, Dar Es Salaam, Tanzania. 23 p.

1   Dasmann, R. F., J. P. Milton, and P. H. Freeman. 1973. Ecological principles for economic development. John Wiley & Sons, New York. 252 p.

6   Dawkins, H. C. 1958. The management of natural tropical high-forest with special reference to Uganda. Institute Paper No. 34. Imperial Forestry Institute, University of Oxford, U.K. 155 p.

6   Dawkins, H. C. 1959. The volume increment of natural tropical high forest and limitations on its improvement. Emp. For. Rev. 38:175-180.

6   Dawkins, H. C. 1964. Productivity of tropical forests and their ultimate value to man. Pages 178-182 *in* The ecology of man in the tropical environment. IUCN Publ., New Series No. 4. IUCN, Morges, Switzerland.

    Denevan, W. M. 1975. The causes and consequences of tropical shifting cultivation. FAO, Rome. 10 p. Multigraphed.

6   Donis, C. 1956. La forêt dense congolaise et sa sylviculture. Bull. Agr. Congo Belge (Bruxelles) 2:261-360.

8   Douglas, J. S. 1973. L'agri-sylviculture: pour accroître la production alimentaire de la nature. Impact Sci. Soc. XXIII(2):127-144.

8   Earl, D. C. 1975. Forest energy and economic development. Clarendon Press, Oxford. 43 p.

3   Easton, J. C., and M. M. McFarlane. 1973. Economics of pulp and paper pollution abatement. FO:MISC/79/9. FAO, Rome, 34 p.

8   Eckholm, E. 1979. Planting for the future: forestry for human needs. Worldwatch Paper 26. Worldwatch Institute, Washington, D.C. 64 p.

3   Erfurth, T. 1976. Product development and the choice and effective application of promotional measures to advance the wider use of products from the tropical moist forests. FO:FDT/76/10(b). FAO, Rome. 10 p.

    Ewel, J., and L. Conde. 1978. Environmental implication of any-species utilization in the moist tropics. Pages 107-123 *in* Proceedings of conference on improved utilization of tropical forests. Forest Products Laboratory, U.S. Forest Service, Madison, Wisconsin.

8   FAO (Food and Agriculture Organization). 1956. Tree planting practices in tropical Africa. FAO, Rome. 302 p.

8   FAO. 1957a. Tree planting practices in tropical Asia. FAO, Rome. 172 p.

6   FAO. 1957b. Tropical silviculture. Vol. 1. FAO, Rome. 190 p.

6   FAO. 1958. Tropical silviculture. Vol. 2. FAO, Rome. 415 p.

2   FAO. 1960. Prácticas de plantación forestal en America Latina. FAO, Rome. 499 p.

6   FAO. 1971. Tropical silviculture. Vol. 3. FAO, Rome. 101 p.

3   FAO. 1973a. Guide for planning pulp and paper enterprises. Forestry and Forest Products Studies No. 18. FAO, Rome. 362 p.

2   FAO. 1973b. A manual of establishment techniques in man-made forests. FO: MISC/73/3. FAO, Rome. 108 p.

    FAO. 1973c. Manual of forest inventory, with special reference to mixed tropical forests. FAO, Rome. 200 p.

5   FAO. 1974a. Employment in forestry. Report on FAO/ILO/SIDA consultation on employment in forestry, Chiang Mai, Thailand, February-March, 1974. FAO/SWE/TF 126, FAO, Rome.

4   FAO. 1974b. Exploitation and transport of logs in dense tropical forests. Forest Development No. 18. FAO, Rome. 100 p.

FAO. 1974c. Lectures presented at FAO/SIDA regional seminar on shifting cultivation and soil conservation in Africa, Ibadan, Nigeria, July 1973. FAO, Rome.

4,8 FAO. 1977. Draft list of large scale forest inventories carried out in the tropics. FO:MISC/77/24, FAO, Rome. 15 p.

8   FAO. 1979. Agris forestry. World catalogue of information and documentation services. FAO Forestry Paper No. 15. FAO, Rome. 135 p.

8   FAO. 1980. Report of FAO/SIDA seminar on forestry in rural community development. FOR:GCP INT 313 (SWE), Rome. 167 p.

2,5 FAO/UNDP (United Nations Development Program). 1971. Demonstration and training in forest range and plantations in peninsular Malaysia. FO:DP/MAL/72/009. Working Paper No. 36. Kuala Lumpur. 205 p.

1,2 FAO/UNEP (United Nations Environmental Program). 1975. The methodology of conservation of forest genetic resources. FO:MISC/78/8. FAO, Rome. 127 p.

8   FAO/World Bank. 1979. Draft report of the Malawi wood energy project. Rept. No. 52/79 MLW4. FAO, Rome. 95 p.

Felker, P., and R. S. Bandurski. 1979. Uses and potential uses of leguminous trees for minimal energy input in agriculture. Econ. Bot. 33(2):172-184.

8   Fleuret, P. C., and A. K. Fleuret. 1978. Fuelwood use in a peasant community. J. Dev. Areas 12(c):315-322.

8   Florence, R. G. 1972. The use and development of forest resources in ASPAC countries. ASPAC Registry of Scientific and Technical Services, Canberra. 51 p.

4   Fontaine, R. G. 1976. The impact upon the environment of forestry practices in tropical moist forests. FO:FDT/76/8(b). FAO, Rome. 20 p.

6   Fraser, A. I. 1975. Technical and economic implications of management systems in moist tropical forests in Asia. FAO, Rome. 13 p.

2   Gallegos, C. M., B. J. Zobel, and W. S. Dvorak. 1980. The combined industry-university-government efforts to farm the Central American and Mexico coniferous resources cooperative. 5 p. Mimeographed.

Garrad, A. 1955. The germination and longevity of seed in an equatorial climate. Gard. Bull. (Singapore) 14:534-545.

7   Golley, F., and E. Farnworth, eds. 1974. Fragile ecosystems: evaluation of research and applications in the neotropics. Springer-Verlag, New York. 258 p.

Goodland, R. J. 1980. Mitigation of deforestation. World Bank, Washington, D.C. Unpublished.

4   Goodland, R. J., and H. S. Irwin. 1975. Amazon jungle: green hell to red desert? Elsevier, Amsterdam. 155 p.

Goodland, R. J., H. S. Irwin, and G. Tillman. 1978. Ecological development for Amazonia. Cienc. Cult. (São Paulo) 30(3):275-289.

2   Grouley, J. 1976. Conversion planting in tropical moist forests. FO:FOT/76/7(b). FAO, Rome.

6   Grubb, P. J. 1977. Control of forest growth and distribution on wet tropical mountains, with special reference to mineral nutrition. Annu. Rev. Ecol. Syst. 8:83-107.

1,6 Hamilton, L. S. 1976. Tropical rain forest use and preservation: a study of problems and practices in Venezuela. Sierra Club Spec. Publ., Inc. Ser. No. 4. Sierra Club, San Francisco, 72 p.

Hartshorn, G. S. 1975. A matrix model of tree population dynamics. Pages 41-51 *in* F. B. Golley and E. Medina, eds. Tropical ecological systems. Springer-Verlag, New York.

Hartshorn, G. S. 1978. Tree falls and tropical forest dynamics. Pages 617-638 *in* P. B. Tomlinson and M. H. Zimmerman, eds. Tropical trees as living systems. Cambridge University Press, Cambridge, U.K.

Hawkes, J. G. 1977. The importance of wild germplasm in plant breeding. Euphytica 26:615-621.

Holling, S. C., ed. 1978. Adaptive environmental assessment. John Wiley & Sons, New York. 377 p.

8   Howe, J. W. 1977. Energy for the village of Africa: recommendations for African governments and outside donors. Overseas Development Council, Washington, D.C.

8   Husch, B. 1971. Planning a forest inventory. FAO Forestry Series No. 4. FAO, Rome. 120 p.

ICRAF (International Council for Research on Agroforestry). 1979. Agroforestry defined. ICRAF Newsletter 1(1):3.

1   IUCN (International Union for the Conservation of Nature and Natural Resources). 1975a. The use of ecological guidelines for development in the American humid tropics. Proceedings of international meeting, Caracas, Venezuela, February 1974. IUCN Publ., New Series No. 31. IUCN, Morges, Switzerland. 249 p.

1   IUCN (International Union for the Conservation of Nature and Natural Resources). 1975b. The use of ecological guidelines for development in tropical forest area of south-east Asia. Proceedings of regional meeting, Bandung, Indonesia, May-June, 1974. IUCN Publ., New Series No. 32. IUCN, Morges, Switzerland. 185 p.

1   IUCN (International Union for the Conservation of Nature and Natural Resources). 1980. World conservation strategy. IUCN, Gland, Switzerland.

7   IUFRO (International Union of Forestry Research Organizations). 1975. Preliminary report, Committee on Tropical Forestry Research. IUFRO, Oslo, Norway. 9 p.

7   Jacobs, M. R. 1972. Research needs in silviculture and forest management. Tech. Rep. No. 1, UNOP/SF Project BRA/45. FAO, Rome. 85 p.

Janos, D. P. 1980a. Vesicular-arbuscular mycorrhizae affect lowland tropical rain forest plant growth. Ecology 61(a):151-162.

Janos, D. P. 1980b. Mycorrhizae influence tropical succession. Biotropica 12:56-64.

Janzen, D. H. 1970. Herbivores and the number of tree species in tropical forests. Am. Nat. 104:501-528.

Janzen, D. H. 1977. Additional land at what price? Responsible use of the tropics in a food-production confrontation. Proc. Am. Phytopathol. Soc. 3:35-39.

2   Johnson, N. E. 1975. Biological opportunities and risks associated with fast growing plantations in the tropics. FAO, Rome. 16 p.

Kadambi, K. 1958. Methods of increasing growth and obtaining regeneration of tropical forests. Pages 67-78 *in* Tropical silviculture. FAO, Rome.

Kartawinata, K. 1979. An overview of the environmental consequences of tree removal from the forest in Indonesia. Pages 129-140 *in* S. G. Boyce, ed. Biological and sociological basis for a rational use of forest resources for energy and organics. Proceedings of international workshop, Michigan State University, East Lansing. May 1979. U.S. Forest Service, Asheville, North Carolina.

King, K. F. S. 1972. A plan of action for the next six years. A summary of the revised FAO study on forest policy, law and administration. *In* Proceedings of 7th World Forestry Congress, October 1972. Liberia del Plata, Buenos Aires, Argentina.

King, K. F. S., and M. T. Chandler. 1978. The wasted lands. International Council for Research on Agroforestry, Nairobi. 36 p.

8   Knowles, R. L. 1972. Farming with forestry: multiple land use. Farm For. 14:61-70.

Kyrklund, B. 1978. Use of mixed tropical hardwoods for pulp manufacture. Pages 309-312 *in* Proceedings of conference on improved utilization of tropical forests. Forest Products Laboratory, U.S. Forest Service, Madison, Wisconsin.

Ladrach, W. E. 1981. Sustained use of tropical forest ecosystems. Seminar presented at U.S. National Academy of Sciences, Washington, D.C., July 1981. 3 p. Mimeographed.

1   Ladrach, W. E., and M. Gutierrez W. 1979. Genetic gains with *Cupressus lusitanica* through six years of tree improvement in Colombia. Cartón de Colombia, Research Report No. 50. Calí, Colombia. 24 p.

2   Lamb, A. F. A. 1972. Tropical pulp and timber plantations: a brief account of forest plantations in the tropics. *In* Proceedings of 7th World Forestry Congress, October 1972. Liberia del Plata, Buenos Aires, Argentina.

6   Lamb, D. 1977. Conservation and management of tropical rain forests: a dilemma of development in Papua New Guinea. Environ. Conserv. 4:121-129.

6   Lamb, D. 1980. Some ecological and social consequences of logging rain forests in Papua New Guinea. *In* J. I. Furtado, ed. Proceedings of 5th international symposium on tropical ecology. International Society for Tropical Ecology, Kuala Lumpur, Malaysia, April 1979.

2   Lanly, J. P., and J. Clement. 1979. Present and future natural forest and plantation areas in tropics. Unasylva 31:12-20.

Lanly, J. P., and M. Gillis. 1980. Provisional results of the FAO/UNEP tropical forest resources assessment project: Tropical America. FAO, Rome. 13 p.

Laundrie, J. F. 1978. Kraft and NSSC pulping of mixed tropical hardwoods. Pages 333-354 *in* Proceedings of conference on improved utilization of tropical forests. Forest Products Laboratory, U.S. Forest Service, Madison, Wisconsin.

6   Lawton, R. M. 1978. The management and regeneration of some Nigerian high forest ecosystems. Pages 580-588 *in* Tropical forest ecosystems. UNESCO, Paris.

6   Leslie, A. 1977. Where contradictory theory and practice coexist. Unasylva 29:2-17.

Litsinger, J. A., and R. Moody. 1976. Integrated pest management in multiple cropping systems. Pages 293-316 *in* R. I. Papendick, ed. Multiple cropping. Spec. Publ. 27. American Society of Agronomy, Madison, Wsiconsin.

Lugo, A. E., and M. M. Brinson. 1978. Calculations of the value of salt water wetlands. Pages 120-130 *in* Wetlands function and value: the state of our understanding. Proceedings of national symposium on wetlands. American Water Resources Association, Minneapolis, Minnesota.

8   MAB (Man and Biosphere Programme). 1970. Management of natural resources in Africa: traditional strategies and modern decision-making. MAB Technical Notes 9. UNESCO, Paris. 81 p.

6   Mazuera, H. 1979. Composition and growth of four to 15 year old natural regeneration in the lower Calima concession. Research Report No. 46. Cartón de Colombia, S.A., Investigación Forestal, Calí, Colombia. 28 p.

6   Meijer, W. 1973. Devastation and regeneration of tropical lowland dipterocarp forest in Southeast Asia. BioScience 23:528-533.

Mikola, P. 1969. Afforestation of treeless areas. Unasylva 23:35-48.

8   Mongi, H. O., and P. A. Huxley. 1979. Soils research in agroforestry. Proceedings of expert consultation held at International Council for Research in Agroforestry (ICRAF), Nairobi, March 1979. ICRAF, Nairobi. 584 p.

Morales, J. O., W. N. Gangham, and M. F. Barrus. 1949. Cultivos intercalados en plantaciones de *Hevea*. Instituto Interamericano de Ciencias Agricolas, Boletin Technico N.I. Turrialba, Costa Rica.

5   Moravscik, M. J. 1981. Scientific and technological assistance and the challenge of the 80's. Science and Public Policy, Feb. 1981:40–44.

8   Muzava, E. M. 1980. Report on village afforestation: lessons of experience in Tanzania. FAO, Rome. 8 p.

1   Myers, N. 1979. The sinking ark. Pergamon Press, New York. 307 p.

Newman, D. 1980. Susceptibility of trees to bagworm (*Oiketicus kirbyi*) defoliation in the Cauca Valley. Research Report No. 63. Cartón de Colombia, Investigación Forestal, Calí, Colombia. 10 p.

NRC (National Research Council). 1977. Methane generation from human, animal, and agricultural wastes. National Academy of Sciences, Washington, D.C. 131 p.

NRC (National Research Council). 1979a. Tropical legumes: resources for the future. National Academy of Sciences, Washington, D.C. 331 p.

NRC (National Research Council). 1979b. Microbial processes: promising technologies for developing countries. National Academy of Sciences, Washington, D.C. 198 p.

NRC (National Research Council). 1980a. Firewood crops—shrubs and tree species for energy production. National Academy Press, Washington, D.C. 237 p.

NRC (National Research Council). 1980b. Conversion of tropical moist forests. National Academy Press, Washington, D.C. 205 p.

NRC (National Research Council). 1980c. Research priorities in tropical biology. National Academy Press, Washington, D.C. 116 p.

6   Nwoboshi, L. C. 1975. Problems and prospects of natural regeneration in the future management of the tropical moist forest for timber production. FAO, Rome.

Okigbo, B. N. 1980. Development of multiple-use management for tropical forests through research in Africa. Pages 26–37 *in* IUFRO/MAB conference: research on multiple use of forest resources, May 1980, Flagstaff, Arizona. Gen. Tech. Rept. WO-25. U.S. Forest Service.

Okigbo, B. N., and R. Lal. 1979. Soil fertility maintenance and conservation for improved agroforestry systems in the lowland humid tropics. Pages 41–47 *in* H. O. Mongi and P. A. Huxley, eds. Soils research in agroforestry. ICRAF001e, Nairobi, Kenya.

8   Olawoye, O. O. 1975. The agri-silvicultural system in Nigeria. Commonw. For. Rev. 54(3–4), No. 161–162:229–236.

8   Openshaw, K., and J. Moris. 1979. The socioeconomics of agroforestry. University of Dar es Salaam, Morogoro, Tanzania. 6 p.

OTA (Office of Technology Assessment). 1981. Impacts of applied genetics: microorganisms, plants, and animals. Congress of the United States, OTA, Washington, D.C. 331 p.

1,6   Ovington, J. D. 1975. Forest management in relation to ecological principles. Pages 111–119 *in* The use of ecological guidelines for development in tropical forest areas of southeast Asia. IUCN Publ., New Series No. 32. IUCN, Morges, Switzerland.

4,6   Palmer, J. R. 1975. Toward more reasonable objectives in tropical high forest management for timber production. Commonw. For. Rev. 53, No. 161–162: 273–289.

1,7   Persson, R. 1974. World forest resources. Review of world's forest resources in the early 1970's. Department of Forest Survey Rep. No. 17. Royal College of Forestry, Stockholm. 261 p.

1,7   Persson, R. 1975. Forest resources of Africa. Rep. No. 18. Royal College of Forestry, Stockholm.

Phillips, F. H., A. F. Logan, and V. Balodis. 1978. Suitability of tropical forests for pulpwood: mixed hardwoods, residues, and reforestation species. Pages 262–278 *in*

Proceedings of conference on improved utilization of tropical forests. Forest products Laboratory, U.S. Forest Service, Madison, Wisconsin.

1 Poore, D. 1976. The values of tropical moist forest ecosystems and the environmental consequences of their removal. FO:FDT/76/8(a). FAO, Rome. 39 p.

Posner, J. L., and M. J. McPherson. 1981. The steep-sloped areas of tropical America: current situation and prospects for the year 2000. Agricultural Sciences Division, The Rockefeller Foundation, New York. Unpublished.

3 Pringle, S. L. 1976. The role of tropical moist forests in world demand, supply and trade of forest products. FO:FOT/76/10(a). FAO, Rome. 22 p.

Qureshi, A., L. S. Hamilton, D. Mueller-Dombois, W. R. H. Penera, and R. A. Carpenter. 1980. Assessing tropical forest lands: their suitability for sustainable uses. East West Center, Honolulu. 69 p.

8 Ranganathan, S. 1979. Agro-forestry: employment for millions. Tata Press, Bombay.

Rathke, J. K., and R. J. Hegstrom. 1975. Strip intercropping for wind protection. *In* Proceedings of the multiple cropping symposium, annual meeting, Knoxville, Tennessee. American Society of Agronomy, Madison, Wsiconsin.

2 Redhead, J. F. 1960. Taungya planting. Niger. For. Inf. Bull. (IBADAN), New Series No. 5:13–16.

7 Roche, L. 1976. Priorities for forestry research and development in the tropics. International Development Research Centre, Ottawa, Canada. 105 p.

8 Roy, S. 1980. Case study on fuelwood collection and problems of rural women. Collected papers from seminar on the role of women in community forestry, December 1980. Forest Research Institute, Dehra Dun, India.

Sanchez, P. A., and J. G. Salinas. 1981. Low input technology for management of oxisols and ultisols in tropical America. Adv. Agron. 34:278–405.

3 Sargent, K. 1975. Factors in the planning of wood based industrial development in the context of southeast Asia. FAO, Rome. 17 p. Multigraphed.

8 Sartorius, P., and H. Henle. 1968. Forestry and economic development. Praeger, New York. 123 p.

Schubart, H. O. R., and E. Salati. 1980. Natural resource for land use in the Amazon region: the natural systems. Paper presented at conference on Amazon land use and agricultural research. Centro Internacional de Agriculture Tropical, Calí, Colombia.

2 Sedjo, R. A. 1980. Forest plantations in Brazil and their possible effects on world pulp markets. J. For. (December, 1980): 702–705.

2 Sedjo, R. A. 1981. The potential of U.S. forestlands in the world context. Paper presented for conference on coping with pressures on U.S. forestlands, March 1981, sponsored by Resources for the Future, Washington, D.C. 31 p.

Sioli, H. 1973. Recent human activities in the Brazilian Amazon region and their ecological effects. Pages 321–334 *in* B. J. Meggers, E. S. Ayensu, and W. D. Duckworth, eds. Tropical forest ecosystems in Africa and South America. Smithsonian Institution, Washington, D.C.

6 Skapski, K. 1971. Intensive forest management. Study paper, Pahang Tenggara regional master planning study for peninsular Malaysia, No. 11. Government of Malaysia, Kuala Lumpur.

8 Smith, N. 1981. Wood: an ancient fuel with a new future. Worldwatch Institute, Washington, D.C.

Smythe, N. 1970. Relationships between fruiting seasons and seed dispersal methods in a neotropical forest. Am. Nat. 104:25–35.

Sommer, A. 1976. Attempt at an assessment of the world's tropical forests. Unasylva 28(112/113):5-27.

8   Spears, J. S. 1980. Small farmers—or the tropical forest ecosystem? Paper presented at international tropical forestry symposium, Yale University, April 1980.

Stover, S. L. 1979. Grazing and exotic forestry: the development of an interculture experiment in New Zealand. Agric. Hist. 53(2):438-450.

Strong, D. R., Jr. 1974. Rapid asymptotic species accumulation in phytophagous insect communities: the pests for cacao. Science 185(4156):1064-1066.

5   Svanqvist, N. 1976. Employment opportunities in the tropical moist forests under alternative silvicultural systems, including agrisilvicultural techniques. FO:FDT/ 76/6(b), FAO, Rome. 107 p.

6   Synnott, T. J., and R. H. Kemp. 1976. The relative merits of natural regeneration, enrichment planting and conversion planting in tropical moist forests, including agrisilvicultural techniques. FO:FDT/76/7(a). FAO, Rome. 12 p.

Toenniessen, G. 1980. Travel diary—Jari project. March 17-21, 1980. Rockefeller Foundation, New York. 11 p.

6   Troup, R. S. 1928. Silvicultural systems. *In* Oxford manuals of forestry. Clarendon Press, Oxford. 199 p.

7   UNESCO (United Nations Educational, Scientific, and Cultural Organization). 1978. Tropical forest ecosystems. A state-of-knowledge report prepared by UNESCO/ UNEP/FAO. Natural Resources Research XIV. UNESCO, Paris. 683 p.

USAID (U.S. Agency for International Development). 1979. Environmental and natural resource management in developing countries. A report to Congress. Vol. I. AID/DOS, Washington, D.C. 184 p.

4,5,8 USDA (United States Department of Agriculture). 1980. Forestry activities and deforestation problems in developing countries. Report to USAID. Forest Products Laboratory, U.S. Forest Service, Madison, Wisconsin. 115 p.

Vandermeer, J. 1981. The interference production principle: an ecological theory for agriculture. BioScience 31(5):361-364.

Vine, H. 1953. Experiments on the maintenance of soil fertility at Ibadan, Nigeria, 1922-1951. Emp. J. Exp. Agric. 21:65-68.

Vine, H. 1968. Developments in the study of soils and shifting agriculture in tropical Africa. Pages 89-119 *in* R. P. Moss, ed. The soil resources of Africa. Cambridge University Press, Cambridge, U.K.

1   Voorhoeve, A. G. 1979. Liberian high forest trees. UNIPUB, New York. 428 p.

1,6 Wadsworth, F. H. 1966. Forest resources of the world. Proc. Sixth World For. Cong. 3:3135-3143. Estrana por Commercial y Artes Traficas, S. A. Barcelona, Spain.

Wadsworth, F. H. 1975. Natural forests in the development of the humid American tropics. Pages 128-138 *in* The use of ecological guidelines for development in the American humid tropics. IUCN Publ., New Series No. 31. IUCN, Morges, Switzerland.

Watters, R. F. 1971. Shifting cultivation in Latin America. FAO Forestry Development Paper No. 17. FAO, Rome. 305 p.

Weber, F. R. 1977. Reforestation in arid lands. Action/Peace Corps Program and Training Journal, Manual Series No. 5, and Volunteer in Technical Assistance, Manual Series No. 37 E. Vita, Mt. Ranier, Maryland. 248 p.

5   Weiss, C., M. Kamenetzky, and J. Ramerk. 1980. Technological capacity as an element of development strategy. Interciencia 5(2):96-100.

1   Whitmore, T. C. 1975. Tropical rainforests of the Far East. Clarendon Press, Oxford. 278 p.

1   Whitmore, T. C. 1976. Conservation review of tropical rain forest, general considerations and Asia. IUCN, Morges, Switzerland. 116 p.

1   Whitmore, T. C. 1980. The conservation of the tropical rain forest. Pages 303–318 *in* M. Soulé and B. Wilcox, eds. Conservation biology: an evolutionary-ecological perspective. Sinhauer Associates, Sunderland, Massachusetts.

     World Bank. 1978. Forestry: sector policy paper. Washington, D.C. 65 p.

8   World Bank. 1979. Burundi forestry project. Staff appraisal report for Eastern Africa Region. Central Agriculture Division. World Bank, Washington, D.C.

8   World Bank. 1980a. Forestry project—case studies. Gujarat community forestry project (first draft May 1980). World Bank, Washington, D.C.

8   World Bank. 1980b. Rwanda integrated forestry and livestock development project. Staff Appraisal Report for Eastern Africa Region, Central Agriculture Division. World Bank, Washington, D.C. 8 p.

8   World Bank. 1980c. Renewable energy task force study, developing countries fuelwood supply/demand analysis, 1980-2000. World Bank, Washington, D.C.

8   World Bank. 1980d. Designing forestry components for inclusion in agricultural and rural development project. World Bank, Washington, D.C.

6   Wyatt-Smith, J. 1963. Manual of Malayan silviculture for inland forests. Malayan Forest No. 23. Kuala Lumpur. 400 p.

4   Zambia Forest Department. 1978. Lusaka fuel wood project. Lusaka, Zambia.

2,3,4 Zobel, B. 1979. The ecological impact of industrial forest management. Res. Rep. No. 52. Cartón de Colombia, S.A., Investigación Forestal. 11 p.

1   Zon, R., and W. N. Sparhawk. 1923. Forest resources of the world. 2 vols. McGraw Hill, New York. 997 p.

7

Soil Management
Considerations

The principal issues here considered are: (1) land resource inventories, (2) choice of land-clearing method, (3) soil management for continuous production of annual food crops, (4) soil managment for persistent grass/ legume pastures and continuous livestock production, and (5) soil management for perennial crop production.

LAND RESOURCE INVENTORIES

The first step is to have available a land resource inventory of the target area, including detailed data on climate, soils, vegetation, and information concerning the infrastructure. The level of detail attainable depends upon the size and intensity of the project. The FAO world soil maps at the scale of 1:5 million provide only a gross estimate. Maps at the 1:1 million scale, such as those produced by the Centro Internacional de Agricultura Tropical (CIAT) Land Resources Evaluation Study (Cochrane *et al.,* 1979; Appendix A) and the RADAM Project of Brazil (Projecto RADAM-Brasil, 1972–1978), provide five times the detail and include, in addition to soils data (see Chapter 2), the needed climatic, vegetation, and communications infrastructure data. For projects with clearly delineated boundaries that involve fairly intensive use of land, a more detailed level of information is usually required (Table 7-1). Soil maps on a scale of 1:20,000 and larger are best for local planning activities (Ranzani, 1978; Morán, 1981).

Class 1 lands are suitable for all uses: high-, medium-, or low-input crop production, improved pastures, forestry, and biological preserves. As the

TABLE 7-1 Land Suitability Classification Framework Used in the Amazon of Brazil for Rainfed Agriculture[a,b]

Land Capability Groups	Annual Crops			Improved Pastures	Forest and/or Natural Pasture	Biological Preserve
	High Input[c]	Medium Input[d]	Low Input[a]	Medium Input[d]	Low Input[e]	No Input
1						
2						
3						
4						
5						
6						

[a]Ramalho et al., 1978.
[b]Blocked area indicates suitability.
[c]Fertilizers; new technology, largely mechanized.
[d]Limited fertilizer, technology, and mechanization.
[e]Primarily manual labor; few purchased inputs.

class number increases, the range in alternatives decreases, because constraints become more severe. Class 6 lands should not be touched at all.

This pattern serves as a logical starting point, but several modifications may be needed. For example, a technology breakthrough of acid-tolerant improved pastures may expand the amount of land assigned to Class 3. Likewise, if biological preserves are limited to land that cannot be used for agriculture or forestry, such as steep lands or swamps, the preservation of genetic diversity will be hampered.

A distinction should be made between single-use development projects and integrated ones. Single-use projects focus on one product, such as rice, beef, rubber, or pulpwood. Integrated projects seek to mesh the best use among the different soils and land systems in the region, including areas that should not be touched. A paddy rice development project should identify poorly drained soils of high native fertility where flooding hazard is low and irrigation water is readily available. A project designed to grow rubber would best be located on well-drained, acid soils, since high soil acidity is needed for high latex yield (Chan, 1979). Those two projects could operate in the same area without impinging on each other. Managers of other single-use projects, such as cassava or cattle production, would prefer working on the best soils, although appropriate pastures and cassava are adapted to acid soils. An integrated approach would recognize that cassava and cattle should not both concentrate on the more fertile soils because such soils could be put to more intensive use.

Efforts should be made to ensure that land suitability classification be made according to up-to-date criteria (Buol *et al.,* 1975; Cochrane *et al.,* 1979; Buringh, 1980; Qureshi *et al.,* 1980). To do so in the humid tropics is seldom easy, because most research programs are isolated.

Local farmers' experience should also be taken into consideration, but under pressure of time urgent decisions made in the capital city often bypass them.

An excellent example of local knowledge is to be found in a survey by Morán (1977) showing the ingenious selection criteria used by shifting cultivators near Altamira, along the Trans-Amazon Highway of Brazil. The *caboclos,* native to the region, select sites with trees of relatively thin trunks, such as acai (*Euterpe aleracea*), babacu (*Orbignya martiana*), and moroco (*Bauhinia macrotachia*). The *colonos,* or new settlers attracted by government colonization projects, looked for virgin forests with thick tree trunks such as acapu (*Vouacapona americana*), caju-acu (*Anacardim giganteum*), and jarana (*Holopyxidium jarana*). After 1 year of similar slash-and-burn practices, the sites chosen by the *caboclos* had a chemical status markedly superior to those of the *colonos.* Table 7-2 suggests that the *caboclos* were able to identify areas of the more fertile Alfisols by vege-

TABLE 7-2 Topsoil (0–10 cm) Properties of Soil Selected by Caboclos and Colonos near Altamira, Pa., Brazil[a,b]

Farmer Type	Indicator Trees (trunk width)	Moist-Soil Color	pH	Org C (%)	Available P (N.C.)[c] (ppm)	Exchangeable Al (meq/100g)	Ca+Mg	K	ECEC[d]	Al Saturation (%)
Caboclo	Thin	10 yr 4/4–3/2	6.2	1.7	26	0	7.1	0.1	8.2	0
Colono	Large	7.5 yr 4/5	4.3	2.3	2	5.5	1.1	0.2	6.8	81

[a]Morán (1977).
[b]Mean of three samples taken a year after felling and burning.
[c]North Carolina extraction method.
[d]Effective cation exchange capacity.

tation, whereas the new settlers selected the acid-infertile Ultisols and Oxisols, where the trees were bigger, perhaps because of a lower tree population per hectare. The *caboclos* also grew mostly cassava, whereas the *colonos* planted rice, corn, and beans, all without fertilization. As a result of the judicious selection of soils and adapted crops by the traditional shifting cultivators, the *caboclos'* farm income was twice that of the new settlers (Morán, 1977). Although indicator species are likely to differ in other regions, this is a good example of accumulated experience as a way to prolong the cropping period. A quantification of these differences in tree species by chemical analysis would be very useful.

LAND-CLEARING METHODS

The choice of land-clearing methods is the first and probably most crucial step affecting the future productivity of farming systems in the humid tropics. Several comparative studies conducted in the Amazon confirm that land-clearing methods that involve burning are superior to mechanical clearing because of the fertilizer value of the ash, soil compaction caused by bulldozing, and topsoil displacement common in mechanized land clearing (Sanchez, 1979).

Fertilizer Value of the Ash

The nutrient content of the ash produced after burning a 17-year-old secondary forest on an Ultisol of Yurimaguas, Peru, has been determined by Seubert *et al.* (1977). On the average, the ash contributed the equivalent of 145 kg/ha of urea, 67 kg/ha of simple superphosphate, 50 kg/ha of muriate of potash, 0.25 ton/ha of dolomitic limestone, and significant quantities of sulfur and such micronutrients as zinc, copper, manganese, and iron. Such ash additions produced major positive changes in the soils during the first year after clearing. Table 7-3 shows that crop yields were always superior in slash-and-burn plots, even those that were fertilized.

Table 7-4 summarizes changes in soil properties in different parts of the Amazon. Variability in the quantity of ash and its nutrient content occurs because of differences in soils, clearing techniques, and the proportion of the forest biomass actually burned. For example, Da Silva (1979) estimated that only 20% of the forest biomass was actually converted to ash when a virgin forest on an Ultisol of southern Bahia, Brazil, was burned. He also analyzed the ash composition of the burned parts of individual tree species and observed very wide ranges in nitrogen, phosphorous, potassium, calcium, and magnesium content. This information suggests that certain species can be considered accumulators of specific nutrients. They should

TABLE 7-3   Effects of Land-Clearing Methods on Crop Yields at Yurimaguas, Peru[a]

Crops[b]	Fertility Levels[c]	Slash and and Burn (tons/ha)[d]	Bulldozed (tons/ha)[d]	Ratio of Bulldozed to Burned (%)
Upland rice (3)	0	1.3	0.7	53
	NPK	3.0	1.5	49
	NPKL	2.9	2.3	80
Corn (1)	0	0.1	0	0
	NPK	0.4	0.04	10
	NPKL	3.1	2.4	76
Soybeans (2)	0	0.7	0.2	24
	NPK	1.0	0.3	34
	NPKL	2.7	1.8	67
Cassava (2)	0	15.4	6.4	42
	NPK	18.9	14.9	78
	NPKL	25.6	24.9	97
Panicum maximum	0	12.3	8.3	68
(6 cuts/year)	NPK	25.2	17.2	68
	NPKL	32.2	24.2	75
Mean relative yields	0			37
	NPK			47
	NPKL			48

[a]Seubert *et al.* (1977).
[b]Yield is the average of the number of harvests in parentheses.
[c]50 kg N/ha, 172 kg P/ha, 40 kg K/ha; L = 4 t/ha of lime.
[d]Grain yields of upland rice, corn, and soybean; fresh root yields of cassava; annual dry matter production of *Panicum maximum*.

be identified. The fertilizer value of the ash is, of course, likely to be of less relative importance in fertile soils (Cordero, 1964).

SOIL COMPACTION

Conventional bulldozing has the obviously detrimental effect of compacting the soil, particularly sandy and loamy Ultisols. Significant decreases in infiltration rates, increases in bulk density, and decreases in porosity have been recorded on such soils in Surinam (Van der Weert, 1974), Peru (Seubert *et al.*, 1977), and Brazil (Schubart, 1977; Da Silva, 1979). The slash-and-burn clearing method had little effect on infiltration rates, but bulldozing decreased them tremendously.

TABLE 7-4 Summary of Changes in Topsoil Chemical Properties Before and Shortly After Burning Tropical Forests in Ultisols and Oxisols of the Amazon[a]

| Soil Property | Timing | Yurimaguas (2 sites) | | Manaus ($\bar{x}$ 7 sites) $(0.5)^b$ | Belem ($\bar{x}$ 60 sites) $(12)^b$ | Barrolandia (1 site) $(1)^b$ |
		I $(1)^b$	II $(3)^b$			
pH (in H_2O)	Before:	4.0	4.0	3.8	4.8	4.6
	After:	4.5	4.8	4.5	4.9	5.2
	Δ	0.5	0.8	0.7	0.1	0.6
Exch. Ca + Mg (me/100 g)	Before:	0.41	1.46	0.35	1.03	1.40
	After:	0.88	4.08	1.25	1.97	4.40
	Δ	0.47	2.62	0.90	0.94	3.00
Exch. K (me/100 g)	Before:	0.10	0.33	0.07	0.12	0.07
	After:	0.32	0.24	0.22	0.12	0.16
	Δ	0.22	(0.09)	0.15	0.00	0.09
Exch. Al (me/100 g)	Before:	2.27	2.15	1.73	1.62	0.75
	After:	1.70	0.65	0.70	0.90	0.28
	Δ	(0.57)	(1.50)	(1.03)	(0.72)	(0.47)
Al satn. (%)	Before:	81	52	80	58	34
	After:	59	12	32	30	5
	Δ	(22)	(40)	(48)	(28)	(29)
Avail. P. (ppm)	Before:	5	15	—	6.3	1.5
	After:	16	23	—	7.5	8.5
	Δ	11	8	—	1.2	7.0

[a] Sanchez (1979).
[b] Months after burning.

TOPSOIL DISPLACEMENT

The third major consideration is the degree of topsoil displacement, not by the bulldozer blade, which is normally kept above the soil, but by dragging uprooted trees and logs. Although no quantitative data are available, topsoil scraping in high spots and accumulation in low spots is common. The better secondary forest regrowth commonly observed near windrows

TABLE 7-5 Effects of Alternative Land-Clearing and Preparation Systems on Soil Properties and Corn Yields in an Alfisol from Ibadan, Nigeria[a]

Land-Clearing Method	Land Preparation Method	Labor Used for Clearing (man-day/ha)	Tractor Time (h/ha)	Erosion Loss (tons/ha)	Runoff Loss (% of rainfall)	Corn Grain Yields (tons/ha)	Topsoil pH	Available P (Bray) (ppm)
Traditional slash-and-burn, incomplete	Hand planting	57	—	0.01	0.6	0.5	6.6	14
Slash-and-burn, complete	Zero tillage	117	—	0.37	3.5	1.6	6.8	13
Slash-and-burn, complete	Conventional tillage	117	—	4.64	12.1	1.6	6.8	19
Bulldozer with shear blade	Zero tillage	—	1.9	3.82	19.1	2.0	6.2	10
Bulldozer with tree pusher and root rake	Zero tillage	—	2.7	15.36	34.2	1.4	6.3	4
Bulldozer with tree pusher and root rake	Conventional tillage	—	2.7	19.57	56.0	1.8	6.5	10

[a]Adapted from IITA (1980).

of felled vegetation suggests that topsoil carryover can substantially reduce yields.

Topsoil displacement by bulldozing carried out by persons more experienced in road construction than in land clearing can reach alarming proportions. It is common to observe large piles of topsoil, deep holes, and complete scraping away of the topsoil. The holes and the scraping expose the less fertile subsoil, which has limited potential for plant growth. It is imperative that bulldozer blades be kept away from contact with the soil. In practice, this is seldom feasible with a conventional blade.

A shearing or "KG-type" floating blade is a generally better tool. Table 7-5 shows results of a recent study conducted on Alfisols of Ibadan, Nigeria, where the traditional incomplete slash-and-burn was compared with a complete slash-and-burn, and bulldozing with a shear blade was compared with bulldozing with a combination tree pusher and root rake. After clearing, maize was planted by hand or by zero tillage techniques developed at the International Institute for Tropical Agriculture (IITA) or by conventional tillage followed by a grain drill. This table shows that erosion and runoff losses with mechanized clearing were much higher than with a slash-and-burn. The best mechanical clearing method was bulldozing with a shear blade followed by zero tillage. Land thus treated suffered runoff and erosion losses similar to those experienced with the slash-and-burn system followed by conventional tillage. Equipping a bulldozer with a combination of tree pusher and root rake tripled erosion and runoff losses, which reached very high levels. Consequently, bulldozing with a shear blade appears to be the least damaging mechanized system. It should be noted that the corn yields reported are all extremely low, whereas the pH of the soil is high. Unfortunately, this makes an adequate assessment of effects of land-clearing methods on crop yields difficult.

ALTERNATIVE LAND-CLEARING METHODS

Da Silva (1979) compared the two extremes, slash-and-burn and bulldozing, with a scheme of removing the marketable trees first, then cutting the rest and burning them. All the advantages of burning to enhance soil fertility were observed in this latter treatment, not significantly different from the conventional slash-and-burn method, but with a substantial increase in income (assuming markets are available). The lack of differences is probably accounted for by the small proportion of the total biomass that is actually burned.

Other alternative methods consist of mechanized clearing followed by burning, using two bulldozers dragging a heavy chain or using large tree-crushing machines that literally "walk over" the felled forest. The last-named method provides a better burn. In the case of the chain-drag system, the remaining logs can be pushed away into windrows with a root rake after burning. These combined operations capitalize on the fertilizer value of the ash, but they still cause some soil compaction and topsoil removal and are often very expensive.

CHANGES IN SOIL PROPERTIES WITH TIME: EFFECTS OF CLEARING AND BURNING

When a tropical forest is cleared and burned, the following changes in soil properties generally occur within the first year:

- Large volatilization losses of biomass nitrogen and sulfur occur upon burning.
- The pH of acid soils increases, aluminum saturation decreases, and availability of nutrients increases, all because of the nutrient content of the ash. These changes are gradually reversed with time, but the actual amount of time is soil-dependent.
- Soil temperatures increase and moisture regimes fluctuate more, because more solar radiation reaches the soil surface than prior to clearing the forests (Sanchez, 1977b).

SOIL MANAGEMENT FOR ANNUAL CROP PRODUCTION

Most of the basic food crops harvested as annuals are produced under shifting cultivation. Examples of these are upland rice, corn, cassava, plantain, yams, cowpea, peanut, and a large variety of vegetables. Although shifting cultivation in its traditional form is an environmentally sound and energy-efficient food production system (Nye and Greenland, 1960), it is also a guarantee of persistent poverty (Alvim, 1978, 1979). Increased population pressures result in shortening the fallow period, which breaks the process of regeneration in soil fertility and introduces erosion hazards and energy inefficiency (because of declining soil productivity).

Continuous crop production in the acid infertile Oxisols and Ultisols of the humid tropics has been considered by many to be impossible in agronomic and economic terms (Goodland and Irwin, 1975; Irion, 1978). Attempts to transplant temperate region technology for annual crop production into the Congo Basin failed (Jurion and Henry, 1969), as have many other attempts either at the research station or on a development project scale. Recent work (Sanchez, 1977a, 1979) shows that continuous cropping of acid-infertile soils is feasible and highly productive under intensively managed rotation systems. This approach requires inputs of fertilizer; economic analysis shows that the system is profitable (Sanchez *et al.,* 1981).

SOIL MANAGEMENT FOR PASTURE AND LIVESTOCK PRODUCTION

Pasture-based beef production is the largest activity on cleared land in the Amazon Basin and is a major source of controversy, particularly in Brazil. There are about 3.7 million ha of cultivated pastures in forest areas of the Amazon, according to estimates by Kirby (1976) and Serrão *et al.,* (1979). Most of them consist of *Panicum maximum,* are not fertilized, and have a carrying capacity of one animal unit/ha, producing about 100 kg/ha of annual liveweight gain. After the first 3 or 4 years, pasture productivity begins to decline, secondary growth invades, and the pasture slowly changes into secondary forest fallow. Serrão *et al.* (1979) estimate that 20% of the area planted to pastures in the Brazilian Amazon is in some state of degradation. This raises serious questions about the value of this important farming system in the Amazon (Goodland and Irwin, 1975; Schubart, 1977; Fearnside, 1978). The Brazilian government has essentially suspended credits for new land clearings for pasture and is concentrating its research efforts on reclamation of the degraded pastures.

A series of studies conducted primarily in the Paragominas area along the Belem–Brasilia Highway, in northern Mato Grosso, and near Belem has provided pertinent information on soil dynamics as a function of time in pasture production (Falesi, 1976; Baena, 1977; Fearnside, 1978; Hecht, 1978; Serrão *et al.,* 1979). These studies show that pastures retard the rate of fertility decline by maintaining constant for several years the benefits of burning the cleared site prior to planting pasture grasses, particularly a high soil pH, elimination of aluminum toxicity, high calcium and magnesium for the first 4 or 5 years, and adequate levels of phosphorus. Serrão·*et al.* (1979) attribute the eventual decline of *Panicum maximum* to phosphorus and nitrogen deficiency and to the poor adaptation of the grass to this environment. In addition, phosphorus deficiency in Oxisols (and Ultisols) increases as a function of topsoil clay content and iron oxides. Hence clayey Oxisols, such as those in Paragominas, evidence degradation earlier than do loamy types, such as those in northern Mato Grosso.

The solution to this troublesome situation is remarkably simple: Clear the jungle of regrowth (*juquira*) by hand, burn the pasture, and broadcast 25 kg P/ha, half of it as simple superphosphate, the remainder as rock phosphate. When Serrão *et al.* (1979) tried this in a 13-year-old degraded pasture at Paragominas, its botanical composition changed from 75% to 80% weeds and jungle regrowth to 90% to 95% *Panicum maximum.* Further experiments suggest that animal liveweight gains increased accordingly.

Many tropical pasture legumes do not persist in Oxisols and Ultisols because of sensitivity to aluminum toxicity. One of the more notorious is *Leucaena leucocephala.*

Those who have misgivings about maintaining high levels of fertilization and about resistance of pastures to pests and diseases question the wisdom of using certain pasture grasses. However, research at CIAT and elsewhere is directed at finding grass and legume species that require lower levels of fertilization, particularly for phosphorus, and are more resistant to pests and diseases. Species thus far selected for trial include: *Brachiaria humidicola, Andropogon gayanus, Pueraria phaseolides,* and *Desmodium ovalifolium.*

At the other extreme of the Amazon, in the rainforest region of Pucallpa, Peru, Toledo and Morales (1979) report that productive grass–legume pastures fertilized with 50 kg P_2O_5/ha/yr as simple superphosphate have persisted for at least 3 years, producing about 377 kg/ha of annual liveweight gains and having a carrying capacity of three animals/ha in mixtures of *Hyparrhenia rufa* and *Stylosanthes guianensis.* Without the legume, *Hyparrhenia rufa* pastures produced a maximum of 148 kg/ha of annual liveweight gain, with a carrying capacity of 2.1 animals/ha.

These data are most encouraging, because they indicate a very high beef production potential in Amazon jungle pastures with minimal inputs. Also, the Brazilian data suggest a significant degree of nutrient recycling in managed pastures.

SOIL MANAGEMENT FOR PERENNIAL CROPS AND TREE PRODUCTION

Production of perennial tree crops is the best known and least controversial of agricultural practices. Several reasons account for the more advanced state of knowledge in this sector, especially the longer history of research efforts in commercial plantations of rubber, oil palm, cacao, coconuts, bananas, and other export crops. Also, when tree crops are established they tend to mimic the rainforest they replaced with some degree of nutrient cycling.

Sustained production of rubber and oil palm on Oxisols and Ultisols of Southeast Asia is widespread (Chan, 1979). These two species are well adapted to these acid infertile soils, where well-managed production systems are notably stable.

Cacao is particularly successful in the more fertile soils, mainly Alfisols, because this species, unlike rubber and oil palm, is sensitive to acid soil infertility. Very profitable cacao plantations have been established throughout the humid tropics of Latin America on Alfisols under intensive management (Alvim, in press).

The management of these three major perennial crops usually includes fertilization but at rates substantially lower than those required for annual crop production because of the small proportion of plant nutrients removed by harvests, which allows a substantial amount of nutrient cycling to take place. In the humid tropical highlands, coffee and tea occupy a similar position. Both species are also tolerant to soil acidity but normally require more intensive fertilization than do the lowland species.

Soil management practices for establishing perennial crop plantations usually involve manual slash-and-burn clearing followed by planting seedlings at the appropriate spacing, with fertilizers applied, and protecting the exposed soil with a rapidly established plant canopy. For shade-tolerant crops, plantains can be used as a canopy; in many cases, annual crops can be grown for a few years until the perennial crop canopy is established.

Table 7-6 shows the effect of different management approaches to long-term oil palm production in an Alfisol of Benin, Nigeria. Kowal and Tinker (1959) found that intercropping with yams, cassava, and corn did not decrease oil palm production. The effects on soil properties indicate that, although under intercropping there is an overall decrease in nutrient availability, this decrease was not a major deterrant to yield, as compared

TABLE 7-6 Total Oil Palm Production as a Function of Establishment Treatments on an Oxisol of Benin, Nigeria, Planted in 1940[a]

Establishment Treatment	Total Fruit Production, 1945–1956 (tons/ha)
Pure stand, normal weed cover	85
2 years of intercropping[b]	87
12 years of intercropping[b]	93
Pure stand, controlled kudzu cover	89
Pure stand, no weeding	75

[a]Adapted from Kowal and Tinker (1959).
[b]With yams, cassava, and corn.

to continuous annual crop production on Ultisols (Seubert *et al.,* 1977) or poorly managed pastures on Oxisols (Serrão *et al.,* 1979).

Plantations of improved forestry species also exist in many areas. The most spectacular project is probably the Jari Florestal Agropecuaria in the Brazilian Amazon. Seven thousand hectares of such acid-tolerant species as *Gmelina arborea, Pinus caribea,* and *Eucalyptus deglupta* have been planted, and significant areas have already undergone the first harvest. In spite of the vast areas involved and the labor demands, the Jari project quickly abandoned bulldozer clearing for the traditional slash-and-burn method. Damaged soil composition, topsoil displacement, and perhaps nutrient deficiency were noted and alleviated by eliminating bulldozer clearing. Thus far no fertilizers have been added to the plantations, which are located in acid infertile Oxisols and Ultisols. Time will tell whether fertilization may be needed for the second harvest of *Gmelina* and other species.

Agroforestry, a combination of annual crops and pastures with trees, either simultaneously or in sequence, is an attractive alternative. This matter is receiving increasing attention, but unfortunately very few hard data are available (Mongi and Huxley, 1979). King (1968), Bishop (in press), and Hecht (in press) have given excellent descriptions of various agroforestry systems in the humid tropics.

PRIORITIES FOR SOIL MANAGEMENT

The soil management approaches here considered focus on the dominant soils of the humid tropics, the acid-infertile Oxisols and Ultisols. Because many of the actual practices discussed are highly site-specific, development planners often need a broader strategy of soil management.

Appropriate Planning and Application of Technology

Despite the environmentally adverse consequences of clearing noted here, agricultural development will continue at increased rates of land clearing to meet basic human needs. Thus the farming systems that replace forests in the humid tropics should be sufficiently intensive, productive, and stable to minimize the amount of virgin forest conversion. Sound development often entails replacing one productive system, the forest, with such other productive systems as annual crops, pastures, tree crops, and so on.

Experience has shown that agricultural development without proper soil management is hardly more than a variant of shifting cultivation (Bruce, 1965). It can lead to soil degradation and economic bankruptcy. Generic examples of these failures are large-scale, mechanized, land-clearing operations for food production that are implemented with little knowledge of what crops, which crop rotations, or which fertilizer-maintenance and pest-management practices to use (UNESCO, 1978). A specific example is the establishment of cattle pastures in certain parts of the Amazon Basin of Brazil. In this case, a major operation foundered for a combination of reasons: choice of unadapted species, absence of legumes, no fertilizer-maintenance program, high stocking rates of cattle, and poor grazing management (Hecht, 1980).

Technology is now available for efficient management of some plantation tree crops and wet rice production (UNESCO, 1978). Such technologies have been widely applied and are continually fine-tuned to specific sites by research and extension agencies (De Datta, 1981; Alvim, in press). In some areas, soil fertility can be maintained under an adequately fertilized and managed grass and legume pasture, if sufficient phosphorus is provided (Bruce, 1965). Technology for continuous cultivation of annual food crops and legume-based pastures in acid soils of the humid tropics have just been developed (Sanchez, 1977a, 1979; G. McIntosh, Central Research Institute for Agriculture, Bogor, Indonesia, unpublished data; Toledo and Serrão, in press). Such practices have to be validated locally at each development project and the adjusted results applied to local farming systems. Many currently negative views with respect to crop and livestock production are likely to be changed when these new technologies are successfully applied.

Development planners should keep the following issues in mind for areas where the decision to clear land for agriculture has already been made:

• Lands most suitable for each designated use, including areas that should not be cleared, should be identified after careful assessment of the soil characteristics and topography.

• In areas with extensive forest lands, large areas should be left intact; cleared areas should be interspersed with untouched forests to form an agriculture–forest mosaic.

• Clearing by manual slash-and-burn is recommended over mechanized operations in order to minimize soil compaction and topsoil displacement and to capitalize on the fertilizer value of the ash. In areas where only mechanized land clearing is possible, an attempt should be made to include burning, keep the bulldozer blade from touching the soil surface, avoid working when the soil moisture is high, and use shear blades instead of conventional blades on bulldozers.

• Annual crop production should be concentrated on fertile soils that are in little danger of flooding. Although many such areas will require maintenance fertilization for sustained production, the level of additional inputs will be minimal. Not all forest on fertile soils should be converted into agriculture, because natural forest reserves are necessary to maintain a reservoir of genetic diversity (see Chapter 3).

• For annual crop production on acid-infertile soils, management should be intensive in order to keep the ground covered throughout the year by crops, either in succession (three crops per year) or through relay cropping. Crop rotation will minimize need for pest control measures. Maintenance fertilization at economically attractive levels is an essential component of such a strategy. Alternatives to such long-term continuous crop production are pasture establishment after 1 or 2 years of cropping and incorporation of trees into the cropping system in order to convert a crop canopy, in time, into a tree canopy.

• Stable pasture systems can be assured through the use of acid-tolerant grass and legume pasture species, adapted to local climatic, soil, and pest conditions; appropriate grazing–management strategies; and livestock breeds adapted to the humid tropics.

RESEARCH NEEDS

• Expand and improve the quality of land-resource evaluation studies. It is recommended that CIAT, which integrates climate, vegetation, and soil constraints into computer-retrievable land systems, be expanded to cover the humid tropics of Asia and Africa. Similar studies at a larger map scale should be conducted for specific areas targeted for development. Soils should be classified according to a quantitative system such as Soil Taxonomy, and its constraints assessed according to the Fertility Capability Classification System or other similar system. Such research would identify areas suitable for crop agriculture, pastures, permanent crops, agroforestry, forestry, and also those areas best left in a natural state.

• Intensify integrated research efforts on land use. At present, few hard research data on how to grow crops, livestock, and trees in the humid tropics are available. Efforts are scattered geographically and are often centered on one discipline, such as ecology or cattle-husbandry. An integrated research effort is needed so that coordinated work on ecology, soils, annual crops, pastures and livestock, perennial crops, agroforestry, and forestry can be conducted at key locations. The U.S. scientific community should foster and help finance the development of a humid tropics research network. The proposed Red de Investigacion Agraria de la Amazonia, an initiative of six Amazonian countries, could thus be strengthened and expanded to Asia and Africa.

SUMMARY

This chapter outlines the principal soil-management considerations for sustained production of annual crops, pastures, and permanent crops in areas where a decision has been made to convert forests into agricultural production. A recommended land-resource evaluation format, including quantitative classification of climate and soil constraints, identifies areas that are suitable for annual crops, pastures, permanent crops, agroforestry, and forestry; it also identifies areas best left in their natural state.

Choice of land-clearing method is crucial in determining future soil productivity. Research conclusively demonstrates that manual slash-and-burn clearing is superior to mechanized land clearing. When manual clearing is unfeasible, mechanized systems should include burning, to take advantage of the fertilizer value of the ash, and the use of a shear blade in order to decrease soil compaction and topsoil loss.

Fertile soils should be given top priority for annual crop production and high-value plantation crops such as cacao. Nutrient dynamics in acid-infertile soils after clearing should be quantified in order to develop a coherent strategy for maintenance of soil fertility. Technology is available at a very limited number of sites for continuous annual crop production in acid-infertile soils on a sustained basis with the judicious use of adapted varieties, rotation schemes, and fertilizer management. Under such systems, soil properties improve with cultivation rather than degrade.

Technology is being developed for sustained legume-based pasture production in which grass and legume species having certain characteristics would be used. These species would be acid-tolerant, would require low levels of available soil phosphorus, would be compatible with one another, and would be tolerant to the chief pests and diseases. The use of such species with judicious grazing management, appropriate tropical cattle breeds (with Zebu and Criollo blood) and maintenance-fertilizer applications, can replace the present highly unstable pasture system with productive sustained use.

These new soil management technologies, both for annual crops and pasture production, must be tested locally in order to validate them and make necessary adjustments. Technologies for permanent crop production are more available and generally known. Given the undesirable ecological consequences of large-scale deforestation in the humid tropics, every hectare that is cleared for agriculture should be managed at a level of intensiveness high enough to guarantee high productivity on a sustained basis.

REFERENCES

Alvim, P. T. 1978. Perspectivas de produção agricola na região amazônica. Interciencia 3(4):243–249.
Alvim, P. T. 1979. Agricultural production potential of the Amazon region. Pages 13–23 *in* P. A. Sanchez and L. E. Tergas, eds. Pasture production in acid soils of the tropics. CIAT, Calí, Colombia.

Alvim, P. T. In press. A perspective appraisal of perennial crops in the Amazon Basin. Proceedings of a conference on Amazon land-use research. CIAT, Calí, Colombia.

Baena, A. R. C. 1977. The effect of pasture (*Panicum maximum*) on the chemical composition of the soil after clearing and burning a typical tropical highland forest. M.S. thesis, Iowa State University, Ames.

Bishop, J. P. In press. Agroforestry systems in the humid tropics east of the Andes. Proceedings of a conference on Amazon land-use research. CIAT, Calí, Colombia.

Bruce, R. C. 1965. Effect of *Centrosema pubescens* Berth. on soil fertility in the humid tropics. Queensl. J. Agric. Anim. Sci. 22:221–226.

Buol, S. W., P. A. Sanchez, R. B. Cate, and M. A. Granger. 1975. Soil fertility capability classification. Pages 126–141 in E. Bornemisza and A. Alvarado, eds. Soil management in tropical America. North Carolina State University Press, Raleigh.

Buringh, P. 1980. Introduction to the study of soils in tropical and subtropical regions. Pudoc, Centre for Agricultural Publishing and Documentation, Wageningen, Netherlands. 114 p.

Chan, H. Y. 1979. Tropical tree crop requirements and land evaluation: a case experience in Malaysia. Rubber Research Institute of Malaysia, Kuala Lumpur. 34 p. Mimeographed.

Cochrane, T. T., J. A. Porras, J. Azevedo, P. G. Jones, and L. F. Sanchez. 1979. An explanatory manual for CIAT's computerized land resource study of tropical America. CIAT, Calí, Colombia. 131 p.

Cordero, A. 1964. The effect of land clearing on soil fertility in the tropical region of Santa Cruz, Bolivia. M.S. thesis, University of Florida, Gainesville.

Da Silva, L. F. 1979. Influência do manejo de um ecossistema nas propiedades edáficas dos Oxissolos de "Tabuleiro." Centro de Pesquisas do Cacau, CEPLAC, Itabuna, Bahia, Brasil.

De Datta, S. K. 1981. Principles and practices of rice production. Wiley, New York.

Falesi, I. C. 1976. Ecosistema de pastagem cultivada na Amazonia brasileira. CPATU Bol. Tec. 1. Centro de Pesquisa Agropecuaria do Tropico Umido, EMBRAPA, Belem, Brasil.

Fearnside, P. M. 1978. Estimation of carrying capacity of human populations in a part of the Transamazonic highway colonization area of Brazil. Ph.D. thesis, University of Michigan, Ann Arbor.

Goodland, R. J. A., and H. S. Irwin. 1975. Amazon jungle: green hell to red desert? Elsevier, Amsterdam. 155 p.

Hecht, S. B. 1978. Soil nutrient dynamics following changes after conversion of a lowland tropical rainforest to artificial pasture. Museo Goeldi, Belem, Brazil. Unpublished.

Hecht, S. B. 1980. Some environmental effects of converting tropical rainforest to pasture in eastern Amazonia. Ph.D. dissertation, Department of Geography, University of California, Berkeley.

Hecht, S. B. In press. Agroforestry in the Amazon Basin. Proceedings of a conference on Amazon land-use research. CIAT, Calí, Colombia.

Irion, G. 1978. Soil infertility in the Amazonian rainforest. Naturwissenschaften 65:515–519.

IITA (International Institute for Tropical Agriculture). 1980. Land clearing and hydrological investigations project. Annual reports. IITA, Ibadan, Nigeria.

Jurion, F., and J. Henry. 1969. Can primitive farming be modernized? INEAC Ser. Hors. 1969. Institut National pour L'Etude Agronomique du Congo, Brussels. 445 p.

King, K. F. S. 1968. Agri-silviculture (the Taungya system). Bull. 1. Department of Forestry, University of Ibadan, Nigeria.

Kirby, J. 1976. Agricultural land use and settlement of Amazonia. Pacific Viewpoint 15:105–132.

Kowal, J. M. L., and P. B. H. Tinker. 1959. Soil changes under a plantation established from high secondary forests. J. West Afr. Inst. Oil Palm Res. 2:376–389.

Mongi, H. O., and P. A. Huxley, eds. 1979. Soils research in agroforestry. ICRAF 001e International Council for Research in Agroforestry, Nairobi. 504 p.

Morán, E. F. 1977. Estrategias de sobrevivencia: o uso de recursos ao longo da rodovia transamazonica. Acta Amazonica 7:363-379.

Morán, E. F. 1981. Developing the Amazon. Indiana University Press, Bloomington. 292 p.

Nye, P. H., and D. J. Greenland. 1960. The soil under shifting cultivation. Commonw. Agric. Bur. Tech. Commun. 51. Harpenden, England. 156 p.

Projeto RADAM-Brasil. 1972-1978. Levantamento de região Amazônica. Vols. 1-12. Ministerio das Minas e Energia, Departamento Nacional da Producao Mineral, Rio de Janeiro, Brasil.

Qureshi, A. H., L. S. Hamilton, D. Mueller Dombois, W. R. H. Perrera, and R. A. Carpenter. 1980. Assessing tropical forest lands: their suitability for sustainable uses. East-West Center, Honolulu. 69 p.

Ramalho, A., E. G. Pereira, and K. J. Beck. 1978. Sistema de availiação da aptidão agrícola das terras. EMBRAPA, Brasilia, Brasil. 70 p.

Ranzani, G. 1978. Alguns solos de transamazônica na região de Marabe. Acta Amazonica 8(3):333-355.

Sanchez, P. A. 1977a. Alternativas al sistema de agricultura migratoria en America Latina. *In* Reunion-Taller sobre Ordenación y Conservación de Suelos en America Latina. FAO/SIDA, Lima, Peru.

Sanchez, P. A. 1977b. Advances in the management of Oxisols and Ultisols in tropical South America. Pages 535-566 *in* Proceedings of international seminar on soil environment and fertility management in intensive agriculture. Society of Soil Science and Manure, Tokyo.

Sanchez, P. A. 1979. Soil fertility and conservation considerations for agroforestry systems in the humid tropics of Latin America. Pages 79-124 *in* H. O. Mongi and P. A. Huxley, eds. Soils research in agroforestry. ICRAF 001e, International Council for Research in Agroforestry, Nairobi.

Sanchez, P. A., D. E. Bandy, and J. H. Villachica. 1981. Soil fertility dynamics after converting a tropical rainforest into continuous production in the Amazon of Peru. North Carolina State University, Raleigh. Unpublished.

Schubart, H. O. R. 1977. Criterios ecológicos para o desenvolvimento agrícola das terras firmes da Amazonia. Acta Amazonica 7(4):559-567.

Serrão, E. A. S., I. C. Falesi, J. B. Veiga, and J. F. Texeira. 1979. Productivity of cultivated pastures in low fertility soils of the Amazon of Brazil. Pages 195-226 *in* P. A. Sanchez and L. E. Tergas, eds. Pasture production in acid soils of the tropics. Centro Internacional de Agricultura Tropical, Calí, Colombia.

Seubert, C. E., P. A. Sanchez, and C. Valverde. 1977. Effects of land clearing methods on soil properties and crop performance in an Ultisol of the Amazon jungle of Peru. Trop. Agric. (Trinidad) 54:307-321.

Toledo, J. M., and V. A. Morales. 1979. Establishment and management of improved pastures in the Peruvian Amazon. Pages 177-194 *in* P. A. Sanchez and L. E. Tergas, eds. Pasture production in acid soils of the tropics. Centro Internacional de Agricultura Tropical, Calí, Colombia.

Toledo, J. M., and E. A. S. Serrão. In press. Pastos y producción animal en la Amazonia. Proceedings of a conference on Amazon land-use research. CIAT, Calí, Colombia.

UNESCO. 1978. Tropical forest ecosystems. A state-of-knowledge report prepared by UNESCO/UNEP/FAO. Paris. 683 p.

Van der Weert, R. 1974. The influence of mechanical forest clearing on soil conditions and resulting effects on root growth. Trop. Agric. (Trinidad) 51:325-331.

8

Surface Water Resources
in the Humid Tropics

INTRODUCTION

Lakes, rivers, and wetlands make up the aquatic systems that form the surface water resources of a given region. The quantity and quality of this water play a vital role in the economic development of any country as well as in the functioning of natural ecosystems.

Although considerable research has been done on the environmental effects of water resource development, detailed knowledge of impacts on lakes, reservoirs, rivers, ponds, and wetlands in the moist tropics deserves special attention. Our somewhat limited understanding of tropical ecosystems as a whole necessitates a particularly careful approach to their utilization and development.

The importance of a thoroughly integrated approach to water resource management in the tropics can scarcely be overemphasized. Every engineering action taken spawns a host of environmental changes. As an example, large hydroelectric power projects have been built or are planned on the Amazon drainage (Goodland, 1980) as well as most of the world's tropical and semitropical rivers. If the river alone is considered, the environmental changes associated with conversion of a river system to a reservoir or series of reservoirs will be far-reaching.

Among the ecological concerns here considered that relate to lakes, reservoirs, rivers, and wetlands in the humid tropics are: (1) lakes—tropical-Temperate-Zone comparisons, responses to stressors, aquaculture; (2) reservoirs—sedimentation, mass wasting, loss of reservoir capacity, fertility, thermal stratification, aquatic plant infestation, fisheries development, diseases, eutrophication, resettlement of human populations, tourism, and environmental impacts; (3) rivers—tropical–Temperate-Zone comparisons, responses to stressors; (4) wetlands—environmental values, classification, structural and functional characteristics, organic matter export, evapotranspiration, responses to stressors.

Developers and ecologists alike must come to an understanding of how these ecosystems function and how they affect adjacent systems. Current knowledge of aquatic ecosystems in the humid tropics is still rudimentary and relies heavily on studies done on Temperate-Zone or dry tropical ecosystems. Should development proceed without adequate knowledge of its potential impacts on aquatic ecosystems, it will be impossible to manage these water resources properly.

Studies of the El Cajon Dam site just below the confluence of the Sulaco and Humuya rivers, above the city of San Pedro Sula in Honduras (Figure 8-1 and Goldman, 1972a), the Purari River Project in Papua New Guinea (Goldman *et al.*, 1973), and the Lokoja, Makurdi, and Ikom projects on

FIGURE 8-1 A narrow valley forms an ideal site for a high-arched, hydroelectric dam on the Sula River at El Cajon, Honduras. Slash-and-burn agriculture has removed much of the topsoil from this area, and the chief agricultural concern is for the fertility of banana plantations and flood control in the Sula Valley below. (Courtesy C. R. Goldman)

the Niger River system in Africa are used throughout this chapter to illustrate many of the principles that should concern ecologists, engineers, foresters, and governments alike. The management principles for tropical wetlands have emerged from experience with mangrove and freshwater wetlands throughout Latin America, with emphasis from studies in the Caribbean.

TROPICAL LAKES

Historically, aquatic ecosystems have provided the medium from which much ecological theory concerning production, nutrient cycling, seasonality, and community dynamics has been formulated. Most of this knowledge has been derived from studies of Temperate-Zone lakes; relatively few comprehensive studies have been conducted on tropical lakes. The social, political, and economic implications of the degradation of regional surface water resources are increasingly well known, but the difficulties of properly managing or restoring these resources are less well recognized. Previous experiences with the management of Temperate-Zone lakes and our relative ignorance of the functioning of tropical bodies of water make it imperative to expand the data base rapidly and to determine to what extent aquatic environmental phenomena differ from those reported for Temperate-Zone systems.

COMPARISON OF TEMPERATE-ZONE AND TROPICAL LAKES

There is no *a priori* reason to expect that the processes characteristic of Temperate-Zone lakes will fundamentally differ from those occurring in the tropics. Furthermore, although the basis for classification of a lake as "tropical" is primarily geographic, the altitudinal, climatic, and watershed differences within these limits make broad generalizations unwise. An aspect common to tropical lakes is higher annual insolation, with relatively smaller seasonal variations than are found in higher latitudes, leading to generally higher water temperatures. Together, high light intensity, warm temperatures, and an extended growing season should give generally higher rates of production in the tropics. Extensive studies of Lake George, Uganda (Ganf and Viner, 1973; Beadle, 1974; Burgis, 1978), have shown this lake to have extremely high stability with respect to standing crops and rates of production. However, as Beadle (1974), Lugo *et al.* (1974), and Burgis (1978) pointed out, this is in fact *not* a common feature of tropical lakes, but is due rather to a fortuitous set of conditions related to the buffering effects of inflows from Lake Edward, the year-long runoff from the Rwenzori Mountains, and to low wind velocities that are unique to Lake George.

Most tropical lakes show significant seasonal differences in the amount of rainfall and in intensity or direction of the wind. These climatic variables are ordinarily the principal factors regulating rates of production, via their control of external (precipitation) and internal (vertical mixing) nutrient supply to the lighted zone of algal and higher aquatic plant growth.

Brylinsky and Mann (1973) applied multiple regression and factorial analysis to data collected from widely ranging latitudinal zones during the International Biological Program and found that solar energy input had the greatest influence on lake production. However, for lakes in a narrower range of latitude, nutrient-related variables became more important. In lakes deep enough to stratify for longer than brief periods, biologically essential nutrients often became depleted in the surface layers. Nutrient depletion results from two processes: (1) the biological uptake of nutrients, which renders them unavailable (at least temporarily) for further production, and (2) the progressive sinking of the planktonic biomass (and detrital particles), which produces a net movement of nutrients to the deep water and sediments where they become spatially isolated from the lighted zone. The first of these processes can occur rapidly (within days or weeks of stratification), whereas the second process is slower and progresses throughout the thermally stratified period. Four mechanisms account for the regeneration of nutrients to the surface layers: (1) turbulent vertical mixing, (2) convective currents, (3) wind-induced upwelling, and (4) excretion by crustaceans and other organisms that are capable of vertical migration through the thermocline.

Talling (1969) reviewed the biological and chemical consequences of vertical mixing in tropical African lakes. Prior to mixing there were sharp vertical gradients of silicon as a result of an impoverished surface layer in Lake Malawi. The vertical distribution became uniform after the onset of mixing. Thus, even in the deep African lakes that are meromictic (Tanganyika and Malawi),* an annual vertical mixing cycle is effective in recirculating nutrients to the surface layers, although the magnitude of the nutrient contribution from the permanently anoxic deep waters is not clear. Lewis (1973), in his study of Lake Lanao, Philippines, found that free nitrate dropped to undetectable levels when the water column stabilized. Dorris (1972) also reported that nitrate reached detectable levels in the

---

*Meromictic lakes do not mix completely, due to a chemical stratification that causes a stagnant, denser (more saline) deep layer that resists wind mixing and traps nutrients in the deepest waters of the lake.

epilimnion only when Lake Atitlan was freely circulating. In Lakes Lanao and Atitlan, seasonal circulation was the main mechanism for distributing nutrients, although the winds accompanying storms can frequently mix to depths where some nutrients are regenerated (Lewis, 1973). Kittel and Richerson (1978) and Richerson et al. (1977) studied the physical limnology of Lake Titicaca, Peru–Bolivia, comparing this lake with other tropical and Temperate-Zone lakes, and concluded that small year-to-year variations in the main heat budget terms would have a greater impact on lowland tropical lakes than on temperate lakes where there are strong, but relatively regular, seasonal changes.

Annual floods, with their associated high sediment and nutrient loads, have been shown responsible for the distinct seasonal regime in the south basin of slightly acid Lake Chad (Beadle, 1974) and for seasonal differences in organic production in several of the humid tropical Amazon Basin lakes (Schmidt, 1973a,b; Fisher, 1979). Melack (1979) reported evidence suggesting that periodic catastrophic changes in the planktonic community in East African soda lakes might be due to subtle changes in salinity induced by changes in lake level. Although salinity changes are less likely to occur in the humid tropics, temperature levels are closer to the upper thermal limits of their biota than in Temperate-Zone lakes. The tolerance of these organisms to environmental change may prove low because of their adaptation to a relatively narrow set of environmental conditions (Sanders, 1968; Odum, 1971).

Talling (1963) also suggested that local cooling due to heat loss to the atmosphere could cause convective currents in Lake Victoria. The colder and denser waters flow downward along the bottom near the shoreline and thus contribute to the exchange between surface and bottom layers. Talling cited Eccles (1962) as detecting a similar phenomenon in Lake Malawi. This differs from vertical mixing in that there is no direct regeneration of nutrients to surface waters, but an upward displacement of the hypolimnion would occur. This inflow near shore also provides a mechanism for supplying oxygen to the monimolimnion of meromictic lakes.

Coulter (1963) suggested another mechanism to prevent major chemical stratification in meromictic lakes and maintain a supply of nutrients to the upper biotic layer. He showed that strong southerly winds on Lake Tanganyika depress the isotherm to the north, resulting in upwelling along the southern shore of deep water deficient in oxygen but rich in nutrients. This phenomenon may be true only for elongated lakes such as Tanganyika and Malawi, which are aligned with strong wind patterns (Talling, 1969). Eccles (1962) stated that the depression of the thermocline in the northern end of Malawi would expose the upper layers to bottom deposits and accelerate the release of nutrients. He added that internal seiches are a further mechanism whereby vertical mixing is maintained when the thermocline is most marked.

As of now there seems to be no published information on the extent of nutrient regeneration by crustaceans in surface water or other organisms in humid tropical lakes, although this process has been shown to contribute effectively to the nitrogen requirements of the epilimnetic phytoplankton in Temperate-Zone lakes (e.g., Axler *et al.,* 1981) and has been judged a major source of regenerate nitrogen and phosphorus in Lake George, Uganda (Ganf and Blazka, 1974), but needs further study. Preliminary studies of nitrogen cycling in Amazon Basin lakes have yielded results similar to those in Temperate-Zone lakes, in that during periods of low external (nitrate) loading, primary producers depend on regenerated nitrogen (ammonium, urea) to satisfy their daily demand (T. R. Fisher and J. M. Melack, University of Maryland and University of California–Santa Barbara, respectively, personal communication, 1981).

The above analysis clearly shows that, although tropical climatic factors are often assumed to be seasonally constant, they are in fact characterized by seasonally distinct meteorology and are often subject to unpredictable storms with violent winds (Lewis, 1973; Beadle, 1974). It is also apparent that primary production in tropical lakes, as in Temperate-Zone lakes, is often regulated by the availability of nutrients and that it is the interaction of physical events with nutrient supplies that is most important in determining rates of aquatic production. As for Temperate-Zone lakes, the amount and distribution of nutrients is linked more to the precipitation and geochemistry of the watershed. The dynamics of nitrogen and phosphorus, the principal limiting nutrients in lakes (Wetzel, 1975), are the least investigated of factors controlling primary production in tropical lakes. Only for Lake George, Uganda, has a relatively large study of these processes been conducted. It is essential to determine the relative importance of external nutrient loading and internal (animal excretion, bacterial remineralization, sediment release) nutrient regeneration to tropical aquatic production and to define differences from Temperate-Zone systems where they exist.

Warmer temperature also affects chemical and biochemical reactions. Solubilities of gases are less at the higher temperatures of tropical waters, which has the effect of reducing oxygen content and increasing planktonic metabolic rates. Thus, fish kills due to low oxygen tension caused by high night-time biological respiration are likely to occur in productive tropical lakes (Beadle, 1974; Johannes and Betzer, 1975). Rates of biological uptake and decomposition in general will increase with rise in temperature and, therefore, will be higher in the tropics. This suggests that tropical organisms may be more sensitive to instantaneous or acute increases in a toxic pollutant (faster uptake), but that the lifetime of the pollutant might be shorter in tropical waters (faster biodegradation). Again, much research is required to test these hypotheses.

RESPONSE OF TROPICAL LAKES TO STRESSORS

Accurate prediction of impacts depends on a clear understanding of the functioning of tropical lakes. It is essential to develop baseline data for a variety of tropical lake types. Impact analysis and lake restoration techniques are still in their infancy so far as Temperate-Zone systems are concerned, even though much more information exists, but the state of the art is sufficient to support certain predictions of the stress-response of tropical lakes, which can then be refined as more information becomes available.

Thermal pollution from power plant cooling has been shown to kill a wide variety of aquatic organisms. There is abundant documentation of this on tropical estuarine and coastal marine communities; one would not expect significant differences in freshwater tropical systems (Farnworth and Golley, 1974; Wood and Johannes, 1975). Higher temperatures tend to enhance the effects of oxygen depletion, which is especially relevant to aquaculture as a protein source in tropical countries. Deleterious effects on fish are also magnified by the interaction of elevated ammonium levels and high pH water common in many African lakes (Beadle, 1974).

Changes in seasonal hydrologic patterns are usually associated with dams or removal of water for irrigation or industrial use (Farnworth and Golley, 1974). It should be noted that the diversity and productivity of many (especially lowland) tropical water bodies depend on fluctuating water levels. High water provides nutrient input and breeding and foraging for a variety of aquatic animals. Swamps along the margins of the Niger River in Nigeria experience extensive lateral fish migration that is greatly reduced by the flow control that dams provide (Goldman, 1978b). Obviously, either a reduction in flow or introduction of pollutants into a system during a natural low-flow period will lead to higher pollutant concentration and thus increase hazards to aquatic life. The increased use of Lake Songkla, Thailand, as a source of water for irrigation was reported to have resulted in increased intrusion of saltwater into this lagoon lake (Limpadanai and Brahamanonda, 1978).

Nutrient enrichment via domestic waste discharge, agricultural and irrigation practices, and erosion would be expected to be fundamentally the same in the tropics as in the Temperate Zone. However, since variations in light and temperature are far less important in controlling annual primary production in tropical lakes, the annual intensity of eutrophication may well be greater. Increased organic loading (e.g., Weiss, 1971) might also somewhat exacerbate low-oxygen effects in the tropics. Despite a number of studies showing the importance of nutrient supply to tropical lakes in Africa and South Africa (Lewis, 1973; Mitchell, 1973; Fittkau *et al.*, 1975; Viner, 1975; Schmidt, 1976), very little is known about internal nutrient cycling and availability or about the consequences of increased nutrient loading. It is only recently that the need for immediate information on these processes has been realized and investigations have now begun on Lake Valencia, Venezuela (W. Lewis, University of Colorado, personal communication), Amazon Basin lakes (T. R. Fisher and J. M. Melack, University of Maryland and University of California–Santa Barbara, respectively, personal communication, 1981), and Lake Titicaca, Peru–Bolivia (P. J. Richerson and T. M. Powell, University of California–Davis, personal communication, 1981).

The same principles that pertain to water pollution by heavy metals, industrial by-product chemicals, and pesticides in Temperate-Zone lakes no doubt apply to tropical systems. However, specific process rates will be higher. Johannes and Betzer (1975) made the generalization that at higher temperatures the biological impact (e.g., poisoning effect) of an assimilated pollutant will be greater at a given concentration, but for similar dilution rates this concentration will decrease faster with time or distance from its source. Studies designed to test these hypotheses are generally lacking, but several research programs are addressing them (e.g., IAEA, 1980, in press).

Careful management seems to be the only feasible approach for the fisheries of large lakes. Inland fisheries production contributes a greater percentage of the catch in many tropical countries than in temperate latitudes (Hickling, 1962), probably because these countries do not have access to oceanic fisheries, which depend on a large capital outlay for equipment. Although direct comparisons of tropical and Temperate-Zone yields from lake fisheries are difficult to make, methods are improving (e.g., Coulter, 1963; Lowe-McConnell, 1975). Melack (1976) used data from African and Indian lakes to show that fish yield increased exponentially with primary productivity.

AQUACULTURE IN THE HUMID TROPICS

Some comparisons of tropical and Temperate-Zone aquaculture production are possible. Fertilization elicited a greater response in the warm waters of Malacca than in European countries (Hickling, 1962). The climate of the tropics can result in greater primary production (Talling,

1969), and it seems reasonable to assume that there is a great potential for increasing fish production in tropical regions through well-planned management.

Mismanagement of tropical lakes is common, as illustrated by the following example. Largemouth bass (*Micropterus salmoides*) were introduced to Lake Atitlan in the 1950's and soon became a predator of the Giant Pied-bill Grebe (*Podilymbus gigas*) chicks, threatening extermination of this rare indigenous bird. Later, black crappie (*Pomoxis nigromaculatus*) and bluegill (*Lepomis macrochirus*) were introduced and may have somewhat reduced the predation pressure on the grebe chicks, but they may also have displaced native species of fish. Ultimately, the maximum yield of a fishery depends on the rate of flux of nutrients through the food web into usable and harvestable fish biomass. Estimation of this theoretical maximum depends on accurate determinations of annual rates of material and energy flow within the individual ecosystem and as such will be highly dependent on the species composition of the system.

Now that development is intense in many areas of the humid tropics, an understanding of tropical lacustrine systems is essential if natural lakes are to endure as water and food resources.

TROPICAL IMPOUNDMENTS

The establishment of man-made "lakes" short-circuits the normal processes of evolution, such that only preadapted organisms, or ones that can quickly adapt to the new environment, can participate in community organization and biogeochemical cycling. Thus, the establishment of reservoirs initiates a new line of ecological succession.

To ignore tropical reservoir ecology as a research tool would be to disregard an important experiment that could lead to a better understanding of plant and animal succession in aquatic ecosystems. It should be possible to predict the characteristics of change on the basis of past examples and histories, provided adequate information exists. Strong emphasis should now be placed on all aspects of reservoir construction and management to optimize resource use, to provide information on the reservoir in question, and to predict ecological interactions in future impoundments.

Sedimentation, Mass Wasting, and Loss of Reservoir Capacity

High sedimentation, as seen in previously studied impoundments (e.g., Banson and Barning, 1969; scope, 1972), is very important to both the longevity and environmental condition of the reservoir. Land-use practices in the period following completion of a reservoir will be a major factor in determining its life expectancy. The extent to which erosion is controlled in the drainage area of the water storage project can greatly influence the sedimentation rate. Figure 8-2 shows an extreme case of bank erosion near the Surinamu Reservoir in Papua New Guinea. In addition to increasing runoff, lack of vegetation cover in the watershed resulting from poor forest practices or overgrazing reduces interception of rain and heightens the impact of rain on soil. This allows large soil particle aggregates to be broken down, after which surface runoff transports the finer particles farther into the reservoir. As a result, the concentration of soil in runoff water is greater, and the turbidity of receiving waters is increased. A detailed study of reservoir longevity as influenced by sedimentation should be a serious concern in planning any dam construction.

Heavy tropical rains, steep valley slopes, and the state of the watershed soils and vegetation all contribute to the rate of sedimentation. Since forest and agricultural development in the tropics, coupled with accelerated run-

FIGURE 8-2 Erosion along roadways, such as this road associated with the Surinamu Reservoir above Port Moresby, Papua New Guinea, can be a serious source of sediment. Particular caution should be exercised in the drainage area during and after construction. (Courtesy, C. R. Goldman)

off from associated roadways, causes high sediment transport by streams, it is important that the reservoir's watershed be managed with special attention to soil conservation and the regeneration of protective forest and associated vegetation. Revegetation and the cessation of human activities that cause erosion can reduce sedimentation and lower the rate at which the reservoir capacity is decreased.

The tendency of the slopes surrounding a reservoir to slump may also be important, as evidenced by the disastrous flood in northern Italy that brought about a massive landslide into a reservoir. Mass wasting following lumbering is likely to occur on sloping land in the tropics and was responsible for the death of thousands during a recent hurricane in Honduras. An earlier hurricane, although of even greater force, was less destructive because the root structure of the cut forest was still intact. The later disaster resulted from incomplete knowledge of erodibility and instability of the slopes and a failure to recognize the soil-stabilizing role of the forest.

THE TROPICAL RESERVOIR

While a reservoir is filling and after filling is completed, it is possible to establish sampling procedures that provide reasonably accurate sedimentation estimates. In order to obtain these estimates, major inflows near their point of entry must be sampled for settleable materials over an entire year. Single-storm events are extremely important, since they may contribute in a few hours most of the sediment discharge recorded over an entire year or, in some extreme cases, several years. All reservoirs eventually fill with silt, and determination of reservoir lifetime is essential in evaluating the economic promise of a project. A detailed sampling program should be initiated prior to dam construction in order to predict realistically the life of the impoundment.

Besides reducing the live storage of an impoundment, large-scale sedimentation can have pronounced effects on the biota and its distribution. Turbidity caused by suspended materials significantly reduces photosynthesis, which usually reduces the productivity of higher trophic levels. In many turbid tropical rivers, however, a sediment- and detritus-based food chain has developed and reduction in sediment transport below the reservoir actually reduces the abundance of important food fish.

The scanning electron microscope has dramatically illustrated the importance of organic and inorganic particles as substrata for aquatic bacteria (Paerl and Goldman, 1972a). The surface of particulate matter provides a site for the attachment of bacteria as well as organics and inorganics that adsorb to these surfaces. Thus sediments stimulate aquatic bacterial growth (Paerl and Goldman, 1972b; Paerl, 1978). In addition to providing food for filter feeders, bacteria and adsorbed organic material may serve as an energy source for mud-feeding fish.

Although drawdown, with consequent exposure of shallow breeding and food-producing areas, is probably the most serious threat of water impoundment to fish (Goldman, 1978a), sedimentation can also destroy potential spawning beds in the shallow littoral zone. Other aspects of sediment deposition include: (1) entrapment of these sediments behind the dam, with resulting loss of live storage of the reservoir and nutrient sources to downstream agriculture and marine fisheries; (2) increase in the ratio of erosion to sedimentation rates along coastal beaches; (3) reduction in deltas that formerly had been replenished during annual floods; and (4) loss of food for downstream detritivores. Reservoirs invariably reduce the volume and alter the pattern of downstream sediment deposition. This aspect of water impoundment in the tropics should receive special consideration during the planning stages.

Water quality following the closing of a dam typically undergoes a transitional period of high organic and inorganic ion concentrations (J. C. Priscu and C. R. Goldman, University of California–Davis, personal communication, 1981) and low hypolimnetic oxygen content. The length of the transitional period depends not only on river water quality, but also on any residual submerged terrestrial vegetation, the thermal profile of the reservoir, the discharge depth, nutrient concentrations of submerged soil, and the rate at which reservoir water is being replaced by inflowing water. Following this transitional period is a state characterized by lower concentrations of minerals and biogenic materials, although nutrient concentrations remain above the levels found in the rivers. This lowering of reservoir fertility may well prove very disadvantageous to a fishery that has developed during the initial period of high fertility. Along these lines, a projection of fish production was made for the proposed Lokoja Reservoir (Goldman, 1978b) just below where the Benue River joins the Niger (Figure 8-3); the projection was based on the Kainji Reservoir fishery on the Niger River.

Decay of submerged terrestrial vegetation and biogenic material will deoxygenate the deeper water of a reservoir and release reduced organic compounds that lower the pH and the oxidizing potential of the water. These conditions favor certain biological reactions, especially the reduction of sulfate to sulfide by the bacterium *Desulfovibrio* (Hutchinson, 1957). In company with microbes that release sulfur from the breakdown of proteins as sulfide, these bacteria can be responsible for increasing the hydrogen sulfide concentration of the waters to a level toxic to fish and poisonous or unpleasant for humans. Since an accumulation of suspended organic matter generally occurs near the impounding dam as a result of

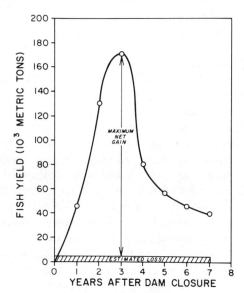

FIGURE 8-3 Estimated annual fish yield of proposed Lokoja Reservoir at the 68-m storage level during first 7 years after dam closure. From Goldman (1978b).

the throughflow characteristics of a reservoir (Priscu *et al.,* in press), these biological reductions will be maximal in the downstream portions of the reservoir. The low-solubility products of sulfide and heavy metal ions can result in large-scale precipitation of metallic sulfides that may interfere with turbine operation. Turbine generator parts that contact H_2S may corrode and malfunction if made of materials that can form metallic sulfides (e.g., copper). Substitutes for, or plating of, these materials may be necessary (Goldman, 1976).

The Byanos Reservoir in Panama was not cleared of trees and vegetation before it was flooded. Figure 8-4 shows the condition of the reservoir in 1979. Although the forest vegetation now inundated has long since died, the dead trunks stand as a reminder that, even in the tropics, decay of hardwoods is a slow process, and oxygen consumption and nutrient release can degrade water quality for many years after a reservoir is completed. The higher aquatic plants, in forming improved habitat for the mosquito vector, caused a resurgence of malaria in the area and even a confirmed case of yellow fever.

With proper watershed control of erosion and sanitation practices, noxious algal blooms are not likely to be troublesome except during the transitional period following dam closure. Eroded materials can serve as a direct source of nutrients if they originate from soils with leachable nitrogen, phosphorus, sulfur, and trace elements. However, even minerals resistant to decomposition can promote growth by providing a substrate on which organic materials can be adsorbed and concentrated. Bacteria colonize these particles and recycle the nutrients for algae by decomposing adsorbed organic matter.

THE FERTILITY OF RESERVOIRS IN THE TROPICS

In contrast to natural lakes, reservoirs have a high water inflow relative to volume so that reservoir productivity is determined to a great extent by the quality of the incoming river water (J. C. Priscu and C. R. Goldman, University of California–Davis, personal communication, 1981). A continuing water quality monitoring program should be established in connection

FIGURE 8-4 Byanos Reservoir in Panama, 1979. (Courtesy, C. R. Goldman)

with any large impoundment project to record important ions as well as sediment in rivers flowing to the proposed reservoir.

Bioassays performed to determine macro- and micronutrients limiting primary productivity are also desirable (Goldman, 1972b), since they can be used to determine the relative fertility of the tributaries and are helpful for identifying watersheds in need of management. The fertilizing effect of river water can be determined in several ways, one of which is to measure essential nutrients directly; another is to add river water to algal cultures and measure the resulting changes in productivity. This latter technique is a bioassay best performed with the natural plankton communities found in the area.

Bioassays to determine the most likely limiting factor can also be helpful in developing management strategy. Combinations of N, P, Si, Fe, and trace elements should be added to water from the inflowing river and subsequent productivity differences measured (Goldman, 1963, 1967). The most likely limiting factor can then be considered when developing strategies for lake management.

THERMAL STRATIFICATION OF RESERVOIRS IN THE TROPICS

Stratification in tropical lakes and reservoirs is still inadequately understood, but is of very great importance. Deep lakes stratify with a warmer surface layer, the epilimnion, at the top and a cooler hypolimnion below. Altitude, wind exposure, basin shape, and the temperature, volume, and turbidity of inflowing waters are all important variables in determining the stability of stratification.

Reservoirs in the tropics with warm water, steep sides, and protection from winds are most likely to be permanently stratified. Mixing of waters may occur, but warm waters have greater resistance to mixing than do cooler waters. As a consequence, slow mixing (low turbulence) and deoxygenation of the hypolimnion may persist from year to year (Beadle, 1966). Cooling of shallow littoral water has been proposed as a slow mixing mechanism in tropical lakes by Beadle (1966) and was shown by Talling (1963) to occur in Lake Albert, Africa.

Modeling of the thermal characteristics of reservoirs has been accomplished in temperate latitudes, and there are excellent prospects for achieving relatively accurate predictions in tropical areas (Goldman, 1978a).

The positioning of dam outlets relative to the stratified layers of the reservoir has important implications for downstream fisheries and aquaculture (Priscu *et al.*, in press). Water from the hypolimnion may be much colder than downstream waters and may shock the fishery below. Epilimnetic waters, on the other hand, may be too warm for some species. It is essential that these potential effects be evaluated so that intake design and reservoir operation can be adjusted appropriately by using variable level discharges.

AQUATIC PLANT INFESTATIONS IN TROPICAL RESERVOIRS

One of the many lessons deriving from experiences with dams in Africa is the seriousness of infestation with higher aquatic plants (C. R. Goldman and J. C. Priscu, University of California–Davis, personal communication, 1981) (Figure 8-5). The water fern (*Salvinia auriculata*) and water lettuce (*Pistia stratiotes*) invaded Lake Kariba on the Zambesi (Zimbabwe and Zambia) shortly after it began to fill in December 1958 (Harding, 1966). Eventually the water fern severely hampered multipurpose use of the lake, and a buoy barrier had to be erected to keep higher aquatic plants away from the turbine inlets (Coche, 1974).

Occasionally, for reasons unknown, a reservoir may remain completely free from macrophytic infestation even though a source of infestation is

FIGURE 8-5   In natural Lake George, Uganda, the floating and emergent vegetation pic-
tured here rarely causes problems to navigation and fisheries. However, if a power plant were
involved, aquatic vegetation such as this could become a severe problem. (Courtesy, C. R.
Goldman)

present and the water appears to resemble that in areas that do suffer. For example, water hyacinth has not colonized certain areas that are apparently suited for it (Little, 1966).

Important factors influencing aquatic weed infestation include: (1) the presence of aquatic weeds in the watershed and within naturally transportable distances, (2) the presence of protected swamps or littoral areas suitable for colonization, (3) the presence of submerged terrestrial vegetation to serve as protection for weed colonies, and (4) sediment accumulation at the head of the reservoir that provides a nutrient-rich, shallow zone for invasion.

Large stands of higher aquatics influence many aspects of reservoir use. One benefit to man is to provide additional food for desirable herbivorous fish or for fish feeding on organisms favored by the protection and food provided by the higher aquatic plant habitat. Dense growth of these macrophytes may also serve to protect fish, particularly smaller fish, from excessive predation.

The negative aspects of aquatic macrophytes, however, overwhelmingly point to the need to control their growth:

• Decomposition of the macrophytes by aerobic bacteria can deoxygenate reservoir waters, with attendant increase in hydrogen sulfide.
• Thick floating mats (sudds), sometimes sufficiently large to support growth of other higher plants (e.g., *Scirpus cubensis* on *Salvinia*), are hazards to navigation and may plug turbine intakes.
• Heavy infestations can interfere with operation of gill nets and seines and seriously hamper commercial and sport fishing.
• Certain disease-bearing species, such as the snail vector of schistosomiasis and the mosquito vector of malaria, find desirable habitats among the macrophytes.
• These plants may reach volumes sufficient to displace significant amounts of water and thus reduce reservoir capacity.
• The macrophytes during periods of rapid growth transpire amounts of water perhaps several times that evaporating from a water surface of equivalent area. For example, the 20% cover of water fern found on Lake Kariba in 1962 probably doubled the evapotranspiration rate.

Since dams disrupt the riparian and watershed habitats, these areas should be studied prior to construction with respect both to the losses in vegetation that would occur and the effects this submerged and decaying vegetation would have on the chemistry of the eventual reservoir. The submergence of vegetation is especially troublesome in the tropics, because tropical forests hold more nutrients relative to the soil than in Temperate-

Zone areas (Freeman, 1974). As the vegetation decays, large amounts of nutrients will be released to the lake and deoxygenation will occur. The Siranumu Dam near Port Moresby, New Guinea, has a hydrogen sulfide-rich outflow, because terrestrial vegetation was not removed before the reservoir filled.

This difficulty is best avoided by direct removal or burning prior to inundation. Burning terrestrial vegetation is generally less desirable than removal, since it will permit nutrients thus released to be quickly utilized by aquatic plants (Ewer, 1966). The cost of removing terrestrial vegetation from the watershed, however, is often prohibitive, and the initial high fertility of the reservoir attributable to easily leached ash may actually be desirable in increasing fish production.

Higher aquatic plants have been controlled by mechanical harvesting, although the equipment, expense, and steep sides of a reservoir make this impractical. Chemical control, especially with 2,4-D, which is harmless to fish, has been used successfully; but the possibility of materials toxic to agriculture moving downstream suggests that it should be used sparingly. Stranding of plants by rapid drawdown is probably one of the more cost-effective approaches.

Biological control of higher aquatic plants is the most desirable method, but experiments with manatees, crayfish, snails, insects, and herbivorous fish have yet to show great promise.

Ideally, infestation by higher plants should be prevented in its earliest stages, since control is expensive or ineffective once exponential growth is well under way. Prevention consists of both limiting sources of infection and controlling the chemical environment. In Ghana, at the Volta Dam, it was recognized that close surveillance was required to prevent infestation (Beadle, 1974). Posters were printed in eight languages displaying papyrus, *Eichornia,* and *Salvinia,* asking that persons seeing these plants report them immediately to the authorities. It was recommended (Goldman, 1972a) that lake patrols be established when the El Cajon Dam in Honduras was completed, in order regularly to survey the reservoir shoreline and remove or kill macrophytes.

It is disastrous to encourage high yield of aquatic macrophytes in the reservoir, unless they can be effectively harvested. In this respect, it should be noted that the Chinese have found water hyacinth and water lettuce to be good duck and pig fodder. Further, the quest for alternative energy sources has stimulated interest in alcohol production from fermentation of various organic materials, including aquatic weeds.

Analysis of wildlife values, including habitats, ranges, migration routes, and the presence of endemic or rare species that might be affected by a proposed dam should be considered. At the El Cajon site in Honduras, it was found that the original biotic communities of the proposed catchment area had already been severely damaged by man, including swidden agriculture, poor forestry practices, and burning (Goldman, 1972a). It was concluded that the biological interests of the area would be best served if swidden agriculture and burning were abandoned and a renewed stand of timber encouraged. It was further recommended in this study that immediate steps be taken to prevent the lumbering or clear-cutting of the few remaining stands of virgin timber in the watershed of the proposed reservoir. Not only would conservation and reestablishment of large tracts of broad-leaf and coniferous forests help to maintain the relatively low sediment levels observed in the Rio Yure, but the forests could serve as sources for faunal and floral repopulation of the watershed.

RESERVOIR FISHERIES

One of the trade-offs in converting a large area of terrestrial habitat to an aquatic one is the potential for viable fisheries. This can be of great importance in areas where the average protein intake is low and where agriculture is marginal. There is, however, a tendency to overestimate production and to overfish the reservoirs. Fish production rose in Lake Kariba along with the total dissolved solids (TDS) during the filling stage, only to decline drastically in 1963 (Balon and Coche, 1974). The decline coincided with a drop in TDS from 81 to 63 ppm. Proposed impoundments in the Amazon Basin will most certainly adversely affect the abundant and commercially important surabi catfish and the beautiful dorado, whereas such fish as the piranha, which do so well in the isolated floodplain ponds, are likely to become dominant in the new lake system. The extremely abundant sabalo, which forms the base of the food chain for many of the larger river carnivores, is certain to find the lake habitat inhospitable. Many of the reservoirs in Brazil, in rather similar watersheds with nearly identical fauna, are now reported to be largely inhabited by the voracious piranha and thus no longer serve as a ready source of protein.

The best way to achieve a high-protein yield from an inland fishery is to promote the growth of species that feed on plants rather than animals. There is great loss in available food energy at each transfer of energy from herbivore through successively larger carnivorous fish.

The importance and complexity of fisheries development merit the formation of some permanent body of advisors to study the various issues and the establishment of regulatory policies to develop and protect the new fishery.

Evaluation of the potential environmental consequence of constructing a dam should not be limited to the catchment area, but should take downstream effects into account as well. The decreased silt load in waters down-stream from the impoundment significantly affects the nutrient load, and hence productivity, of these waters.

Nutrients contained in or bound to river-borne particulate matter have a fertilizing effect on the land and on ocean waters near rivers. This may contribute significantly to the productivity of existing coastal fisheries and forms an essential part of the riverine detrital food chain. Removal of this silt by a reservoir can decrease phytoplankton photosynthesis in the estuary, which in turn decreases fish productivity in nearby coastal waters. An example of this is to be found in the eastern Mediterranean, where sardine catches were much smaller after the closure of the Aswan High Dam (Walton, 1981).

A similar situation exists regarding the effects of reduced sediment load on the fertilization of river valley agricultural lands. Floodplains are normally very rich, but fertility can be slowly lost if nutrients are not renewed by flooding. A decrease in traditional agriculture has been reported in the floodplains below the Volta Dam (Hilton and Kown-tsei, 1972), and Lake Kariba apparently does not produce the protein that the area was capable of producing before the dam was built.

Only actual surveys of downstream and coastal fisheries and wildlife resources make it possible to plan and implement protective measures before completion of the dam, and such surveys are strongly recommended. For example, the rich fishery potential of the Gulf of New Guinea could be greatly changed should the Purari River system be completely developed for hydroelectric purposes.

The effect of impoundment on coastal wildlife resources also deserves special attention, since these coastal areas are essential to the maintenance and reproduction of many valuable and endangered wildlife species.

Deltas and their associated estuaries are especially rich areas in which sediment loads are deposited, resuspended, and redeposited (Mikhailov, 1964; Tison, 1964). Altered flow rates and sediment loads can have dramatic effects in these areas, particularly in relation to the distance of saltwater intrusion (Goldman, 1971). The estuarine environment and associated mangroves and rice terraces remain among the richest of all ecosystems. Any alteration of their fertility should be viewed with great concern, and the long-term cost-benefits should be reviewed with care.

DISEASES AND THEIR VECTORS

An increase in health hazards often accompanies the creation of large reservoirs. The high concentration of people and the inadequate sanitation common to work camps of a dam labor force often create an ideal environment for the spread of malaria, dysentery, tuberculosis, venereal disease, and other maladies. Workers are a source of new disease, and they and their families are highly susceptible to endemic diseases. The large population entering a previously sparsely inhabited region provides high host densities, thereby increasing the likelihood of the spread of many diseases. At different stages of dam construction in the tropics, increases and decreases in malaria, dysentery, schistosomiasis, and onchocerciasis have been reported (Kershaw, 1966; Waddy, 1966; Obeng, 1969; Paperna, 1969; Warmann, 1969).

Factors relevant to vector ecology should receive special attention. Water-related disease-causing agents, vectors, and the nutritional status of the people are important variables in health and should be considered in evaluating the impact of hydroelectric dam projects. Methods of reducing health hazards associated with the project must be developed at an early stage in the planning process.

Health records in the El Cajon area reveal that, aside from basic malnutrition, the most prevelant health problems in the area are tuberculosis, typhoid, dysentery, and malaria. In the Purari delta area and coast, gastrointestinal diseases, malaria, and tuberculosis are common.

It has been found in Africa that the stress associated with resettlement of the people inhabiting a project site significantly increases disease and mortality, particularly among the very young and the very old. Therefore, it can be expected that the incidence of any diseases occurring at the site is likely to increase, and steps should be taken to offset this.

Aside from the necessity of an intensive health survey of the area and an inoculation program, it should be pointed out that, in the period of transition, because normal cultivation will be interrupted, the people's food supply will be more uncertain than ever. Therefore, it is essential that they receive adequate nourishment during this transitional period, until new communities are established.

Malaria is endemic in most tropical areas of the world and has had a resurgence in recent years. Submerged trees and swampy habitats of aquatic plants encourage the development of *Anopheles* mosquitoes, certain species of which serve as vectors. Creation of mosquito habitats obviously must be avoided in constructing the reservoir; it is likely that the steep reservoir sides and foraging fish population will provide adequate control over much of the area. In view of the relatively high human population densities that the building of the dam will introduce into parts of the catchment area, antimalarial prophylactic measures must be stringently applied.

Schistosomiasis bears certain ecological similarities to malaria, since snail vectors (such as *Bulinus* and *Biomphalaria*) of the parasitic blood fluke (*Schistosoma* spp.) are favored by submerged trees and higher aquatic plants. Transmission takes place when the free-swimming cercaria stage of the fluke penetrates the skin. Although no cases were reported in Honduras, *Biomphalaria*-bearing *Schistosoma mansoni* does occur in South America and the Caribbean. Schistosomiasis has increased in association with water development in Rhodesia (Schiff, 1972) and Ghana (Paperna, 1969). Preventive measures include the destruction of terrestrial vegetation and control of higher aquatic vegetation. If schistosomiasis is not endemic to the area under consideration, detailed medical examinations should be performed on all persons associated with the dam project who will be entering the watershed, in order to prevent its introduction. In addition, a careful survey should be made of aquatic habitats in the vicinity for snail hosts.

Onchocerciasis, or "river blindness," is a disease caused by the nematode *Onchocerca,* which is transmitted to humans by the black fly (*Simulium* spp). the common name of the disease derives from the fact that some victims become blind. These black flies can breed effectively only in swiftly flowing and well-oxygenated waters, an environment that characterizes the catchment area rivers and will decrease in extent as the reservoir basin fills (Waddy, 1966). In other words, the likelihood of onchocerciasis will diminish as a new dam slows the movement of water into the area and decaying vegetation promotes deoxygenation. However, spillways may provide an ideal microhabitat for the larvae and may require special attention. In one instance, DDT was used to control *Simulium* larvae during construction on the Volta River. Attention to areas below the dam is, of course, warranted, because the lowered sediment transport may cause them to become a greater menace as *Simulium* habitat. Further, there is the possibility that migrant laborers could bring the disease into the area.

Gastrointestinal troubles (such as dysentery) attributable to water-borne pathogens continue to be common in the tropics. Although the inevitable increase in human contact with the surface waters of the catchment area following completion of the dam will introduce protozoa and bacteria, the removal from the watershed of people not involved with construction would reduce human sources of infestation. This tactic should be combined with adequate treatment of drinking water supplies and treatment or diversion of human wastes. This is an instance where a small investment in education can bring a large payoff in reduction of water-related diseases.

EUTROPHICATION OF RESERVOIRS

The past history of watershed management provides impressive evidence of the need to anticipate sewage-treatment requirements. Lack of such foresight has repeatedly brought on undesirable eutrophication and loss of sanitary water supplies. Therefore, a wastewater treatment study should be initiated looking to satisfactory treatment facilities for future watershed populations. A series of strategically located small secondary treatment plants and septic tanks near population centers is indicated by past experience to be an absolutely necessary, albeit costly, investment.

RESETTLEMENT OF RESERVOIR BASIN POPULATIONS

Impoundment projects often necessitate the relocation or resettlement of people. Whenever possible, large-scale resettlement schemes should be avoided, but, if resettlement is essential, several factors must be considered. In any case it is important that population relocation be recognized as an integral part of the hydroelectric project and that local people be actively involved in planning it.

The proposed Wabo Dam Project in Papua New Guinea is a good example of a large hydroelectric scheme that would involve a relatively minor resettlement. Between 300 and 500 people in three villages would be displaced. A thorough understanding of their social structure and careful consideration of their views were required in formulating relocation plans. Assessment of their spiritual and physical attachments to the land would minimize resentment during and after evacuation. Just how the government handles these people will be a major factor in determining their future relationship with the government and in the social success or failure of the entire project. This project stands in sharp contrast to the Lokoja Project in Nigeria, which would require resettlement of about 225,000 people.

TOURISM

Careful consideration should be given to the touristic value of the impoundment area as compared with that of the proposed reservoir. The recreational use of an area is usually, but not always, enhanced. Care must therefore be exercised in promoting a hydroelectric project on the strength of its recreational benefits.

The two most important issues associated with the watershed are likely to be control of erosion and pollution, plus the need to protect developing fisheries. Tourist and recreational development should be postponed until the reservoir has been filled for several years, water quality has stabilized, and characteristics of the new fish population are known. When this information is in hand, recreational facilities can be more wisely developed.

The possibility that valuable archaeological sites exist in the area to be flooded should be investigated carefully, to ensure that they can be excavated by a trained team of archaeologists well in advance of inundation.

ANCILLARY ENVIRONMENTAL IMPACTS

The secondary impacts of impoundment made possible by the availability of electric power and the potential for industrial development are of considerable importance. Industry associated with a new source of energy generally brings about an influx of people and increased demand for food and services.

Evaluation of the long-range effects of a project is at best speculative. Nonetheless, attention must be focused on the more likely environmental impacts in order to facilitate dealing with them in the future and to contribute to making the project a rational component of future development.

Such natural resources as timber and mineral or petroleum reserves are usually much more effectively exploited if electrical power is available. If an industrial complex is included as part of a new dam project, it should be described, and brief descriptions of the potential impacts of alternative plans for use of these resources should be made. Initial impacts of the complex will include the construction of facilities on natural areas, pollution, and increased use of renewable and nonrenewable resources.

Certain impacts are peculiar to construction itself. For example, road building causes a series of environmental impacts, including increased erosion, and the road serves as an avenue for the transport of diseases and pests.

Diversion of water for irrigation and subsequent changes in agriculture impact on environment and social life. The decision to embark on comprehensive development of an area should be based on a careful study of the advantages and disadvantages of replacing existing ecosystems with man-made ones. Effects on the nation's health, nutrition, style and standard of living, land-use patterns, and population growth rate should receive special attention. In every case, it is essential that local leaders be involved at an early stage and that they understand the broad spectrum of impacts that are likely to result.

TROPICAL RIVERS

COMPARISON WITH TEMPERATE-ZONE RIVERS

Because of the great range of conditions encountered and because the data base is very limited, few generalizations about tropical river systems can be made. Tropical and Temperate-Zone rivers may differ greatly as to temperature, substrate, chemical composition, flow rate, and turbidity. Organic matter derived from the watershed makes up a significant, if not major, part of the organic material transported by rivers. In the tropics, the seasonality of these inputs is less, and the more uniform annual insolation is more conducive to year-round biological production of organic matter in the larger, slower moving rivers. This effect will be mitigated to the extent that riparian vegetation reduces direct insolation and by periods of higher rainfall and increased flushing (Whitton, 1975).

The pioneering work of Sioli's group (Sioli, 1964, 1975; Fittkau et al., 1975) was based on a recognition of the role of bedrock in stream watersheds in producing a characteristic runoff within the Amazon Basin. Their work categorized the major water sources as (1) clear waters from areas of low relief; (2) black waters, from low-relief areas, that are clear but stained by humic organic materials and are otherwise nutrient impoverished; (3) white waters from high-relief areas of large flow and heavy sediment and salt load; and (4) "decanted" white water in river embayments, or low-flow channels where the silt load has settled out. Gibbs' (1967, 1972) outstanding study of the Amazon River system was also based on attention to the sources of the dissolved and suspended matter. He studied the main tributaries of the river and estimated their respective discharges. The concentration of suspended solids varied seasonally and with distance from the ocean. Organic matter also changed in the different "environments"; the highest percentage was reported from the most "tropical" environments. Gibbs concluded that 84% of the total dissolved salts and suspended solids discharged from the Amazon was eroded from the 12% of the basin that consists of mountainous Andean environment. Relief was the most significant factor (of nine factors considered) determining the geochemistry of the river system.

In Temperate-Zone rivers, the concentrations of the principal plant growth nutrients, N and P, will be determined by the relative rates of leaching or erosion from the watershed, precipitation inputs, internal decomposition of organic matter, biological N_2-fixation, and biological assimilation (Likens et al., 1977). The need for quantitative budgets of nutrient inputs (via streams and rivers) of African, South American, and Asian lakes has arisen concomitantly with discovery of the widespread occurrence of nutrient-limited primary production in those lakes. [See studies by Talling (1969), Africa; Lewis (1973), the Philippines; and Lewis and Weibezahn (1976), Venezuela.]

The distribution of organisms in running waters has been shown to be largely a function of water temperature, substrate structure, and flow regime (Hynes, 1970). Although literature is scanty regarding tropical ecosystems, there appear to be no substantive differences (Beadle, 1974). Work by Cummins et al. (1973), Cummins (1973), and Merritt and Cummins (1978) developed the concept of invertebrate functional-feeding groups (e.g., shredders, collectors, scrapers, grazers, predators), by which stream organisms (largely macroinvertebrates) could be categorized on the basis of morphological adaptations to food acquisition. This scheme has provided a conceptual basis for examining the effects that environmental changes can have on the organisms in a stream or river.

RESPONSES TO STRESSORS

The range of predictable human-related perturbations on tropical riverine systems is very broad, ranging from the introduction of exotic species that have no direct physical or chemical effect on water quality, to more drastic changes involving impoundment and conversion of riverine habitat to a reservoir. Davies (1979) stated that all major rivers in South Africa were already impounded without the preimpoundment data having been collected, which makes it extremely difficult to document subsequent changes. Nevertheless, it is possible to draw on the literature available from studies in the Temperate Zone to predict the consequences of various watershed development schemes on tropical rivers.

Disruption of riparian vegetation can be expected to have a major impact on the ecology of the adjacent river. This community has been shown to have a major influence on the quantity and composition of organic matter entering the stream and on plant productivity in the system (Fisher and Likens, 1973; Sedell *et al.*, 1978; Cummins and Klug, 1979). Removal of this community, and of watershed vegetation, will tend to increase the sediment entering the river. The amount of increase will depend on the timing of vegetation removal (with respect to seasonal rainfall), the extent of plant recolonization, and the specific nature of the topsoils in the watershed. The volume of water directly entering the river will also increase, causing additional sheet erosion (Hynes, 1970; Whitton, 1975). The nutrient levels of stream inflows will also be increased (Likens *et al.*, 1977), depending on the extent to which the vegetation is actually exported. Sediment load, if severe, alters the ecosystem by preventing light from reaching algae and attached plants, suffocating invertebrates or clogging their feeding apparatus, covering up attached algae and higher aquatic plants, overlaying the substrate, and enriching the water with nutrients (especially adsorbed phosphate). Boon (1979) reported that in the Tuntang River, Java, changes in a dam outflow brought about significant changes in size of suspended particles and in turbidity.

Increased thermal loading due either to direct injection of hot water from power plants or to release of surface water from upstream impoundments can have deleterious effects on organisms if the temperature approaches their lethal limits. It may also affect egg development time, maturation, and other biological processes keyed to seasonal river temperature. This has been particularly well documented in numerous Temperate-Zone studies (Smith, 1972; Ward and Stanford, 1979). Higher water temperature will also influence the productivity and species composition of downstream fisheries (see preceding section on tropical reservoirs). Indirect effects of temperature, discussed earlier in relation to impoundment, include changes in metabolic rates, changes in responses to toxicants, and changes in dissolved oxygen concentrations.

Major environmental perturbations can result from such alterations as small-scale flood control measures, channelization, or from impoundment near the headwaters (Cummins, 1979). Flow rates are integrally related to virtually all other river characteristics, controlling the residence time of a volume of water in a region, dilution of tributary inputs, basin erosion and scouring, invertebrate and vertebrate distribution, degree of plant and bacterial growth, silt deposition, oxygen concentration, and the degree of salinity intrusion into coastal rivers (Ward and Stanford, 1979). Seasonal alterations in flow regimes can disrupt the ecological communities adapted to the original flow patterns (Beadle, 1974; Davies, 1979).

In summary, the quality of tropical river water resources can be expected to deteriorate significantly if not properly managed. The river system is a key link between the various regional sources of water such as lakes, reservoirs, and wetlands. As such, its degradation will automatically confer deterioration to downstream water resources. Criteria for river water quality, whether based on immediate use for human consumption, irrigation, fishery, or industry, must necessarily take into consideration current and future downstream use.

FORESTED WETLANDS

Forested wetlands make up a small part of the total area of tropical forests. Of an estimated $19,271 \times 10^3$ km^2 of tropical forests (Persson, 1974), only about 9,700 km^2 has been attributed to forested wetlands, including saltwater mangroves. However, their ecological value and importance cannot be measured simply by the area.

Forested wetlands are important because they are closely related to terrestrial, coastal, and marine ecosystems as a result of the flow of water, nutrients, and organic matter and production of commercially important organisms. In Papua New Guinea, crocodile farming in forested wetlands has become increasingly important as a cash crop. Mature female crocodiles lay large clutches of eggs that are gathered by villagers, who raise the young in pens for later extraction of skins. Crocodile farming also serves to protect crocodillians, a major group of endangered species, by fostering preservation of habitats and animals as a source of eggs for hatching.

Also, coastal mangroves prevent shoreline erosion and serve as breeding and nursery areas for fish and shellfish. Shrimp and crabs are especially important inhabitants of mangrove swamps.

A qualitative list of values of wetlands follows (Lugo and Brinson, 1978):

Water: Storage of floodwaters; conservation of water during droughts; desalination of salty water

Organic productivity: High primary productivity; high secondary productivity (e.g., commercial and sport fisheries); high export of organic foods to other ecosystems; high wood production (in forested saltwater wetlands)

Biogeochemical values: High capacity to recycle nutrients; high storage of organic matter and CO_2 sink; net oxygen production; closure of many biogeochemical cycles by reducing N, C, S, Fe, etc., in anaerobic muds; sequestering heavy metals, radioactive isotopes, and other poisonous chemicals in anaerobic muds

Geomorphological values: High potential for erosion control; protection of coastlines against storms, tides, and winds; high potential for building land

Biotic values: Locations for fisheries nurseries, bird rookeries, and refuges for terrestrial animals; gene banks for haline and euryhaline plant and animal species

Other values: Natural laboratories for teaching and research; locations for recreation and relaxation; rich organic soils (used for agriculture or aquaculture or as fuel); locations for solid-waste disposal or construction activities; importance as natural heritage

CLASSIFICATION OF WETLANDS

Saltwater forested wetlands in New World topics are usually pure or mixed stands of red (*Rhizophora mangle*), black (*Avicennia germinans*), or white (*Laguncularia racemosa*) mangroves. Lugo and Snedaker (1974) classified mangroves into six types on the basis of the geomorphological characteristics of the site: (1) fringe forests, (2) riverine forests, (3) overwash forests, (4) hammock forests, (5) basin forests, and (6) dwarf (or scrub) forests. The sixth type consists of sites in which all mangrove species can be present; the structural development is poor and probably nutrient-limited (Lugo and Snedaker, 1974).

Brown *et al.* (1978) reported finding 12 different classification schemes for freshwater wetlands. These were based on such characteristics as floristic composition, topographic location, and such environmental parameters as hydroperiod and water quality. Odum *et al.* (1974) classified coastal ecosystems according to the intensity and pattern of delivery of all the energy flows that converged on them. The sum of all the energy sources converging on an ecosystem, expressed in equal energy units, is termed the energy signature (Odum *et al.*, 1977). The main component of the energy

ECOLOGICAL CONCEPT

MANGROVE WETLANDS

Mangroves grow along coastlines and estuaries in dry-to-moist tropical, subtropical, and warm temperate bioclimates. Their maximum growth, however, is in the moist tropics, where the abundant flow of fresh water from humid watersheds creates optimal conditions. Initially, mangroves attracted scientific attention because they are trees that grow in salt water and because of their "unusual" adaptations, such as seeds that germinate on the tree, specialized roots for gas exchange, and leaves with salt-excreting glands.

Recent studies have shown that mangroves are very productive ecosystems that allocate a significant part of this production to leaf production. Leaf fall in mangroves is high, averaging about 7.3 t/ha/yr, and is proportional to rainfall. Mangrove leaf litter has special ecological importance, because it serves as the base of food chains that support most estuarine and estuarine-dependent marine commercial fisheries. Mangrove leaves find their way to these economically valuable fisheries by two principal pathways: (1) leaf fragmentation into detritus that is colonized by fungi and bacteria that, in turn, are ingested by fish, and (2) dissolution into organic matter that floculates in the estuary, is colonized by bacteria and fungi, and is finally ingested by fish. Production and export of detritus particles predominate in mangroves growing adjacent to the water edge, whereas production and export of dissolved organic matter predominate in the mangroves that grow far from the water's edge. Both mechanisms are critical for the functioning of estuaries and the production of fish protein. Because of their high net primary production and the predominance of oxygen-free muds, mangroves are also important regulators of water quality. They process sewage, absorb nutrients and heavy metals, and precipitate sediments. In many areas, mangroves protect people from storm waves, swash, and river floods.

signature to a wetland is water input. Brown *et al.* (1978) divided wetlands into two categories on the basis of the delivery of water: flowing-water and still-water forested wetlands, which system is used in this report.

Riverine mangrove forests and flowing-water freshwater forests are essentially parallel types. Both generally develop along the edges of rivers. In riverine mangroves there is some vertical movement, due to tide, but the dominant direction of water movement is lateral. The term reverine wetlands is thus used to refer to both the saltwater and freshwater forested wetlands that are subject to lateral water movement. On the periphery of riverine saltwater forests, red mangrove dominates, whereas black and while mangroves dominate the inner areas. Riverine freshwater wetlands in the tropics support higher species diversity, but there are exceptions, such as those dominated by palm or *Pterocarpus* in Central America.

Basin mangrove forests are comparable to still-water freshwater forests. Inputs of water to black mangroves are from freshwater runoff, rainfall, and tidal exchanges of salt water. Water is generally stagnant or slowly moving as sheet flow over very small topographic gradients. In still-water freshwater wetlands the inputs of water are from surface runoff and rainfall, and floodwaters are stagnant. The term basin wetlands is thus used to refer to both freshwater and saltwater forests where the waters are stagnant or very slowly flowing. Basin saltwater forests are dominated by black, or by a mixture of black and white, mangroves.

The freshwater counterpart to a fringing mangrove is the forested wetlands that grow around the edge of tropical lakes. However, there have been no studies on the latter. In a review of mangroves by Cintron *et al.* (1980), overwash mangroves were grouped with fringing mangroves on the basis of similarities in their structural and functional characteristics.

In scrub saltwater and freshwater forests, nutrient limitation or other stressors, rather than the pattern of water delivery, appear to be the cause of the scrubbiness. However, in the scrub forests the main source of water is rainfall, and floodwaters tend to be stagnant and generally shallow. In examples taken from southern Florida, scrub saltwater forest is dominated by red mangrove and scrub freshwater forest by pondcypress. Other saltwater species (e.g., black mangroves) may assume scrubby characteristics under the influence of such environmental stressors as salinity.

Water flow or lack thereof appear to be appropriate criteria by which wetlands can be grouped. In flowing-water (riverine) conditions, dissolved oxygen is usually fairly constant, roots and sediments are well ventilated, input and export of materials tend to be high, and reduced and toxic substances are removed. In the saltwater environment, these benefits from flowing water are particularly important so far as the salt budget of the ecosystem is concerned.

Under still-water (basin) conditions, the above characteristics tend to be reversed, so that there is a greater probability of physical and chemical fluctuation. For example, dissolved oxygen tends to be depleted rapidly, reduced and toxic substances accumulate, and redox potentials will be low. There is less opportunity for the import of materials from other ecosystems and for the export of materials downstream. Because export of materials tends to be low, basin wetlands accumulate organic matter (Brown *et al.*, 1978). The greater possibility of increasing soil salinity when the floodwaters are stagnant or very slowly flowing and when freshwater inputs are reduced is important to basin mangroves.

Structural Characteristics

Freshwater forests are more diverse and more complex and have higher above-ground biomass than do their saltwater counterparts. In both freshwater and saltwater forested wetlands, biomass and other indices of forest structure, except stem density, decrease in order from riverine to basin to scrub. The trend in stem density is almost a reverse of this pattern in both freshwater and saltwater forested wetlands. If one looks at water movement gradients within a given type of forested wetland, it is clear that water movement or lack of it correlates with the differences in the structural features. The saltwater wetlands are generally lower than those of freshwater wetlands. Thus, the response of these two types of forested wetlands to environmental gradients follows a parallel course, but to different degree. Given the same water flow, one might expect nutrient inputs to be similar; the only difference, therefore, would be presence or absence of salt. The lower values of structural indices in the saltwater wetlands are therefore a measure of the "cost" of producing adaptations to overcome salt.

Functional Characteristics

Gross (GPP) and Net Primary Productivity (NPP) decrease in this order, riverine–basin–scrub, in both saltwater and freshwater forested wetlands. Respiration in freshwater forests follows the same trend, but respiration in saltwater wetlands is highest in the basin forests. Absolute rates of GPP are higher in freshwater forests, but NPP is generally higher in saltwater forests. Litter production is highest in the riverine, followed by the basin and then by the scrub in both freshwater and saltwater forested wetlands, but the absolute magnitudes are generally higher in the saltwater forests.

Application of sewage effluent to saltwater forested wetlands appears to increase wood production only, but in freshwater forested wetlands both litter production and wood production increase. It is possible that, because saltwater forests produce litter at some of the fastest rates reported for forests, increasing rates of litter production following enrichment are not possible unless a new structural balance develops.

Export of Organic Matter

Wetlands often have drainage patterns that act to export materials downstream. Only those freshwater forested wetlands that border streams generally export organic matter, unless a basin forest forms the headwaters of a river. However, both basin and riverine saltwater forested wetlands are capable of exporting materials because they are flushed by the tides. Few data on the export of materials are available for either freshwater or saltwater forested wetlands. However, waters draining watersheds that are covered with significant areas of wetlands have higher concentrations of dissolved organic matter than do waters draining upland forested watersheds (Brinson *et al.*, 1981). For example, concentrations of organic carbon in waters draining wetland watersheds ranged from 2 to 36 mg/l, whereas concentrations in water draining upland watersheds ranged from 1 to 5 mg/l (Brinson *et al.*, in press). Richey *et al.* (1980) estimated a total export of organic carbon from the Amazon Basin of 0.1 billion t/yr, contributed largely by the riverine freshwater forests of the Amazon River. The export of organic matter appears to be linearly related to stream discharge (Lugo, 1980a, using data from Malcom and Duram, 1976). Therefore, when sampling for organic matter export, it is important that high stream discharge conditions be sampled as well as low stream discharge conditions. For example, Lugo *et al.* (in press) found that 10% of the annual discharge of water and 70% of the annual export of sediments in a tropical watershed occurred during a single storm.

Data on absolute amounts of organic carbon exported from forested wetlands are scarce. However, from the few data available, basin saltwater forests appear to export more organic matter than do riverine freshwater forests (Table 8-1). Preliminary calculations suggest that most of the export in

TABLE 8-1   Export of Total Organic Carbon (TOC) from Forested Wetlands

Type	Concentration (mg/C/l)	Export (TOC) (g C/m^2/yr)	Source
Saltwater			
South Florida (basin)	22.8 (TOC) 18.8 (DOC)	58.1	Lugo *et al.*, 1980c
Freshwater			
Louisiana (riverine)	11.7 (DOC)	10.4	Day *et al.*, 1977
North Carolina (riverine)	147[a] (DOC)	4.0[a]	Mulholland and Kuenzler, 1979
Louisiana (riverine)	—	8.0[b]	Hern and Lambou, 1979
Palm forest in Puerto Rico	2-35 (TOC)	35.0	Frangi and Lugo, unpublished

[a] Mean of eight sites; includes only dissolved organic carbon (DOC).
[b] Mean of two sites; includes only dissolved organic carbon (DOC).

the basin saltwater forest resulted from tidal exchange (55%, Lugo et al., 1980). Export from the saltwater forest due only to freshwater runoff and seepage (26 g C/m^2/yr) is still higher than from the freshwater forests. Most of the exported organic carbon in the basin freshwater and saltwater wetlands is in dissolved form (Hern and Lambou, 1979; Lugo et al., 1980). Hern and Lambou (1979) found that particulate organic carbon (POC) content decreased between import and export waters due to conversion to DOC by the detritus-based food chains in freshwater forested wetlands.

The higher export of organic matter from saltwater wetlands is to be expected, because litter production in these wetlands is higher than in freshwater wetlands. Tidal exchange provides an additional transporting mechanism. Riverine saltwater wetlands should export even more organic matter than basin ones, because litter production is higher there, and tidal flushing and freshwater runoff are also higher. However, in terms of absolute amounts of organic matter export, basin saltwater wetlands may be more important to the organisms in the estuary than riverine wetlands, because generally the basin wetlands are more extensive. In addition, Lugo et al. (1980) found that black mangrove leaves formed a more nutritious detritus (C:N = 23) than red mangrove leaves (C:N = 43) during decomposition.

EVAPOTRANSPIRATION

Evapotranspiration rates for freshwater and saltwater forested wetlands are shown in Table 8-2. However, data for both freshwater and saltwater forests were available only for basin forested wetlands. Evapotranspiration from basin saltwater forests was comparable to that from freshwater forests, and both were lower than evaporation from open water (Brown, 1978). Evapotranspiration from the riverine freshwater forest, on the other hand, was higher than for open water (Brown, 1978). Evapotranspiration from the scrub freshwater forest was the lowest.

The transpiration ratios of the riverine and scrub freshwater forests are similar to those of basin freshwater forests (Brown, 1978). However, the low evapotranspiration of scrub freshwater forest appears to be mostly a function of poor canopy development (leaf area index of less than 1; Brown, 1978) resulting from poor site conditions. In the riverine forest, the absolute amount of water transpired is high, but, because water is not potentially limiting, structural adaptations to limit water loss are not formed and primary productivity is maximized (Brown, 1978).

Unfortunately, transpiration data for riverine saltwater forests are not available. Since these wetlands tend to be dominated by red mangroves, data for a fringing red mangrove site may provide insight about the water

TABLE 8-2 Evapotranspirational Rates of Saltwater and Freshwater Forested Wetlands

Type	Evapotranspiration (mm)		Source
	Daily	Annual	
Riverine			
Freshwater			
Florida	5.6	—	Brown, 1978
Basin			
Saltwater			
Southern Florida	1.6[a]	—	Lugo et al., 1975
Southern Florida	2.1 (3.4)[b]	753	Lugo et al., 1980
Southern Florida	2.8 (4.4)[b]	1,010	Lugo et al., 1980
Freshwater			
Florida	3.8	—	Brown, 1978
Florida	2.6 (4.5)[b]	965	Heimburg, 1976
Palm forest in Puerto Rico	1.6	584	Frangi and Lugo, unpublished
Scrub (palm forest)			
Freshwater			
Southern Florida	0.9 (1.3)[c]	—	Brown et al., in press

[a]Transpiration only.
[b]Daily rate obtained by dividing annual rate by 365. Number in parenthesis is average summer (June–August) rate.
[c]First number, transpiration when forest was flooded; second number, evapotranspiration when forest was dry.

relations one might expect in a riverine saltwater forest. Brown and Lugo calculated a transpiration ratio for red mangroves from data in Lugo *et al.* (1975) of 249 g water/g organic matter, which is 1.5 times higher than the ratio for black mangroves. Red mangroves tend to live in less saline conditions than black mangroves, and red mangroves exclude salt in the root zone. Because reds transpire more water per unit of organic matter fixed than black mangroves, it is suggested that salt exclusion is not as energy-expensive when salinities are lower (in red mangrove sites) as it is in the higher-salinity black mangrove environments.

RESPONSE OF FORESTED WETLANDS TO STRESSORS

Wetland ecosystems are often subjected to environmental impacts (Figure 8-6). Because the water regime is the chief component of the energy struc-

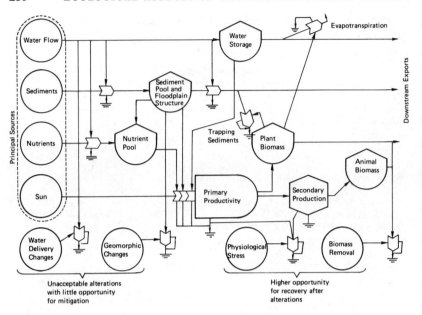

FIGURE 8-6   Diagram showing the major flows of energy and nutrients in wetlands and the locations where human interventions affect these flows. Adapted from Brown *et al.*, 1978; Brinson *et al.*, 1981.

ture of a wetland, any impacts that alter this factor seriously impair the structural and functional characteristics of the ecosystem. Thus, the brackets in the lower part of the diagram identify interventions that allow few opportunities for mitigation (on the left-hand side) and others that allow higher opportunities for mitigation (right-hand side). The basis for the differences is that interventions that affect the major sources of nutrients, water, or energy (i.e., those that alter the hydrology or the geomorphology of the wetlands) rapidly affect the whole ecosystem, because they reduce primary production. Rapid ecosystem deterioration follows, a deterioration that is irreversible until natural water flows and geomorphology are reconstituted.

Human interventions on downstream compartments (such as biomass removal or physiological stress on plants, microbes, or animals) can be alleviated more easily, because the wetland maintains its vigor and capacity to grow as long as its primary sources of energy and resources remain intact. Thus, the resources to overcome stress can be made available, and the system can recover more easily provided the intervention is not chronic or of greater intensity than the wetland's natural capacity to heal (Lugo, 1980b).

Impounding water in a freshwater wetland has serious consequences for the structural and thus functional characteristics of the system. The structure of a riverine freshwater forested wetland that is subjected to impoundment at a mean depth of flooding of 60 cm deteriorates rapidly; above 60 cm, chronic increases in flooding produce significant reductions in the complexity of the forest brought about by the death of many trees. When a riverine freshwater forested wetland is subject to other stressors, such as a shorter growing season or exposure to colder temperatures, and is subjected to spring flooding rather than summer flooding, its response to impoundment is faster than that of a riverine forest without these additional stressors (Figure 8-7).

Decreases in net biomass production have been measured in an impounded riverine freshwater forested wetland that was permanently flooded (Conner *et al.,* in press). Leaf-litter production in the impounded forest was 3.3 t/ha/yr, whereas, in a nearby naturally flooded forest, leaf-litter production was 4.2 t/ha/yr. Comparable values for wood production in the impounded are 5.6 t/ha/yr and 7.49 t/ha/yr in the naturally flooded forest.

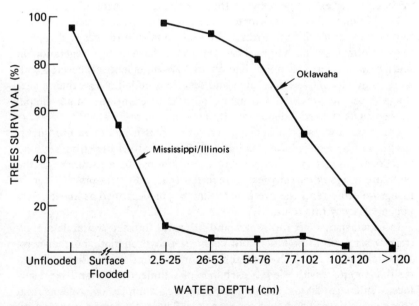

FIGURE 8-7 Survivorship curve for trees in riverine freshwater forested wetlands subject to impoundment. The top curve is for a forest in Florida that has been subjected to 5 continuous years of flooding; the bottom curve is for a forest in Illinois that has been subjected to 7 years of continuous flooding and other stressors. From Lugo and Brown (in press).

Draining wetlands also has serious consequences for the structural and functional characteristics of riverine freshwater forested wetlands (Figure 8-6). Burns (1978) found that total biomass (above-ground and below-ground) of a drained forest was approximately half that of a nearby undrained forest, reductions occuring in all biomass compartments. The following factors are noted for biomass production: litter production was similar in drained and undrained forest; wood production in the drained forest was about half that of the undrained forest; and root production in the drained forest was about 25% that of the undrained forest (Burns, 1978).

Chronic impoundment of saltwater forests also leads to dramatic changes in structural and functional characteristics of the ecosystem. For example, in Sanibel Island, Florida, R. Twilley, A. Lugo, and W. Khoon (personal communication, 1980) found that, after 16 years of impoundment, a mangrove stand had (1) a complete change in species dominance (from red to white mangrove), (2) lower stand height (4.9 versus 6.8 m), (3) lower basal area (10.5 versus 17.6 m²/ha), (4) lower complexity index (4.9 versus 7.4), and (5) a higher accumulation of loose litter on the forest floor (3,737 versus 639 g/m²). In Puerto Rico, Patterson-Zucca (1978) described extensive mangrove mortalities that resulted from construction of a road that impeded water exchange between the forest and the surrounding ocean.

In addition to their sensitivity to alterations in the hydroperiod, saltwater forests are very sensitive to stressors that interfere with the gas exchange of roots, sediments, and stems. For example, a basin forest vegetation in southwestern Puerto Rico that had about 10% of its lenticels covered with oil from an oil spill was defoliated and died in a period of less than a year (Lugo et al., in press-a). A fringing forest affected by the same oil spill showed signs of partial defoliation (Lugo et al., in press-a).

Other stressors, such as low temperature, excessive temperature fluctuations, and hot water have also been reported to affect the structural and functional characteristics of mangrove ecosystems. In a summary of the literature, Lugo et al. (in press-a) reported that most stressors that act on mangrove ecosystems elicit responses that can be described as linear or exponential decay functions.

In conclusion, both freshwater and saltwater forested wetlands are extremely sensitive to pollution and changes in hydroperiod. Furthermore, saltwater forests and perhaps freshwater forests are very sensitive to stressors that interfere with the gas exchange of sediment, root, and stem surfaces. Drainage diking and impounding are examples of stressors that change hydroperiod and alter gas exchange. These stressors cannot be mitigated (Brown et al., 1978). Both types of forested wetlands are adapted to such natural stressors as periodic flooding and anoxic soil conditions, and saltwater forests also tolerate salinity. Such human-induced stressors as those discussed above, plus harvesting and addition of toxic substances, heat, or sediments, are instances of energy drains on forested wetlands beyond those to which they are already adapted.

SUMMARY

Natural lakes, reservoirs, ponds, and rivers constitute the surface aquatic resources of the humid tropics. Although less studied than their counterparts in Temperate-Zone and even arid tropical systems, they are similar to them in many respects, differing chiefly in their higher temperatures and frequently in their low dissolved-salt content. The multiple use of water for hydroelectric generation, irrigation, fish and shellfish production, and waste disposal necessitates a thoroughly integrated approach to its management.

The higher temperatures encountered in these systems tend to intensify the short-term impact of chemical pollution, while at the same time causing a more rapid degradation of organic pollutants. Since many organisms are near the upper limits of temperature tolerance, they may be highly sensitive to thermal pollution. The proliferation of reservoirs in the tropics necessitates development of improved management strategies encompassing a variety of disciplines. Planning discharge levels, erosion control of the watershed, and clearing of the basin prior to flooding are extremely important considerations. Fisheries and aquatic weed management in new reservoirs is also important and should benefit greatly from a combination of research and monitoring.

Public health aspects of water-associated diseases and vectors require increased attention in the humid tropics. It is important to recognize that wetland forests and especially coastal mangroves form important, fragile, buffer zones between the land and sea. Because of their contribution to coastal and riverine fish and shellfish production and to wastewater treatment, they must be protected.

REFERENCES

Axler, R. P., G. W. Redfield, and C. R. Goldman. 1981. The importance of regenerated nitrogen to phytoplankton productivity in a subalpine lake ecology. Ecology 62:345–354.

Balon, E. K., and A. G. Coche, eds. 1974. Lake Kariba: a man-made tropical ecosystem in Central Africa. Dr. W. Junk Publishers, The Hague, Netherlands. 767 p.

Banson, J. K. A., and K. Barning. 1969. Probable sedimentation and seismic effect on the Volta River. *In* L. Obeng, ed. Man-made lakes. Ghana University Press, Accra. 397 p.

Beadle, L. C. 1966. Prolonged stratification and deoxygenation in tropical lakes I. Crater Lake, Nkugute, Uganda, compared with Lakes Bunyoni and Edward. Limnol. Oceanogr. 11(2):152–163.

Beadle, L. C. 1974. The inland waters of tropical Africa. Longman, London. 365 p.

Boon, P. J. 1979. Adaptive strategies of *Amphipsyche* larvae (*Trichoptera: Hydropsychidae*) downstream of a tropical impoundment. Pages 237-256 in J. V. Ward and J. A. Stanford, eds. The ecology of regulated streams. Plenum, New York.

Brinson, M. M., B. L. Swift, R. C. Plantico, and J. S. Barclay. 1981. Riparian ecosystems: their ecology and status. U.S. Fish and Wildlife Service, Office of Biological Services. FWS/OBS-81/17. Washington, D.C. 154 p.

Brinson, M. M., A. E. Lugo, and S. Brown. In press. Primary and secondary productivity in wetlands. Ann. Rev. Ecol. Syst.

Brown, S. 1978. A comparison of cypress ecosystems in the landscape of Florida. Ph.D. dissertation, University of Florida, Gainesville.

Brown, S., M. M. Brinson, and A. E. Lugo. 1978. Structure and function of riparian wetlands. Pages 17-31 in R. R. Johnson and J. F. McCormick (tech. coord.) Strategies for protection and management of floodplain wetlands and other riparian ecosystems. Gen. Tech. Rep. WO-12. U.S. Forest Service, Washington, D.C.

Brown, S., E. Flohrschutz, and H. T. Odum. In press. Structure, productivity, and phosphorus cycling of the scrub cypress ecosystem. In K. C. Ewel and H. T. Odum, eds. Cypress swamps. University Press of Florida, Gainesville.

Brylinsky, M., and K. H. Mann. 1973. An analysis of factors governing productivity in lakes and reservoirs. Limnol. Oceanogr. 18:1-14.

Burgis, M. J. 1978. The Lake George ecosystem. Verh. Int. Verein. Limnol. 20:1139-1152.

Burns, L. A. 1978. Productivity, biomass and water relations in a Florida cypress forest. Ph.D. dissertation, University of North Carolina, Chapel Hill.

Cintron, G., A. E. Lugo, and R. Martinez. 1980. Structural and functional properties of mangrove forests. Paper presented at the symposium signaling the completion of the *Flora of Panama*. April 14-17, 1980, Panama City, Panama. Available from A. E. Lugo, Institute of Tropical Forestry, P.O. Box AQ, Rio Piedras, Puerto Rico.

Coche, A. G. 1974. Limnological study of tropical reservoirs. Pages 1-246 in E. K. Balon and A. G. Coche, eds. Lake Kariba: a man-made tropical ecosystem in Central Africa. Dr. W. Junk Publishers, The Hague, Netherlands.

Conner, W. H., J. G. Gosselink, and R. T. Parrondo. Comparison of the vegetation of three Louisiana swamp sites with different flooding regimes. Am. J. Bot. 68:320-331.

Coulter, G. W. 1963. Hydrological changes in relation to biological production in southern Lake Tanganyika. Limnol. Oceanogr. 8:463-471.

Cummins, K. W. 1973. Trophic relations of aquatic insects. Annu. Rev. Entomol. 18:183-206.

Cummins, K. W. 1979. The natural stream ecosystem. Pages 7-24 in J. V. Ward and J. A. Stanford, eds. The ecology of regulated streams. Plenum, New York.

Cummins, K. W., and M. J. Klug. 1979. Feeding ecology of stream invertebrates. Annu. Rev. Ecol. Syst. 10:147-172.

Cummins, K. W., R. C. Petersen, F. O. Howard, J. C. Wrycheck, and V. I. Holt. 1973. The utilization of leaf litter by stream detritivores. Ecology 54:336-345.

Davies, B. R. 1979. Stream regulation in Africa: a review. Pages 113-142 in J. V. Ward and J. A. Stanford, eds. The ecology of regulated streams. Plenum, New York.

Day, J. W., Jr., T. J. Butler, and W. H. Conner. 1977. Productivity and nutrient export studies in a cypress swamp and lake system in Louisiana. Pages 255-269 in M. Wiley, ed. Estuarine processes. Vol. 2, Circulation, sediments, and transfer of material in the estuary. Academic Press, New York.

Dorris, T. C. 1972. La ecología y la pesca del Lago de Atitlán. E. V. Publicación Especial I, El Centro de Investigación de Embalse de la Universidad Estatal de Oklahoma.

Eccles, D. H. 1962. An internal wave in Lake Nyasa and its probable significance in the nutrient cycle. Nature 194:832–833.

Ewer, D. W. 1966. Biological investigations on the Volta Lake, May 1964 to May 1965. Pages 21–31, in R. H. Lowe-McConnell, ed. Man-made lakes. Academic Press, New York.

Farnworth, E. G., and F. B. Golley, eds. 1974. Fragile ecosystems—evaluation of research and applications in the neotropics. Springer-Verlag, New York, 258 p.

Fisher, S. G., and G. E. Likens. 1973. Energy flow in Bear Brook, New Hampshire: an integrative approach to stream ecosystem metabolism. Ecol. Monogr. 43:421–439.

Fisher, T. R. 1979. Plankton and primary production in aquatic systems of the central Amazon Basin. Pages 31–38 in A. Riggs, ed. The Amazon Alpha Helix expedition to the Amazon for the study of fish blood and hemoglobin. J. Comp. Biochem. Physiol. A, v. 62.

Fittkau, E. J., J. Irmler, W. J. Junk, F. Reiss, and G. W. Schmidt. 1975. Productivity, biomass, and population dynamics in Amazonian water bodies. Pages 289–311 in F. B. Golley and E. Medina, eds. Tropical ecological systems. Springer-Verlag, New York.

Freeman, P. H. 1974. The environmental impact of tropical dams. Guidelines for impact assessment based upon a case study of Volta Lake. Smithsonian Institution, Washington, D.C.

Ganf, G. G., and P. Blazka. 1974. Oxygen uptake, ammonia and phosphate excretion by zooplankton of a shallow equatorial lake (Lake George, Uganda). Limnol. Oceanogr. 19:313–325.

Ganf, G. G., and A. B. Viner. 1973. Ecological stability in a shallow equatorial lake (L. George, Uganda). Proc. R. Soc. Lond., Ser. B. 184:321–346.

Gibbs, R. J. 1967. The geochemistry of the Amazon river system. Part I: The factors that control the salinity and the composition and concentrations of the suspended solids. Geol. Soc. Am. Bull. 78:1203–1232.

Gibbs, R. J. 1972. Water chemistry of the Amazon River. Geochim. Cosmochim. Acta 36:1061–1066.

Goldman, C. R. 1963. The measurement of primary productivity and limiting factors in freshwater with Carbon 14. Pages 103–113 in M. S. Doty, ed. Proceedings of conference on primary productivity measurement, marine and freshwater. U.S. Atomic Energy Commission, TID-7633, Washington, D.C.

Goldman, C. R. 1967. Integration of field and laboratory experiments in productivity studies. Pages 346–352 in G. H. Lauff, ed. Estuaries. Publ. No. 83. American Association for the Advancement of Science, Washington, D.C.

Goldman, C. R. 1971. Reduced flows and the future ecology of the San Francisco-Bay Delta system. Proc. Symp. Hydrobiol. (Miami, Fla.) 8:174–190.

Goldman, C. R. 1972a. El Cajon project. Feasibility study 5; ecology. Prepared for Motor Columbus Consulting Engineers, Inc. and the World Bank with the support of Empresa National de Energia Electrica, Tagucigalpa, Honduras. 59 p.

Goldman, C. R. 1972b. The role of minor nutrients in limiting the productivity of aquatic ecosystems. Pages 21–33 in G. E. Likens, ed. Nutrients and eutrophication. Am. Soc. Limnol. Oceanogr. Spec. Symp. No. 1.

Goldman, C. R. 1978a. Ecological aspects of water impoundment in the tropics. Rev. Biol. Trop. 24 (Suppl. 1):87–112.

Goldman, C. R. 1978b. Environmental impact assessment. Chapter 10 in Lokoja hydroelectric project. IV: Secondary impacts. Report for National Electric Power Authority, Lagos, Nigeria.

Goldman, C. R., R. W. Hoffman, and A. Allison. 1973. Environmental studies design,

Purari River development, Papua New Guinea. United Nations Development Program, New York.

Goodland, R. J. A. 1980. Environmental ranking of Amazonian development projects in Brazil. Environ. Conserv. 7(1):9-26.

Harding, D. 1966. Lake Kariba—the hydrology and development of fisheries. Pages 7-20 in R. H. Lowe-McConnell, ed. Man-made lakes. Academic Press, New York, London.

Heimburg, K. 1976. Hydrology of some north-central Florida cypress domes. Thesis. University of Florida, Gainesville.

Hern, S. C., and V. W. Lambou. 1979. Productivity responses to changes in hydrological regimes in the Atchafalaya Basin, Louisiana. Pages 93-102 in Proceedings of an international symposium, environmental effects of hydrological engineering works. Tennessee Valley Authority, Knoxville, Tenn.

Hickling, C. F. 1962. Fish culture. Faber and Faber, London. 295 p.

Hilton, T. E., and J. Y. Kown-tsei. 1972. The impact of the Volta scheme on the lower Volta flood plains. J. Trop. Geogr. 1972:29-37.

Hutchinson, G. E. 1957. A treatise on limnology. Vol. 1. John Wiley & Sons, New York. 1015 p.

Hynes, H. B. N. 1970. The ecology of running waters. University of Toronto Press, Toronto. 555 p.

IAEA (International Atomic Energy Agency). 1980. Agrochemical residue: biota interactions in soil and aquatic ecosystems. IAEA, Vienna, Austria, 1978.

IAEA (International Atomic Energy Agency). In press. Agrochemical residue—biota interactions in soil and aquatic ecosystems. IAEA, Burnaby, B.C., Canada.

Johannes, R. E., and S. B. Betzer. 1975. Marine communities respond differently to pollution in the tropics than at higher latitudes. Pages 1-12 in E. J. F. Wood and R. E. Johannes, eds. Tropical marine pollution. Elsevier Publ., Amsterdam.

Kershaw, W. E. 1966. The Simulium problem and fishery development in the proposed Niger Lake. Pages 95-98 in R. H. Lowe-McConnell, ed. Man-made lakes. Academic Press, New York, London.

Kittel, T., and P. J. Richerson. 1978. The heat budget of a large tropical lake, Lake Titicaca (Peru-Bolivia). Verh. Int. Verein. Limnol. 20:1203-1209.

Lewis, W. M. 1973. The thermal regime of Lake Lanao (Philippines) and its theoretical implications for tropical lakes. Limnol. Oceanogr. 18:200-217.

Lewis, W. M. 1974. Primary production in the plankton community of a tropical lake. Geol. Monogr. 44:377-409.

Lewis, W. M., Jr., and F. H. Weibezahn. 1976. Chemistry, energy flow, and community structure in some Venezuelan freshwaters. Arch. Hydrobiol. (Suppl.) 50:145-207.

Likens, G. E., F. H. Bormann, R. S. Pierce, J. S. Eaton, and N. M. Johnson. 1977. Biogeochemistry of a forested ecosystem. Springer-Verlag, New York. 146 p.

Limpadanai, D., and P. Brahamanonda. 1978. Salinity intrusion into Lake Songkla, a lagoonal lake of southern Thailand. Verh. Int. Verein. Limnol. 20:1111-1115.

Little, E. C. S. 1966. The invasion of man-made lakes by plants. Pages 75-86 in R. H. Lowe-McConnell, ed. Man-made lakes. Academic Press, New York, London.

Lowe-McConnell, R. H. 1975. Fish communities in tropical freshwaters: their distribution, ecology, and evolution. Longman, London. 478 p.

Lugo, A. E. 1978. Stress and ecosystems. Pages 62-101 in J. H. Thorp and J. W. Gibbons, eds. Energy and environmental stress in aquatic systems. U.S. Dept. Energy Symp. Series, CONF-771114. National Technical Information Service, Springfield, Virginia.

Lugo, A. E. 1980a. Are tropical forests sources or sinks of carbon? Pages 1-19 in S. Brown,

A. E. Lugo, and B. Llegel eds. The role of tropical forests in the global carbon cycle. CONF-800350. Office of Environment, U.S. Department of Energy, Washington, D.C.

Lugo, A. E. 1980b. Mangrove ecosystems: succession or steady state? Biotropica, Tropical Succession: 65–72.

Lugo, A. E., and M. M. Brinson. 1978. Calculation of the value of salt water wetlands. Pages 120–130 *in* P. E. Greeson, J. R. Clark, and J. E. Clark, eds. Wetlands functions and values: the state of our understanding. American Water Resources Association, Minneapolis, Minnesota.

Lugo, A. E., and S. Brown. In press. The Ocklawaha River forested wetlands and their response to chronic flooding. *In* K. C. Ewel and H. T. Odum, eds. Cypress swamps. University Presses of Florida, Gainesville.

Lugo, A. E., and S. C. Snedaker. 1974. The ecology of mangroves. Ann. Rev. Ecol. Syst. 5:39–64.

Lugo, A. E., M. Brinson, M. Cerame Vivas, C. Gist, R. Inger, C. Jordan, H. Lieth, W. Milstead, P. Murphy, N. Smythe, S. Snedacker, R. Johannes, and W. Lewis. 1974. Tropical ecosystem structure and function. Pages 67–112 *in* E. G. Farnworth and F. B. Golley, eds. Fragile ecosystems. Springer-Verlag, New York.

Lugo, A. E., G. Evink, M. Brinson, A. Broces, and S. C. Snedaker. 1975. Diurnal rates of photosynthesis, respiration and transpiration in mangrove forests of South Florida. Pages 335–350 *in* F. B. Golley and E. Medina, eds. Tropical ecological systems. Springer-Verlag, New York.

Lugo, A. E., R. R. Twilley, and C. Patterson-Zucca. 1980. The role of black mangrove forests in the productivity of coastal ecosystems in South Florida. Final report to U.S. Environmental Protection Agency, Corvallis Environmental Research Laboratory, Corvallis, Oregon. Center for Wetlands, University of Florida, Gainesville.

Lugo, A. E., G. Cintron, and C. Goenaga. In press-a. Mangrove ecosystems under stress. *In* G. W. Barrett and R. Rosenberg, eds. Stress effects on natural ecosystems. J. Wiley & Sons, New York.

Lugo, A. E., F. Quinones-Marquez, and P. L. Weaver. In press-b. La erosión y sedimentación en Puerto Rico. Caribb. J. Sci.

Melack, J. M. 1976. Primary productivity and fish yields in tropical lakes. Trans. Am. Fish. Soc. 105:575–580.

Melack, J. M. 1979. Photosynthesis and growth of *Spirulina plantensis* (Cyanophyta) in an equatorial lake (Lake Simbi, Kenya). Limnol. Oceanogr. 24:753–760.

Merritt, R. W., and K. W. Cummins, eds. 1978. An introduction to the aquatic insects of North America. Kendall-Hunt, Dubuque, Iowa. 441 p.

Mikhailov, V. M. 1964. Hydrology and formation of river-mouth bass. Humid Trop. Res. UNESCO 24(2):59–64.

Mitchell, D. S. 1973. Supply of plant nutrient chemicals in Lake Kariba. Pages 165–169 *in* W. C. Ackerman, G. F. White, and E. B. Worthington, eds. Man-made lakes: their problems and their environmental effects. Geophys. Monogr. Ser., Vol. 17.

Mulholland, P. J., and E. J. Kuenzler. 1979. Organic carbon export from upland and forested wetland watersheds. Limnol. Oceanogr. 24:960–966.

Obeng, L. E. 1969. The invertebrate fauna of aquatic plants of the Volta Lake in relation to the spread of helminth parasites. Pages 320–325 *in* L. E. Obeng, ed. Man-made lakes. Ghana University Press, Accra.

Odum, E. P. 1971. Fundamentals of ecology. W. B. Saunders, Philadelphia. 574 p.

Odum, H. T., B. J. Copeland, and E. A. McMahan. 1974. Coastal ecological systems of the United States. The Conservation Foundation, Washington, D.C.

Odum, H. T., W. Kemp, M. Sell, W. Boynton, and M. Lehman. 1977. Energy analysis and the coupling of man and estuaries. Environ. Manage. 1:297-315.

Paerl, H. W. 1978. Microbial organic carbon recovery in aquatic ecosystems. Limnol. Oceanog. 23:920-926.

Paerl, H. W., and C. R. Goldman. 1972a. Heterotrophic assays in the detection of water masses at Lake Tahoe, California. Limnol. Oceanog. 17(1):145-148.

Paerl, H. W., and C. R. Goldman. 1972b. Stimulation of heterotrophic and autotrophic activities of a planktonic microbial community by siltation at Lake Tahoe, California. Mem. Inst. Hydrobiol. 29 (Suppl.):129-147.

Paperna, I. 1969. Snail vectors of human schistosomiasis in the newly formed Volta Lake. Pages 326-330 in L. E. Obeng, ed. Man-made lakes. Ghana University Press, Accra.

Patterson-Zucca, C. 1978. The effects of road construction on a mangrove ecosystem. Thesis. University of Puerto Rico, Rio Piedras.

Persson, R. 1974. World forest resources. Review of the world's forest resources in the early 1970's. Department of Forest Survey, Royal College of Forestry, Stockholm, Sweden.

Priscu, J. C., J. Verduin, and J. E. Deacon. In press. The fate of biogenic suspensoids in a desert reservoir. Proceedings of symposium on surface water impoundments. American Water Resources Association, Minneapolis, Minnesota.

Richerson, P. J., C. Widmer, and T. Kittel. 1977. The limnology of Lake Titicaca (Peru–Bolivia), a large, high altitude, tropical lake. Publ. 14. Institute of Ecology, University of California—Davis. 78 p.

Richey, J. E., J. T. Brock, R. J. Maiman, R. C. Wissmar, and R. F. Stallard. 1980. Organic carbon: oxidation and transport in the Amazon River. Science 207:1348-1351.

Sanders, H. L. 1968. Marine benthic diversity: a comparative study. Am. Nat. 102:243-282.

Schiff, C. J. 1972. The impact of agricultural development on aquatic systems and its effects on the epidemiology of schistosomiasis in Rhodesia. Pages 102-108 in M. T. Farvar and J. P. Milton, eds. The careless technology. Natural History Press, Garden City, New York.

Schmidt, G. W. 1973a. Primary production in the three types of Amazonian waters. II: The limnology of a tropical flood plain lake in central Amazonia (Lago do Castanho). Amazonia 4:139-203.

Schmidt, G. W. 1973b. Primary production in the three types of Amazonian waters. III: Primary productivity of phytoplankton in a tropical flood plain lake of central Amazonia (Lago do Castanho, Amazonas, Brazil). Amazonia 4:375-404.

Schmidt, G. W. 1976. Primary production of phytoplankton in the three types of Amazonian waters. IV: On the primary productivity of phytoplankton in a bay of the lower Rio Negro (Amazonas, Brazil). Amazonia 5:517-528.

SCOPE (Scientific Committee on Problems of the Environment). 1972. Man-made lakes as modified ecosystems. Report 2. International Council of Scientific Unions, Paris. 76 p.

Sedell, J. R., R. J. Naiman, K. W. Cummins, G. W. Minshall, and R. L. Vannote. 1978. Transport of particulate organic material in streams as a function of physical processes. Verh. Int. Verein. Limnol. 20:1366-1376.

Sioli, H. 1964. General features of the limnology of Amazonia. Verh. Int. Verein. Limnol. 15:1053-1058.

Sioli, H. 1975. Tropical river: the Amazon. Pages 461-488 in B. A. Whitton, ed. River ecology. University of California Press, Los Angeles.

Smith, K. 1972. River water temperatures: an environmental review. Scott. Geogr. Mag. 88:211-220.

Talling, J. F. 1963. Origin of stratification in an African rift lake. Limnol. Oceanog. 8(1):68-78.

Talling, J. F. 1969. The incidence of vertical mixing, and some biological and chemical con sequences in tropical African lakes. Verh. Inter. Verein. Limnol. 17:998–1012.

Tison, L. J. 1964. Problems de sedimentation dans les deltas. Humid Trop. Res. UNESCO 24(2):57.

Viner, A. B. 1975. The supply of minerals to tropical rivers and lakes (Uganda). Pages 227–261 *in* A. D. Hasler, ed. Coupling of land and water systems. Springer-Verlag, New York.

Waddy, B. B. 1966. Medical problems arising from the making of lakes in the tropics. Pages 87–94 *in* R. H. Lowe-McConnell, ed. Man-made lakes. Academic Press, London, New York.

Walton, S. 1981. U.S.–Egypt Nile project studies high dam's effects. BioScience 31(1):9–13.

Ward, J. V., and J. A. Stanford. 1979. Ecological factors controlling stream zoobenthos with emphasis on thermal modifications of regulated streams. Pages 35–36 *in* J. V. Ward and J. A. Stanford, eds. The ecology of regulated streams. Plenum, New York.

Warmann, J. St. G. 1969. Onchocerciasis and the Volta Dam construction. Page 352 *in* L. E. Obeng, ed. Man-made lakes. Ghana University Press, Accra.

Weiss, C. M. 1971. Water quality investigations, Guatemala: Lake Atitlan 1968–1970. ESE Publ. 274. University of North Carolina, Chapel Hill. 175 p.

Wetzel, R. G. 1975. Limnology. W. B. Saunders, Philadelphia. 743 p.

Whitton, B. A., ed. 1975. River ecology. Blackwell Scientific Publications, Oxford, U.K.

Wood, E. J. F., and R. G. Johannes. 1975. Tropical marine pollution. Elsevier Publ., Amsterdam. 192 p.

APPENDIXES

A

Land Resource
Base Data*

Land resource information is put into a comparable geographic base by delineating land systems (areas that have a repetitive pattern of climate, landscape, and soils) directly onto satellite and radar imagery. Although the work has mainly been an exercise in collating existing information, field work is carried out to help fill in knowledge gaps and standardize criteria. Following the collection, revision, and mapping of the climate, landscape, and soil information, the data are coded and recorded in a computerized data storage–retrieval–analytical map and data printout system to facilitate speedy analyses. In the case of the Amazonia study, long-term climatic data were obtained from 1,144 stations throughout tropical America, including 107 stations in Amazonia, and were compiled by Hancock *et al.* (1979).

Potential evapotranspiration (PET) is calculated to assess the amount of energy available for plant growth and to determine the water balance and growing seasons. Hargreaves' (1977b) equation is used; it is based mainly on solar radiation and temperature. The precipitation deficit (DEF PREC) is the difference between the mean precipitation and the PET. The dependable precipitation (DEP PREC) reflects the 75% probability level of precipitation occurrence—that is, the amount of precipitation that will be equaled or exceeded in 3 out of 4 years. The moisture availability index (MAI) is a moisture adequacy index at the 75% probability level of precipitation occurrence, computed by dividing DEP PREC by PET. Hargreaves (1977a) has further shown that the relationship between the MAI and annual crop pro-

---

*SOURCE: Cochrane and Sanchez, 1981.

duction is satisfactory when soil moisture storage is adequate for a week or more. He suggested that MAI values lower than 0.33 define a dry month, but this level may be too high for soils that have very low moisture-holding capacities. The wet season, therefore, is defined as that part of the year with MAI values larger than 0.33. Total wet-season evapotranspiration (WSPET) is calculated as the sum of PET during wet months or parts thereof. Since PET is temperature-dependent, it is related to the energy available for photosynthesis during the period when moisture is not limiting. Wet-season mean temperature (WSMT) is calculated in a similar manner.

Vegetation classes are identified in accordance with the criteria of Eyre (1968) for tropical forests. Correlations between physiognomic vegetation types and climatic parameters were made for well-drained soil sites with more than 20 years of climatic data. Climatic subregions are identified as a result of such analysis.

Subdivided land systems that make up the landscape are delineated on satellite and side-looking radar imagery (Projeto RADAMbrasil, 1972–78; U.S. Geological Survey 1977). Maps are collated, drawn at a scale of 1:1,000,000, and computerized in 4-minute by 4-minute units (about 6,800 ha) to serve as the basis for thematic map production. Field work must be carried out, wherever feasible, to provide on-the-ground information to help standardize descriptive criteria and study the variation of landscape features. These variations, although not mapped (because of scale limitations), are described as land facets, and the proportion of each land facet within the land systems is estimated. In this way, selected landscape features are computed on the basis of the land facet subdivision. It should be noted that, since the smallest mapping unit is the land system, thematic mapping for a given characteristic generally represents the rating of the main land facet.

The subdivision of land systems into land facets is especially useful in bridging the gap between land systems and soil units. Obviously, land facets will contain soils with a variation in properties, but some level of generalization must be accepted in making an inventory of land resources. The most extensive soils in each land facet are first classified into the great categories of the Soil Taxonomy system (Soil Survey Staff, 1975), then described in terms of their physical and chemical properties. Areal estimates for each great group are made according to topographic divisions along climatic subregions.

Several physical and chemical properties of the topsoil (0–20 cm deep) and subsoil (21–50 cm deep) are recorded, tabulated, and coded. Physical properties of soil include slope, texture, presence of coarse material, depth, initial infiltration rate, hydraulic conductivity, drainage, moisture-holding capacity, temperature regime, moisture regime, and the presence of expanding clays. Chemical properties include pH; percentage Al satu ration; exchangeable Al, Ca, Mg, K, and Na; total exchangeable bases (TEB); effective cation-exchange capacity (ECEC); OM; available P; P fixation; available Mn, S, Zn, Fe, Cu, B, and Mo; free carbonates; salinity; percentage Na saturation; presence of cat clays; x-ray amorphism; and elements of importance to animal nutrition. (The Bray, Olsen, and Truog methodologies were used in estimating data on available P. Assured values were derived by the method described by Vettori (1969).)

The quantity and quality of the available data varied considerably from region to region. They are tabulated according to the Fertility Capability Soil Classification system (FCC) described by Buol et al. (1975) and modified by Sanchez et al. (1980). FCC units were incorporated into the computer programs to permit production of thematic maps. Other parameters not included in the FCC system may be divided into arbitrary classes.

The interpretation of the data generated by the Centro Internacional de Agricultura Tropical land evaluation study are developed in terms of soil properties, constraints, dynamics, and management under main farming systems.

REFERENCES

Buol, S. W., P. A. Sanchez, R. B. Cate, and M. A. Granger. 1975. Soil fertility capability classification: a technical soil classification for fertility management. Pages 126–141 *in* E. Bornemisza and A. Alvarado, eds. Soil management in tropical America. North Carolina State University, Raleigh.

Cochrane, T. T., and P. A. Sanchez. 1981. Land resources, soil properties and their management in the Amazon region: a state of knowledge report. Proceedings of conference on Amazon land use research. Centro Internacional de Agricultura Tropical (CIAT), Calí, Colombia.

Eiten, G. 1972. The cerrado vegetation of Brazil. Bot. Rev. 38(2):201–341.

Eyre, S. R. 1968. Vegetation and soils. Aldine, Chicago. 323 p.

Hancock, J. K., R. W. Hill, and G. H. Hargreaves. 1979. Potential evapotranspiration and precipitation deficits for tropical America: a resume of the preliminary climatic data used for land resources evaluation study of tropical America. Centro Internacional de Agricultura Tropical (CIAT), Calí, Colombia. 398 p.

Hargreaves, G. H. 1977a. Consumptive use of water and irrigation water requirements. J. Irrigation Drainage Div. Am. Soc. Civ. Eng. 103(2):287–290.

Hargreaves, G. H. 1977b. World water for agriculture: climate, precipitation probabilities, and adequacies for rainfed agriculture. Utah State University, Logan.

Projecto RADAMbrasil. 1972–1978. Levantamento da região Amazônica. Vols. 1–12. Ministerio das Minas e Energia, Departamento da Produção Mineral, Rio de Janeiro, Brasil.

Sanchez, P. A., S. W. Buol, and W. Couto. 1980. The fertility capability classification system and its application to land evaluation guidelines. Tropical Soils Program, North Carolina State University, Raleigh. Manuscript. 30 p.

Soil Survey Staff. 1975. Soil taxonomy: a basic system of soil classification for making and interpreting soil surveys. U.S. Dept. Agr. Handb. 436. U.S. Department of Agriculture, Washington, D.C.

U.S. Geological Survey. 1977. EROS data center. U.S. Government Printing Office, Washington, D.C. 28 p.

Vettori, L. 1969. Metodo de analise de solo. Bol. Tec. 7, Equipe de Pedologia e Fertilidade do Solo. Rio de Janeiro, Brasil.

B
Appendix

Ecological Evaluation of
Natural Environments:
Instructions to Observers*

THE SITE

In the first instance sites should be chosen within a uniform vegetation type and uniform terrain (land forms, slope, altitudinal range, soil drainage, degree of disturbance, and so on). Then other sites—those that contain irregular features but are considered important as habitats—should be examined. Such sites may represent early successional stages, forest edge, ecotone, firebreaks, or other disturbed areas of the forest. The *minimum* area of each site inspected should be 1,000 m². Some time should be spent walking about on the site noting features before data forms are filled in. Survey of the area by aircraft or from a lookout also permits its relationship with surrounding areas to be determined and provides information about canopy features.

SCORING OF FEATURES

Except when measurements or brief descriptions are called for, the necessary notations consist of indicating pertinent choices by a simple checkmark on the form, or estimating prominence of a given feature on a 4-point scale (0–3). The relative frequency of occurrence is noted on this scale as 0

*These instructions refer to detailed record forms to be found in J. Kikkawa and L. J. Webb (1976).

(not evident), 1 (rare and/or inconspicuous), 2 (occasional or rare but conspicious) and 3 (common, either uniformly or in patches). Some indication of the *range of abundance* of features is necessary; otherwise observers tend to overestimate.

Observations at a site should preferably be made by two observers working independently. Field glasses make observations of canopy features easier. No data form can list all the features that may seem relevant to an observer, so full use should be made of the blank sections for "prominent features not included." If the features involved in the questions to be checked "yes" are found to include more than one alternative, multiple answers should be checked accordingly.

STRUCTURE AND LIFE FORMS

EXTERNAL FEATURES

A "more or less even" canopy surface refers to a surface having a range in canopy height of less than one-fourth of the maximum height (excluding emergents if present); "uneven" surface refers to a surface having a range of one-fourth to one-half of the maximum height; and "very broken" surface refers to a surface having a range of more than one-half of the maximum height. If more than one type of canopy surface occurs at the site, the alternatives should be checked appropriately. "Canopy" is defined as a more or less continuous layer of tree crowns. "Emergents" are outstanding trees whose crowns are exposed on all sides above the main canopy.

INTERNAL FEATURES

Leaf size refers to trees and vines in the canopy, excluding palms, tree ferns, and other special life forms noted in the immediately following section of the data form. Leaves fallen to the forest floor are a convenient guide to leaf size, provided some allowance is made for exaggeration due to shade leaves in the understory, which are generally larger than more exposed sun leaves.

"Plank" buttresses are parallel-sided and relatively thin triangular flanges or "fins" that generally extend at least 1–2 m up the trunk.

Numbers of trees in the upper tree layer (canopy) and in the lower tree layer(s) control the density of the total canopy. The number of stems is conveniently counted on a 20-m × 20-m quadrat, the boundaries of which can be estimated after some practice. Several quadrats should be chosen to cover the range of canopy density from most dense to most sparse.

ILLUSTRATIONS FOR TRAINING OBSERVERS

Diagrams and photographs to illustrate various life forms and structural features are useful as supplements to field instructors in training of non-botanical observers, who may not know, for example, how to differentiate life forms such as ferns, palms, and pandans. Such illustrations are given in Webb *et al.* (1976).

NICHE OCCUPATION TYPES OF LAND BIRDS (BASED ON FEEDING AND NESTING HABITS)

1. insectivorous species that normally feed in trees and shrubs, but may also feed on the ground or in the air, and that nest in trees, shrubs, or human artifacts

2. tree-nesting herbivorous species that normally feed on nectar, flowers, fruit, leaves, etc., in trees and may also feed on fruit, etc., on the ground

3. tree-nesting omnivorous species that normally feed on nectar, fruit, insects, spiders, etc., in trees and may also feed on the ground or in the air

3a. species that are insectivorous or omnivorous during the breeding season but feed exclusively or nearly exclusively on fruit or seeds, or both, during the nonbreeding period

4. small predators and scavengers including large omnivorous species that normally feed on the ground or in trees and nest in trees, banks, or termite mounds

5. mainly insectivorous species that feed on the ground or in grass and nest in trees, shrubs, or grass

5a. species that habitually accompany army ants

6. mainly herbivorous species that feed on the ground or in grass and nest in trees, shrubs, or grass

7. ground-feeding species, either insectivorous or herbivorous, that nest on the ground

7a. species smaller than the House Sparrow

7b. species of the size range between the House Sparrow and Rock Pigeon

7c. species larger than the Rock Pigeon

8. diurnal and nocturnal aerial-feeding species that nest in trees or on the ground

9. large diurnal and nocturnal predators and scavengers that nest in trees

10. parasitic breeders
10a. omnivorous parasitic breeders

SPECIES LIST: Attach species lists of birds of the site or region if available.

DATA ANALYSIS

Details of data analysis are provided by Webb *et al.* (1976) for structural forest features. The same analytical method is used for data on birds. Essentially, the program (MULCLAS for a Cyber 75 computer) is designed to cluster sites in a hierarchical fashion on the basis of similarities in the analyzed features coded on the data form. In an example provided by

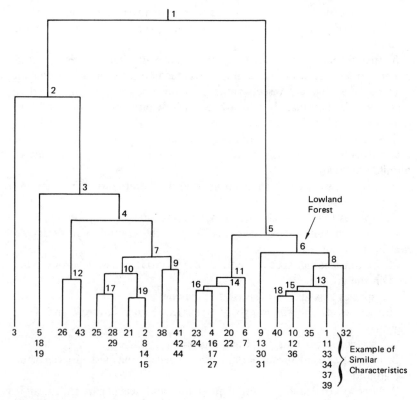

APPENDIX FIGURE 1   Dendrogram of MULCLAS classification for 32 sites in New Guinea. From Webb *et al.* (1976).

Webb *et al.*, 32 sites in New Guinea were analyzed to produce the accompanying dendrogram (Appendix Figure 1).

The dendrogram indicates that sites 1, 11, 33, 34, 37, and 39 are identical for all practical purposes. For example, all the sites have a similar environment with high rainfall on well-drained sandy soil and major plant association that sorts out on the same "branch" of the dendrogram. By this means, any tropical forest site in the world may be fitted into the system and compared with another in terms of complexity. Secondary forests and disturbed situations also will sort out appropriately with this program. In this regard, the data charts provide a fairly quick and fairly clean assessment of vegetational and animal complexity and diversity at any site. Site-by-site comparisons may then be clustered for a large study area, and potential impacts may be assessed. The alternatives to this kind of methodology for preliminary assessment are either ineffective short-term environmental-impact studies or long-term in-depth studies that may incur inordinate delay in development planning.

REFERENCES

Kikkawa, J., and L. J. Webb. 1976. Identification and classification of wildlife habitats. Pages 744-762 *in* XVI IUFRO World Congress Division I. Oslo, Norway.

Webb, L. J., J. G. Tracey, and W. T. Williams. 1976. The value of structural features in tropical forest typology. Austr. J. Ecol. 1:3-28.

SUGGESTED READING

Webb, L. J., J. G. Tracey, J. Kikkawa, and W. T. Williams. 1973. Techniques for selecting and allocating land for nature conservation in Australia. Pages 39-52, *in* Nature conservation in the Pacific. ANUPress, Canberra.

C
Appendix

Large-Scale
Forest Inventories

Appendix Table 1 (page 252) lists large-scale forest inventories that have been carried out in the humid tropics (FAO, 1977). The list was compiled on the basis of information available in the Forestry Department of the Food and Agriculture Organization and is not intended to be complete. The inventories were carried out between 1955 and 1977 and were concerned with forested areas larger than 20,000 ha.

The inventories were conventionally designated as four main types:

RECONNAISSANCE: These surveys generally cover large areas (several hundred thousand hectares). Field-sampling intensity is very low and precision is never very high. The surveys are often carried out for a first rough appraisal to permit selection of priority areas; sometimes the field sampling is no more than collection of ground truth data for establishing the photo-interpretation keys, the whole survey being basically a small-scale mapping exercise.

NATIONAL: These surveys cover the whole country (or at least the forested part of it) and aim at providing precise information on the important parameters for the whole country or large parts of it (states, provinces). With very few exceptions, they are not continuous.

SUBNATIONAL: Same as national; although they do not cover the whole forested part of a country, they are carried out on a significant part of it.

PREINVESTMENT: These surveys provide the information needed for the granting of a large logging concession or for a feasibility study linked with the creation of a wood industry complex. They generally cover areas between 50,000 hectares and a few hundred thousand hectares.

Tactical inventories (i.e., those necessary for detailed working plans and short-term harvesting planning) are not included in the list. For this reason, many countries where intensive surveys were and are being carried out, sometimes on a large total area, do not appear on the list.

REFERENCE

FAO (Food and Agriculture Organization). 1977. Draft list of large scale forest inventories carried out in the tropics. FO:MISC/77/24. FAO, Rome. 15 p.

D
Appendix

Soil Constraints Analysis

The soil is one of the more critical factors affecting the outcome of development projects in the humid tropics. Many misconceptions exist about what happens to soils when tropical forests are harvested or converted to agriculture. It is widely believed that, when they are cleared, soils under humid tropical forests will rapidly degrade, erode, or transform themselves into laterite, making crop or livestock production impossible and causing a negative environmental impact. Such concerns are often discussed within a highly emotional context and carry political overtones. Technical assistance agencies need a quantitative assessment of the principal soils of the humid tropics and guidelines for managing and conserving them. An analysis of soil constraints is a good way to establish practical limits within which to work in projects concerned with agriculture, forestry, or pasture lands.

Chapter 2 of this report provides a broad picture of the kinds of soils that exist in the humid tropics. But because soils are mapped and classified as natural bodies rather than according to potential for a specific use, that chapter included little by way of practical advice. Soil survey information can be interpreted in terms of constraints to agricultural development by drawing from data in soil taxonomy and considering many properties of the topsoil layer.

Soil classification systems, including soil taxonomy, do not include many of the transient properties of topsoils, because they are subject to change by management. To have a proper interpretation of major constraints, it is essential to consider the measurable parameters that indicate the kinds of difficulties that may arise. The Fertility Capability Classification System (FCC) is one way to quantify such soil constraints (Appendix Table 2, page 264).*

If a sufficiently detailed data base is used, a meaningful interpretation can be made for planning and assessment. This has been done for the Amazon by Cochrane and Sanchez (1981) at a scale of 1:1,000,000 and serves as an example of the kind of information that may be useful for other regions.

The first step was to subdivide the target area into major climatic subdivisions. Cochrane and Jones (1980) found that wet-season evapotranspiration could be used to categorize native vegetation types very well. This parameter reflects the energy available for photosynthesis when there is plenty of water. The Amazon was then divided into four major climatic regions: tropical rainforest, semievergreen seasonal forest, and two types of savannas (Appendix Table 3, page 265).† The second step was to subdivide each climatic region into topographical positions, separating the flat, poorly drained areas from upland areas in three different slope categories (Appendix Table 4, page 265).‡ These were further subdivided into land systems—that is, areas in which there is a recurring pattern of climate, landscape, and soil (Cochrane, 1979).

The properties of the main soils of each land system were then compiled and classified according to the FCC system. Appendix Table 5 (Page 266)§ shows the main soil constraints in the Amazon as a whole. The more widespread ones are chemical rather than physical.

Phosphorus is deficient in about 90% of the Amazon; the degree of this deficiency depends on which crops are to be grown. Aluminum toxicity, the main result of soil acidity, extends over about 75% of the region. Thus about 27% of the Amazon is not troublesomely acid; this is primarily in the alluvial areas and in the well-drained high-base-status soils.

Low potassium reserves are widespread in about 56% of the region, which suggests a need for potassium fertilization in about half the Amazon.

Poor drainage and flooding characterize one-fourth of the region, including alluvial areas (*varzeas*) and inland swamps (*aguajales*); the remainder is well drained. Many of the *varzeas* are not severely threatened by floods and have a high production potential.

About 16% of Amazon soils, mainly the Oxisols and Ultisols of clayey topsoil texture, can fix large quantities of phosphorus. This value, when considered against the 90% of the Amazon that suffers from phosphorus

*Buol *et al.*, 1975.
†Cochrane and Sanchez, 1981.
‡*Ibid.*
§*Ibid.*

deficiency (Appendix Table 5), suggests that most can be successfully treated without resort to large quantities of phosphorus fertilizers. This situation is much more favorable than the ones in the Llanos and Cerrado savannas, where high phosphorus fixation is very widespread. Research conducted on phosphorus fertilization in the Amazon confirms this supposition (Sanchez, 1977; Serrão *et al.*, 1979). Nevertheless, there are 77 million ha of soils that are both deficient in phosphorus and have a high fixation capacity. Most of these are Oxisols with clayey topsoil texture.

About 15% (64 million ha) of the Amazon has effective cation exchange capacity (CEC) values below 4 meq/100 g. Low cation exchange capacity means that there are few negative charges in the soils capable of retaining such nutrient cations as calcium, magnesium, and potassium. Consequently, these nutrients can be rapidly lost by leaching, particularly in the well-drained soils. Also, low-CEC soils are poorly buffered, meaning that changes in fertilizer and lime applications may affect the behavior of other nutrients. In Yurimaguas, Peru, for example, potassium applications can cause magnesium deficiency because of an imbalance between these two cations (Villachica, 1978).

Appendix Table 5 also indicates that only about 8% of the Amazon is such as to suggest severe erosion hazard. This is due partly to the overall level-to-gentle (0%–8%) slopes found in 72% of the Amazon, and partly to the favorable soil structure of many Oxisols and Ultisols. The 39 million ha of highly erodible soils are found on steep slopes, particularly where the soils show a rapid clay increase with depth. The deep soils, mostly classified as Ultisols or Alfisols, are generally very subject to erosion unless protected by a plant canopy during periods of heavy rains. In the rest of the Amazon, erosion is not likely to be an overwhelming issue because of a favorable combination of gentle slope and uniform texture with depth.

Among the three climatic subregions, the seasonal forested region has the highest proportion of highly erodible soils (10%), as compared with 6% in the rainforest and only 3% in the savanna region (Cochrane and Sanchez, 1981).

The above statements do not imply that erosion is of no consequence in the Amazon; any soil can be eroded by mismanagement, and sheet erosion commonly occurs in nearly level, well-drained Oxisols and Ultisols. Rather, they imply that, compared to other parts of the world, the erodibility of the main soils of the Amazon is not high. Most of the gully erosion that one sees is caused by civil engineering, rather than agriculture. The overall situation, however, could change drastically in the event plant cover is removed and not replaced rather promptly. This seldom happens in the forested regions of the Amazon, because, when crops or pastures fail, weeds and secondary forest regrowth generally produce a plant canopy rapidly. Gullying along cattle trails in overgrazed pastures, however, is increasingly serious. Also, sheet erosion had been reported in poorly managed pastures at the beginning of the rainy season in the seasonal forest area.

Appendix Table 5 shows that only 4% of the Amazon is subject to laterite formation. This percentage reflects the 21 million ha of soils with soft plinthite in the topsoil (technically known as Plinthaquox, Plinthaquults, and Plinthudults). This point deserves emphasis, given the currency of broad generalizations to the effect that Amazon soils once cleared will be irreversibly transformed into hardened plinthite or laterite. These three great groups are the only soils in which this phenomenon can occur. But as the soft plinthite is in the subsoil, the topsoil must first be removed by erosion before hardening to ironstone can take place. Since these soils occur mainly on flat, poorly drained landscapes, erosion is unlikely to be extensive.

Hardened laterite outcrops occur in geomorphically predictable positions in parts of Amazonia geologically affected by the Guayanan and Brazilian shields, sometimes mixed with soil materials as *Latosol Concrecionario*. These geological outcrops are an asset to development, because they provide excellent low-cost roadbuilding materials. The lack of plinthite or laterite in upper Amazon areas not affected by the Precambrian shields is a definite constraint to roadbuilding. Many poorly drained subsoils of these areas have mottled colors resembling plinthite, but are in fact mixtures of kaolinite and montmorillonite clay minerals (Sanchez and Buol, 1974; Tyler *et al.*, 1978). These materials make low-cost roads very difficult to maintain, in contrast to the favorable characteristics of plinthite for road construction.

Only about 6% of the Amazon has soils with no major limitations. These are the well-drained soils high in native fertility, classified mainly as Alfisols, Mollisols, Vertisols, and well-drained Inceptisols and Entisols. Nevertheless, they represent a total of 31 million ha. Where they occur, permanent agriculture has a better chance of success, particularly in the Terra Roxa soils, which combine high native fertility with excellent physical properties. Many of the successful cacao plantations are in such soils. Examples of high-base-status soils are found near Altamira, Porto Velho, and Rio Branco in Brazil, in the Oriente of Ecuador (associated with relatively volcanic deposits), and in parts of the high selva of Peru. The data base for a similar analysis of soil constraints in humid tropical regions outside the Amazon is not available.

REFERENCES

Buol, S. W., P. A. Sanchez, R. B. Cate, Jr., and M. A. Granger. 1975. Soil fertility capability classification. Pages 126–144 *in* E. Bornemisza and A. Alvarado, eds. Soil management in tropical America. North Carolina State University Press, Raleigh.

Cochrane, T. T. 1979. An ongoing appraisal of the savanna ecosystems of tropical America for beef cattle production. Pages 1-12 *in* P. A. Sanchez and L. E. Tergas, eds. Pasture production in acid soils of the tropics. Centro Internacional de Agricultura Tropical (CIAT), Calí, Colombia.

Cochrane, T. T., and P. G. Jones. 1980. Clima e vegetacao na America do Sul tropical. Um estudio computarizado dos recursos das terras. *In* Anais do XXXI Congresso Nacional de Botanica. Ilheus, Itabuna, Brasil.

Cochrane, T. T., and P. A. Sanchez. 1981. Land resources, soil properties and their management in the Amazon region: a state of knowledge report. Proceedings of conference on Amazon land use research. Centro Internacional de Agricultura Tropical (CIAT), Calí, Colombia.

Sanchez, P. A. 1977. Alternativas al sistema de agricultura migratoria en America Latina. *In* FAO/SIDA—Reunion—Taller Sobre Ordenación y Conservación de Suelos en America Latina. Lima, Peru.

Sanchez, P. A., and S. W. Buol. 1974. Properties of some soils of the Amazon Basin of Peru. Soil Sci. Soc. Am. Proc. 38:117-121.

Serrão, E. A. S., I. C. Falesi, J. B. Veiga, and J. F. Texeira. 1979. Productivity of cultivated pastures in low fertility soils of the Amazon of Brazil. Pages 195-226 *in* P. A. Sanchez and L. E. Tergas, eds. Pasture production in acid soils of the tropics. Centro Internacional de Agricultura Tropical (CIAT), Calí, Colombia.

Tyler, E. J., S. W. Buol, and P. A. Sanchez. 1978. Generic association of properties of soils of an area of the upper Amazon of Peru. Soil Sci. Soc. Am. J. 42:771-776.

Villachica, J. H. 1978. Maintenance of soil fertility under continuous cropping in an Ultisol of the Amazon jungle of Peru. Ph.D. Thesis. North Carolina State University, Raleigh. 269 p.

E
Appendix

Methods for Conducting
Baseline Studies

ENVIRONMENTAL PROFILES

As background for a local baseline study, knowledge of the overall environment, biota, in-country experts (individuals and agencies), and impediments to environmentally sound programs is essential. Thus, the environmental profile studies instituted by the U.S. Agency for International Development (AID) are very useful sources of data. Examples of AID reports are those dealing with Bolivia (Freeman *et al.*, 1980) and the Dominican Republic (Hartshorn *et al.*, 1981). The former provides an overview of the state of the environment and natural resources, based on an initial desk study prepared by the Library of Congress. A team of experts then updated and expanded the desk study on the basis of field experience. Similar studies are planned for other countries receiving AID support.

The AID profiles are required reading for all workers responsible for determining factors that must be considered in preparing baseline reports on specific in-country sites. In addition they identify scientists, ecologists, and institutions in the country who can provide expertise in planning and analyzing baseline studies.

Ideally, the environmental profile for a country provides a clear documentation of the milieu within which development must work. Minimal components for countries having territory in the humid tropics include the following:

general environmental charac-   water resources
    teristics   water impoundments
soil resources   natural forests

plantation forests	pollution
agroforests	weeds, pests, and diseases
wildlife resources	health impacts and epidemiol-
freshwater fisheries	ogy
soil erosion and watershed con-	current and potential recre-
ditions	ational attributes
parks, reserves, and wildlife	environmental scientists
refuges	institutional perspectives
human cultures	literature sources

The profile should summarize what is known in these areas. It should also clearly identify major gaps in knowledge where additional study is required prior to planning specific development projects. Definitive environmental planning must be site-specific, but many difficulties can be mitigated by producing a high-quality profile report.

FACTORS AFFECTING BASELINE STUDIES

SCALE OF PROPOSED PROJECT

Baseline studies are usually designed to evaluate large-scale projects, such as watershed management, production forests, resettlement projects, hydropower development, and establishment of a national park. Small-scale projects, such as those at a local or village level, usually do not involve enough land to warrant the expense of a baseline study approach. Where small-scale projects are to be developed, another approach must be found. In some situations an appropriate procedure can be worked out by modifying the third of the three protocol approaches described later in this section.

OPTIONS FOR DEVELOPMENT

Six options are available to development planners in the humid tropics. The options (after Dasmann *et al.,* 1973) are:

• The area in question may be left in an undisturbed state and reserved for watershed protection, or for its contribution to landscape stability, or as a forest preserve, wildlife refuge, or scientific study site, or for educational use.

• The area may be developed as a national park or similar reserve. In this case, a large part is left undisturbed (as above), but other parts, selected for esthetic appeal, serve recreation and tourism.

• The area may be used for limited harvest of its native plants (especially trees), wildlife, and fish, but maintained in an essentially natural state that contributes to landscape stability and allows some scientific, educational, recreational, and tourism activities.

• The area may be used for a more intensive harvest of natural products, as in forest production, pastures for livestock, and hunting and fishing. The area may also be used for scientific experiments and associated educational activities, but becomes of less interest for recreation and tourism. It has a changed role in maintaining landscape stability and watershed protection, but this role should not be overlooked in planning.

• The area may be used for intensive cultivation of forest plantations, pastures, or food crops, or for a combination of these. A substantial amount of the natural vegetation and animal life will be harvested in this process and will not be maintained. However, populations of other plants (weeds) and animals (pests) will increase in these modified areas, and outbreaks of weeds, parasites, and diseases affecting the native and introduced biota (trees, pastures, crops, and livestock) may create difficulties.

• The area may be used for intensive urban, industrial, or transportation purposes, involving the nearly complete removal of natural vegetation and animal life.

UNDERSTANDING ECOSYSTEMS

Key ecological factors of significance in planning include (after Bene *et al.*, 1977), but are not restricted to:

• determination of hydrologic cycles, biogeochemical cycles, energy flow patterns, food chains, and biotic interrelationships within the ecosystem
• definition of regulatory functions within the ecosystem, especially succession, predator/prey relations, and biotic factors affecting nutrient and energy balance
• study of destabilization or irreversible effects produced, by analyzing various kinds of resource use
• selection of ecologically sound development concordant with the principle of long-term, sustainable resource production
• establishment of linkages between the specific project site and a regional development perspective

In many cases, the detailed research required for such an in-depth analysis of the environment is not attainable. The ecological baseline study must therefore provide a framework of data that will allow comparison of the site to similar areas where research is more advanced. The baseline study should provide data to make possible a reasonable assessment of the basic characteristics of the on-site ecosystem, without the complex, long-term, in-depth research effort required for full understanding. For this reason, the baseline sample sites should be monitored during the period of project development to alert project management to possible unexpected adverse environmental impacts. Less frequent but long-term monitoring after completion of project development would furnish the same result over a longer period and provide data of assistance in evaluating plans for similar projects in their early planning stages.

MANAGEMENT ZONES

From the ecological point of view, areas for development may be grouped into five major zones on the basis of location, proposed use, and the results of the baseline study (Miller, 1972):

1. critical zones approaching or on the threshold of irreversibility, characterized principally by such physical changes as accelerated erosion, expanding landslides or mass earth movements, uncontrolled stream flow, volcanic and earthquake activity, rapid lateritization, flooding, and silting
2. unique zones supporting outstanding or unusual examples of forest or other vegetation, fauna, scenery, indigenous cultures (World Bank, 1981), and archaeological or other cultural values
3. multipurpose zones where permanent vegetation must be maintained on slopes, river catchments, swamps, potential floodplains, streambanks, and easily eroded soils, but where other parts of the area may be used to produce such goods or services as food, timber, water, minerals, wildlife, hunting, fishing, and tourism
4. holding zones not under pressure for development at present and not qualifying as unique, but with potential for future development
5. agricultural and agroforestry zones having high potential as sources of to-be-developed food, fiber, and timber crops and livestock, where physical and biotic damage to environment and production can be substantially controlled

Areas falling into zones 1 and 2 should be kept free of development until the risks and opportunities can be fully evaluated. Areas of the zone 4 type may be subjected to detailed and long-term evaluation concerning potential uses, because there is no appreciable pressure to develop them.

Areas in zones 3 and 5 are the most critical, because they cannot normally be subjected to long-term study, strong pressures already exist for their development, and they are logical as development sites. In the past, most developmental projects in the humid tropics have been undertaken in areas of the zone 3 and 5 type that were already substantially changed with respect to the original vegetation and its geographic extent. Today, however, new population and societal pressures are encouraging development projects of the multipurpose and agroforestry/agriculture type in extensive tracts of relatively undisturbed natural vegetation (NRC, 1980). This situation forces the planner to evaluate proposed projects on the basis of minimal baseline data and by interpolating from similar sites that are better known. Although this procedure increases the risk of underestimating difficulties, the continued in-process and post-completion monitoring reduces this element of concern. For this reason, three protocols for baseline studies are outlined below. The first (I) is applicable to areas falling within zones 1 and 4, where detailed evaluation is necessary because of previous critical ecologic damage (zone 1) or because adequate time is available before decisions about ultimate use have to be made (zone 4).

The second protocol (II) should be applied to areas in zone 2, where preservation of natural features, flora, and fauna or other unique aspects is of great concern. In these cases, only minimal initial data on physical and geochemical parameters and regulatory functions are necessary, but substantial evaluation of the unique resources that will be preserved is required. In the case of national parks, forest reserves, and wildlife refuges, strong emphasis must be given to evaluating floral, faunal, and habitat diversity in relation to biotic interactions.

The third protocol (III) should be applied to areas lying in zones 3 and 5. In these zones, relatively undisturbed areas of natural vegetation often are under consideration for conversion within a very short period. In consequence, this protocol centers on a series of particularly strong ecological indicators that will provide maximum information. It would be very helpful if forest ecologists devised simple methods for obtaining data on the key physical, geochemical, hydric, and biotic components and grouping them into a relatively small number of predictive indicators. The scheme here suggested is a first effort to this end, but it should not be in lieu of protocols I and II, when time permits their use.

DATA BASES FOR PLANNING

The essence of any ecological baseline study is to provide data on the characteristics, status, and processes operating within an ecosystem that will serve to improve development projects and resource management. The baseline study provides data on how the ecosystem functions, its sensitivity to change, its ability to recover from impacts, and the degree to which the project design must be adapted to ensure long-term stable and sustained resource production.

The protocols presented here are based on four ecological guidelines recommended in a UNESCO (1978) report and summarized below:

• A vegetative cover must be maintained to provide effective protection against deterioration and erosion.

• A balanced nutrient cycle must be maintained, preferably without the addition of chemically based fertilizers.

• Agroforest and forest crops introduced into the area must have nutrient demands compatible with nutrient inputs from rain, dust, decomposition, fixation, and weathering.

• The spectrum of biotic diversity of physiognomy, trophic levels, life forms, life history, species composition, and age distribution must be maintained above any level at which weeds, pests, parasites, diseases, and other ecological risks become a serious adverse economic or ecological factor.

All three protocols require certain base data in common, including information on the physical setting of the area, its climate, and the kinds and amount of vegetative cover.

Minimal information about the area to be analyzed includes: site identification (country, province, locality), location (coordinates), altitude, areal extent, land form(s) of area and adjacent areas, principal geologic formations, major drainage relations, and a history of previous human uses of the area.

In the preliminary stages of the study, data on climate should be analyzed (from nearby weather stations, if necessary) to determine mean monthly and mean annual temperatures, temperature extremes, and major seasonal fluctuations; mean monthly and annual precipitation, rainfall extremes, and major fluctuations; and data on winds, including periods of strong winds and their prevailing direction. In the baseline study itself, daily means, maxima, and minima for temperature and wind force should be obtained, as well as daily values for precipitation, at several sites.

Information on vegetation type and cover is of great importance. For development projects where relatively small areas will be affected, much information on vegetation may be obtained by conventional air photography. Whenever possible, especially where a substantial land area is involved, remote-sensing techniques of air radar photography and satellite photography should be used. The preferred radar technique is Side Looking Air-Borne Radar (SLAR), which has been used for mapping vegetation, especially forests, in eastern Panama, Nicaragua, New Guinea, Indonesia,

Ecuador, and Brazil (UNESCO, 1978). ERTS and LANDSAT (satellite) programs provide a basis for satellite assessment of vegetational features (Talbot and Pettinger, 1981). These systems take photographs in the visible and near infra-red spectrum that may be reproduced for visual analysis in false color or color images. The system may also be used for automatic computer interpretation to assign photographed areas by vegetation type.

An especially significant approach for evaluating land resources on a broad geographic scale has been developed by Cochrane (see Cochrane and Sanchez, 1980). This method provides a geographic synthesis of the land resource base especially for topography, climate, water, and soils (Appendix A).

BASELINE STUDY GUIDE FOR CRITICAL AND HOLDING ZONES (FIRST PROTOCOL)

In addition to the basic data on the physical setting and climate of the area under review, an ideal baseline study should evaluate the many kinds of inputs and outputs of energy and materials and the direction of their flow as shown in Figure 2-8. The baseline study should be conducted over at least a 12-month period to obtain an idea of the influence of possible seasonal fluctuations, and it must involve a series of sample site stations if the area to be studied is larger than a few hundred hectares. The following are essential features for analysis:

• data on soils, including soil temperatures and their daily and seasonal fluctuations; soil structure and porosity; hydrodynamic properties; chemical properties, with particular attention to organic nitrogen, sulphur, and phosphorus in order to assess the potential fertility of the soil and estimate its capacity for the storage and cycling of organic nutrients and the potential impact of the removal of vegetation on these features (See Appendix D for recommended soil constraints analysis.)

• data on water resource inputs and outputs, including rainfall; effects of winds, fogs, and cloud cover; throughfall (rain reaching ground); interception (amount of rain held by vegetation but not reaching ground); evapotranspiration (evaporation and transpiration through plants); runoff; and available soil water, to estimate the availability of water in the system for plant growth, the critical features of the hydrologic cycle, the rates of leaching and erosion, the interactive relations between water and soil, and the impact of vegetation removal on these figures

• quantitative data on the organization, structure, and stratification of the vegetation, including composition, height classes, main dimensions of trees, development of root systems, buttresses and aerial roots, and lianes and epiphytes; population densities, spatial distribution, species diversity, and biomass estimates to determine the complexity in three dimensions of the vegetational component

• data on successional stages, especially those developing from shifting agriculture, burning, exploitation, flooding, and erosion to evaluate regeneration patterns and to determine possible utilization of marginal forest lands

• quantitative data on net primary production and the rates of litter production and tree growth and regeneration

• quantitative data on the composition and ecological role of the animal component, especially species diversity, population densities, interspecies interactions, and positions in the food web and life histories of particularly significant herbivores and high-level predators

• assessment of potential increases in weeds, pests, parasites, and diseases associated with modification of the ecosystem

• data on biogeochemical cycling, especially litter decomposition, the plant nutrient pool and its exchanges, and recovery and flow patterns, with special attention to the regulatory features of the food web in nutrient cycling and maintenance of environmental balance and stability

• determination of human uses, population densities, and societal needs that have contributed to the environmental crisis typical of zone 1 areas

• determination of current human uses of the ecosystem by people living in the area, especially tribal groups (World Bank, 1981)

BASELINE STUDY GUIDE FOR UNIQUE ZONES
(SECOND PROTOCOL)

The information required for a baseline analysis of the ecology of unique areas will vary substantially with the size and planned use of the area. Unique zones that support archaeologic finds, sites of historical monuments, buildings, and the like require an evaluation different from one required for a site of a national park or for the preservation of indigenous cultures. Except where substantial environmental disturbance is necessary to make an archaeological, historic, or cultural site accessible, the two types of unique zones have little in common. For this reason, the second protocol aims at analysis of areas that are unique in natural qualities (vegetation, fauna, scenery, or indigenous cultures). It may also be used for evaluating potential impacts on the natural environment when a sizeable area is to be set aside for archaeological study requiring disruption in the course of excavation or restoration. Essentially, this protocol will be followed for preliminary assessment of areas that are to be preserved as natural forest reserves, national parks, wildlife refuges, indigenous culture reserves, and key archaeologic sites.

The second protocol centers on the evaluation of three aspects of the environment that will provide maximum information about the complexity, diversity, and uniqueness of an area. These features are based on the complex interactions among the physiochemical (abiotic) factors of the humid tropical environment as exemplified by the soil, vegetational physiognomy and plant diversity, and the diversity of animal species. The relationship of soil to vegetation is reviewed elsewhere in this report. Three correlates express well this interaction: (1) vegetation types within one geologic formation, especially in humid tropical forests, are strongly correlated with physiography; (2) soil nutrient characteristics, primarily the availability of phosphorus, are the major determinants of forest composition; (3) soil physical properties and drainage are the primary determinants of forest physiognomy. Vegetational complexity, stratification, and species diversity are greatest on nutrient-rich soils with high rainfall and little seasonality. Vegetational differences (in complexity, structure, stratification, and species diversity) are apparently due to the interaction of amount and seasonal pattern of rainfall, the temperature regimen, and soil characteristics. Animal diversity, in turn, is strongly correlated with the structural complexity of vegetation in humid tropical sites (Cody and Diamond, 1975).

For these reasons, maximal information is required on physiography and soils, structure and physiognomy of vegetation, plant species diversity, and the ecological roles and species diversity of the animal component. These features contain key dominant variables that can serve as predictive indicators of ecological conditions. In most cases, a survey or baseline study of a unique area will require several man-years to complete. Inventories of species and data on their life histories and ecological roles are especially difficult to obtain. It is thus essential that the initial baseline study concentrate on a few significant and predictive components of the environment and its biota.

As a means of obtaining information of this type, a modified version of the data form designed by Kikkawa and Webb (1976) has been adopted for use in zone 2 areas containing unique natural features (see Appendix B). The modified form emphasizes three specific environmental components:

- substratum (physiography and soil)
- vegetation (structure and life forms) and tree-species diversity
- animal diversity, estimated by an ecological census of the bird fauna

Use of the modified form involves a system of field-data collection that can be sorted out by numerical (computer-assisted) analysis. The data on physiography and soils are standard. Use of a consistent and standardized scoring of the features of structure and physiognomy of vegetation (Webb *et al.*, 1976) allows assessment of the study area and comparison with other tropical sites. An estimate of plant species diversity, especially for tree species, in association with their ecologic position is provided by the form.

Probably the most important departure from most Temperate-Zone baseline studies in the modified form is the use of the bird fauna as an indicator of total faunal diversity. Most baseline studies in temperate areas attempt to assess quantitatively the faunal component by various trap or recapture methods. Usually, invertebrates, birds, and small mammals are selectively studied. The variety and taxonomic confusion characteristic of most tropical invertebrate groups make them unlikely candidates to be used as predictive indicators of ecologic conditions. Studies of small-mammal populations are also difficult because of low species densities, the inability of the worker to trap except on the substrate, and uncertainties in identification.

Birds, on the other hand, are conspicuous, noisy components of the environment, whose abundance, ecological roles, and species diversity have been shown to be correlated with the structure and diversity of the vegetation and substrate (Kikkawa, 1968; James and Shugart, 1970; Karr, 1971; Lovejoy, 1975). In addition, birds include many nesting and feeding types that use a wide variety of materials and food from the environment. The more structurally complex and more productive environments have the greatest variety of bird ecological roles and the greatest bird-species diversity. Another advantage is that almost every tropical country has residents who can readily identify bird species in the field by sight and sound. The taxonomy of birds is very stable and well known, as are their ecological roles, especially nesting and feeding habits.

The appeal of the modified form is that a substantial amount of data can be obtained within a very short time. The vegetation structure and life-form data for a locality in a proposed park or reserve may be recorded in an hour, such that several sites may be visited in 1 day. The rapidity of data collection by observers without taxonomic knowledge, once they have been briefed on using the form, is also an advantage. Similarly, the bird data may be recorded within a period of several days when mornings are clear. Visits to the same site at different times of the year for the bird census are usually necessary. Numerical analysis of the data provides, through clustering techniques, a classification of sites and a ranking of structural attributes (plants) and ecological roles (birds) that can be used for comparison with other sites. The availability of computer processing usually is required in this analysis.

A final advantage for the modified form is that its basic components are included in the IUFRO form (Kikkawa and Webb, 1976) now in use throughout the world. Comparable data from many sites are thus available to ascertain the relative distinctness, species diversity, and environmental complexity of any proposed natural forest reserve, national park, wildlife refuge, or similar unique area in humid tropical countries.

BASELINE STUDY GUIDE FOR MULTIPURPOSE, AGRICULTURAL, AND AGROFORESTRY ZONES (THIRD PROTOCOL)

The ecological baseline study of these kinds of areas, ranging from nearly undisturbed environments to ones where substantial ecological modification has already taken place, are among the more difficult to implement. It is usually in these areas that strong human-population or economic pressures require a guide assessment. Ideally, a study similar to the one outlined in the first protocol is desirable, but such a study is infeasible for these areas.

This protocol is aimed at obtaining maximal data on ecological conditions and the potential effects of their disturbance in a minimal time period (6 months). In consequence, the field studies should be carried out by an experienced and knowledgeable team of environmental scientists brought together for the specific purpose of studying a specific project site. The following elements require analysis:

• physiographic data obtained by mapping, in which air photography or remote sensing (or both) should be used
• data on soils—discussed above (first protocol)
• data on water resources—discussed above (first protocol)
• quantitative data on vegetation—discussed above (second protocol)
• quantitative data on the bird component of the fauna—discussed above (second protocol)
• assessment of potential increases in populations or incidence of weeds, pests, parasites, and diseases after modification of the environment

Because areas in zones 3 and 5 are usually heterogeneous with respect to current human use, a series of sites on a transect through relatively undisturbed, partly disturbed, and heavily impacted environments should be sampled. If possible, several successional stages should be sampled. In this way, the field data will allow interpretation of the impact of various degrees of vegetation removal on the environment and allow better planning.

REFERENCES

Bene, J. G., H. Beall, and A. Cote. 1977. Trees, food and people: land management in the tropics. IDRC-084e. International Development Research Centre, Ottawa, 52 p.

Cochrane, T. T., and P. A. Sanchez. 1980. Land resources, soil properties and their management in the Amazon region: a state of knowledge report. Paper presented at international conference on Amazon land use and agricultural research, April 1980. Centro Internacional de Agricultural Tropical (CIAT), Calí, Colombia.

Cody, M. L., and J. M. Diamond, eds. 1975. Ecology and evolution of communities. Harvard University Press, Cambridge, Massachusetts. 838 p.

Dasmann, R. F., J. P. Milton, and P. H. Freeman. 1973. Ecological principles for economic development. John Wiley & Sons, New York, 252 p.

Freeman, P. H., B. Cross, R. D. Flannery, D. A. Harcharik, G. S. Hartshorn, G. Simmonds, and J. D. Williams. 1980. Bolivia. State of the environment and natural resources. A field study. JRB Associates, McLean, Virginia.

Hartshorn, G. S., G. Antonini, R. DuBois, D. Harcharik, S. Heckadon, H. Newton, C. Quesada, J. Shores, and O. Staples. 1981. The Dominican Republic: country environmental profile. A field study. JRB Associates, McLean, Virginia. 118 p.

James F. C., and H. H. Shugart. 1970. A quantitative method of habitat description. Audubon Field Notes 24:727-736.

Karr, J. R. 1971. Structure of avian communities in selected Panama and Illinois habitats. Ecol. Monogr. 41:207-233.

Kikkawa, J. 1968. Ecological classification of bird species and habitats in eastern Australia. J. Anim. Ecol. 37:143-165.

Kikkawa, J., and L. J. Webb. 1976. Identification and classification of wildlife habitats. Pages 747-762 in XVI IUFRO World Congress, Division 1. Oslo, Norway.

Lovejoy, T. E. 1975. Bird diversity and abundance in Amazon forest communities. The Living Bird 13:127-191.

Miller, K. 1972. Conservation and development of tropical rainforest areas. In 11th General Assembly and 12th Technical Meeting of International Union for Conservation of Nature and Natural Resources, Banff, Canada. IUCN, Washington, D.C.

NRC (National Research Council). 1980. Conversion of tropical moist forests. National Academy of Sciences, Washington, D.C. 205 p.

Talbot, J. J., and L. R. Pettinger. 1981. Use of remote sensing for monitoring deforestation in tropical and subtropical latitudes. Cienc. Interam. 21(1-4):63-71.

UNESCO (United Nations Educational, Scientific and Culture Organization). 1978. Tropical forest ecosystems. A state-of-knowledge report prepared by UNESCO/UNEP/FAO. Natural Resources Research XIV, UNESCO, Paris. 683 p.

Webb, L. J., J. G. Tracey, and W. T. Williams. 1976. The value of structural features in tropical forest typology. Austr. J. Ecol. 1:3-28.

World Bank. 1981. Economic development and tribal peoples: human ecologic considerations. Office of Environmental Affairs, World Bank, Washington, D.C. 103 p.

APPENDIX
TABLES

APPENDIX TABLE 1 Selected List of Large-Scale Forest Inventories Carried Out in the Humid Tropics[d] (Supplements Appendix C)

Country	Type of Inventory and General Location	Approximate Area (ha)		Executing Agency or Company[b]	Date	Remarks
		Total	Forest			
AFRICA						
Cameroon	Subnational	2,200,000	1,850,000	CTFT	1966–67	Inventory units: forest zones of 500–800,000 ha
	Boumba-Ngoko					
	Haut-Nyong					
	Preinvestment	500,000		CTFT	1965	Inventory units: 5–30,000 ha; 27 species
	Deng-Deng	500,000	300,000	Govt. and FAO	1970–71	Secondary species; down to 10 cm d.b.h.
	Edea	100,000	100,000	CTFT	1969	Inventory units: 5,000 ha; all species D > 10 cm
	West Cameroon	300,000	300,000	CTFT	1973	
Central African Empire	Preinvestment					
	Lobaye	110,000	110,000	Govt.	1961–62	Inventory units: 10–20,000 ha; all species D > 20 cm
	Haute-Sangha		450,000	CTFT	1963–64	Inventory units: 10–30,000 ha; all species D > 20 cm
	Bimbo		55,000	CTFT	1968	All species D > 20 cm
	Subnational					
	Secteur de Nola	835,000	785,000	CTFT	1967	Inventory units: 50–80,000 ha; 70 species D > 20 cm

Country	Location	Area	Area	Agency	Year	Remarks
Gabon	Reconnaissance First and second zones	(20,150,000)^c	(15,515,000)	Govt. and FAO (CTFT)	1969–70	No field sampling; rough photointerpretation; mostly data collation
	First zone	(several million hectares along the project railway)		CTFT	1971	No field sampling or photointerpretation; only data collation
	Subnational Lambarene	785,000	700,000	CTFT	1969	All trees D >60 cm; selected list of species for D >20; inventory units: 250,000 and 500,000 ha
	Third zone (part)	2,800,000	2,500,000	Govt. and FAO (CTFT)	1969–70	Id-sampling intensity 0.03%
	Preinvestment Complementary pulp and paper	70,000	70,000	CTFT (SOGACEL)	1969	All species D >15 cm; inventory units: 30,000 and 40,000 ha
	Third zone (part)	250,000	250,000	FAO (CTFT) and Govt.	1970–73	All species D >60 cm; inventory units: 100–200,000 ha and selected species D >20 cm
						Inventories for working plans only
Ghana						
Ivory Coast	National	(1)13,090,000	12,190,000	CTFT	1965–67	43 species; photointerpretation
		(2)12,580,000	2,500,000	DRC	1965–67	All trees D >10 cm; photointerpretation
	Preinvestment San Pedro	250,000	250,000	CTFT	1972	All species D >15 cm

APPENDIX TABLE 1 (Continued)

Country	Type of Inventory and General Location	Approximate Area (ha)		Executing Agency or Company[b]	Date	Remarks
		Total	Forest			
Kenya	Preinvestment		1,240,000	Schultz (CIDA)	1963-68	Including mangroves and plantations 1,500,000 ha; photographed and mapped in toto
Liberia	National		2,500,000	German mission	1960-68	Several types of field designs
Madagascar	Reconnaissance (national)	(25,000,000)		Govt. and FAO	1971	Accessibility and density mapping at 1:500,000
Nigeria	Preinvestment Subnational (Calabar State)	(several blocks of 50,000 ha) 400,000	370,000	Schultz (CIDA)	1968-71 1965-67	No photointerpretation; point sampling; all species D >30 cm
	National Forest reserves of all other states	1,700,000		Govt. and FAO	1973-77	
People's Republic of the Congo	Reconnaissance Nord-Congo	10,890,000	10,480,000	Govt. and FAO	1962-63	Photointerpretation and vegetation mapping
	Preinvestment Ouesso	1,180,000	1,170,000	CTFT	1970-71	All species D >60 cm; 40 species of D >20 cm; inventory units: 40-75,000 ha
	Sibiti-Zanaga	980,000	830,000	Govt. and FAO (CTFT)	1971-72	All species D >60 cm; 40 species D >20 cm; inventory units: 5,000, 30,000, and 60,000 ha

Sierra Leone	Preinvestment	60,000	25,000	Govt. and FAO	1959–63	Tama-Tonkoli forest reserves
		75,000	40,000			Gola forest reserves
Tanzania	Subnational		7,100,000	Govt. and FAO	1969–71	
Uganda	Preinvestment		60,000	Govt. and CIDA	1971–73	
Zaire	Preinvestment	5,000,000		Govt. and CIDA	1970–72	
	Lopori-Maringa		5,000,000 (est.)	Govt. and CIDA	1974–72	0.2% sampling intensity
AMERICAS						
Bolivia	Preinvestment		930,000	Govt.	1967–69	Done by the Forest Service and Service of Soils
Brazil						
Amazonas	Reconnaissance	(450,000,000)	(350,000,000)	Projecto RADAM	1971–77	Broad vegetation mapping plus some ground-truth data collection
	Reconnaissance		589,000	SUFRAMA/ PROFLAMA	1972	
	Zona Franca de Manaus					
	Xingu		5,700,000	SUDAM/ Sondotecnica	1974–75	
	Transamazonica (Araquaia-Tapajós)		20,000,000 (est.)	IBDF		
	Marajo Island	1,500,000		IDESP	1975	

APPENDIX TABLE 1 *(Continued)*

Country	Type of Inventory and General Location	Approximate Area (ha)		Executing Agency or Company[b]	Date	Remarks
		Total	Forest			
	Preinvestment					
	Tapajós forest reserve	165,000	160,000	IBDF	1977	Typical preinvestment survey for feasibility study
	Tapajós-Xingú		2,250,000	Govt. and FAO	1954-56	
	Xingu-Tocantins		1,770,000	Govt. and FAO	1956-57	
	Tapajós-Madeira		2,960,000	Govt. and FAO	1956-57	
	Tocantins-Guamá		3,300,000	Govt. and FAO	1957	
	Caete-Maracassumé		445,000	Govt. and FAO	1958	
	Ucuuba		350,000	Govt. and FAO	1962	
	State of Goiás		260,000	Govt. and FAO	1962	
	Road BR 14		2,200,000	Govt. and FAO	1959-60	Extrapolation from 900,000 to 2,200,000 by photointerpretation
	Amapá		50,000	Govt. and FAO	1963(64?)	
	Benjamin Constant		20,000	Govt. and FAO	1963(64?)	
Alagoas	Reconnaissance	530,000	115,000	Govt. and FAO	1968	
Parana area	**Preinvestment** Santa Catarina	560,000	60,000	Govt. and FAO	1960	
Colombia	Reconnaissance Magdalena-Sinu	15,000,000	3,210,000 (1965 est.)	Govt. and FAO	1965	Photointerpretation mainly, plus ground checks
	Preinvestment Serrania de San Lucas	1,020,000	920,000	Govt. and FAO	1966-69	
	Rio Carare		35,000	Govt.	1964	

Country	Project	Area	Area	Agency	Date	Remarks
	Rio San Juan	290,000		Govt. (I.G.)	1969	
	Barbacoas		275,000	Govt.	1970–	
	Teresita		100,000	Govt.	1970–	
	Solano (Caquetá)		50,000	Govt.	1972	
	Jugadó-Antadó (Chocó)		125,000	INDERENA	1975	Area covered not known
	Reconnaissance (national)		?	INDERENA	1976-77	General vegetation mapping
Costa Rica	Reconnaissance (national)	(5,090,000)	(2,600,000)			
	Preinvestment					
	Rio Machó	60,000	30,000	Govt. and FAO	1965-67	
	Versante atlantico		?	JAPDEVA/ SWEDFOREST	1974-76	Area covered not known
Dominican Republic	Reconnaissance (national)	4,840,000	555,000	OEA	1966	Interpretation of 1958 aerial mosaics
	Subnational	2,400,000	350,000 (1966 est.)	FAO	1968-71	
Ecuador	Preinvestment					
	Esmeralda	1,295,000	825,000	FAO	1964-68	
	Guayas		275,000	T. Ingledow & Assoc. / CEDEGE	1969(?)	
	Zamora Chinchipe/ Morona Santiago		1,600,000	CTFT	1975-77	
	Machala-Ora-Loja		180,000	CTFT	1975-77	
El Salvador	Subnational					
	(northern zone)	200,000	20,000	Govt. and FAO	1973	Also study of forest depletion between 1963 and 1973
French Guyana	Preinvestment					
	La Palma		10,000	Govt. and FAO	1973	
	Subnational	4,000,000 (est.)	4,000,000 (est.)	ONF	1964-70	
	Preinvestment		350,000	CTFT	1973-74	
			20,000	CTFT	1974	

APPENDIX TABLE 1 (Continued)

Country	Type of Inventory and General Location	Approximate Area (ha)		Executing Agency or Company[b]	Date	Remarks
		Total	Forest			
Guatemala	Reconnaissance					
	El Peten	3,740,000	3,610,000	Govt. and FAO	1964–68	
	Preinvestment	465,000	400,000	Govt. and FAO	1964–68	
	Salama	45,000	45,000	Govt. and FAO	1964–68	
	Finca San Jerónimo	40,000	20,000	Govt. and FAO	1975–77	
	Subnational Altiplano Occidental	1,300,000	500,000	Govt.	1977–	This inventory will be continued until 1980 to cover a total of 1,250,000 ha of forest
Guyana	Reconnaissance	4,870,000	4,500,000	Govt. and FAO	1968–69	Only area information by forest type
	Southern part	10,100,000		Govt. and FAO	1969–70	Precision ± 15% on total volume per forest type
	Preinvestment Ebini-Itaka	125,000	125,000	Govt. and FAO	1968–69	
	Northwest district	75,000	75,000	Govt. and FAO	1970	Inventory limited to two riverine swamp forest types
	Great Falls		235,000	Govt.	1970	
Haiti	Reconnaissance Pine forests	80,000	65,000	Govt. and British...	1975–76	

Country							Remarks
Honduras	Subnational Preinvestment		2,600,000	2,195,000	Govt. and FAO	1963-65	Essentially pine forests
	Olancho		1,435,000	720,000	Copino	1969	Area more or less already covered by the govt./FAO subnational inventory of pine forests (1963-65); Olancho area was assessed at least five times
Mexico	Subnational States of Chihuahua, Durango, and Sonora		19,600,000	8,600,000 (field) 19,600,000 (map)	Govt. and FAO	1961-64	Only the 8,600,000 ha of pine forest were inventoried
	National Other states		196,389,000	44,700,000	Govt.	1963-76	It was intended to complete the first cycle of the national forest inventory in 1976; CFI started in 1976; CFI started in areas not under concession
Nicaragua	Preinvestment Rosita		110,000	110,000	Govt. and FAO	1968	Mixed forests
	—		100,000	100,000	Govt. and FAO	1970-71	Mixed forests ± 6% error (0.95) on total volume
	Puerto Cabezas Reconnaissance		345,000	310,000	Govt. and FAO	1973	Pine forests
	Nueva Segovia Reconnaissance (national)		250,000 (13,000,000)	85,000	Huntings/ Westinghouse	1977 1971-73	Broad vegetation and land-use mapping
Panama	Reconnaissance Darien		2,615,000	2,370,000	Green Acres	1962	

APPENDIX TABLE 1 (Continued)

Country	Type of Inventory and General Location	Approximate Area (ha)		Executing Agency or Company[b]	Date	Remarks
		Total	Forest			
	Whole country	7,710,000	4,165,000	FAO (CTFT)	1971–72	Mainly photointerpretation, with two-stage field sampling
	Preinvestment					
	Donoso	185,000	155,000	Govt. and FAO	1969	
	Azuero	230,000	160,000	FAO (CTFT)	1972	
Peru	Reconnaissance (national)	(128,521,500)	(79,683,000)	Universidad Nacional Agraria	1969–76	General forest mapping (1:1,000,000)
	Reconnaissance Muallaga–Chiriyam	3,360,000	2,700,000	Govt. and FAO		
	Rio Nievas	12,000,000		Govt.	1958	Information on the numerous reconnaissance inventories is given in "Inventario de los estudios y disponibilidades de los recursos forestales del Peru"—2nd ed., 1971.
	Preinvestment	200,000		Govt. and FAO (Forestal)	1974–75	0.2% sampling intensity
	San Ignacio		180,000	Govt.	1974	
Surinam	Preinvestment Coastal zone	260,000	195,000 (est.)	Govt.	1949–59	2% sampling intensity in mixed forests
	Intermediate zone		333,000	Govt. and FAO	1972–74	Same methods as in Guyana mixed forests

Venezuela	Reconnaissance Imataca		405,000	Govt. and FAO	1964–67	
ASIA–OCEANIA						
Fiji	National		?	British Aid (LRD)	1966–69	
India	Preinvestment	4,715,000	3,060,000	Govt. and FAO	1965–68	Preinvestment survey is going on under Indian operation
Indonesia	Preinvestment Tarakan	29,000,000	? · 260,000	Govt. (PIS) · Govt. (Imhutani) and FAO	1969– · 1965– 1977–78	Specifications unknown · Austro-Indonesian pulp mill project
Kampuchea	National	3,400,000 (est.)		USAID	1960–62	
	Subnational East Mekong	5,520,000	3,875,000	Govt. and FAO	1957–61	± 15% for volume per forest type, diameter class, and group of species
	Cardamones	490,000	425,000	Govt. and FAO	1965–69	± 10% for total volume on the whole area
Laos	Preinvestment	880,000	615,000	CIDA USAID	1965–69	Three areas around Vientiane, Savannakhet, and Pakse
Malaysia Peninsular	Reconnaissance (national)	13,210,000 (whole country)	8,320,000 (63%)	Govt. (FRRS)	1962–69	Photointerpretation with minimal ground checking

APPENDIX TABLE 1 (Continued)

Country	Type of Inventory and General Location	Approximate Area (ha) Total	Approximate Area (ha) Forest	Executing Agency or Company[b]	Date	Remarks
	National	13,210,000	8,320,000	Govt. and FAO	1970–72	± 10% (0.95) on gross volume; all species D >45 cm by industry planning unit (six planning units in total)
	Preinvestment Pahang Tengara	925,000		CIDA		
	Johore Tengah	200,000		British aid		
Sarawak	Reconnaissance	650,000		British aid	1955–56	Aerial survey and mapping
	Preinvestment	1,240,000	1,160,000	Govt. and FAO	1969–71	Precise results at 100,000–150,000 ha unit level (hill forests)
		1,000,000 (est.)		Govt.	1961–	Swamp forests
Sabah	National	4,600,000 (est.)		CIDA	1969–72	
New Caledonia	Reconnaissance (national)	1,640,000		CTFT	1972–74	
	Preinvestment		255,000	CTFT	1972–	
Papua New Guinea	Reconnaissance	6,800,000		Australian govt.	74–70	
Philippines	National	30,000,000 (est.)	17,150,000	Govt. and USAID	1962–68	

Sri Lanka (Ceylon)	National	6,400,000	2,900,000	CIDA	1959–60	FAO inventories (about 1968) are not mentioned because they were performed on a small area (less than 50,000 ha) for working plans
Thailand	Subnational					
	Northern teak-bearing provinces	6,000,000	3,280,000	Govt. and FAO	1956–57	
	Northeastern	17,000,000	7,820,000	Govt. and FAO	1961–62	
	National					
	1st national	34,500,000		Govt.	1962–70	Less northeastern
	2nd national	51,500,000		Govt.	1970–77	

[a]SOURCE: Food and Agricultural Organization. 1977. Draft list of large-scale forest inventories carried out in the tropics. FAO, Rome. Mimeographed.

[b]Abbreviations: AID, Agency for International Development (United States); CEDEGE, Comision de estudios para el desarollo de la cuenca del Río Guayas (Ecuador); CFI, Commonwealth Forestry Institute (United Kingdom); CIDA, Canadian International Development Agency; CTFT, Centre Tecnique Forestier Tropical (France); DRC, Development and Resource Corporation (United States); FAO, Food and Agriculture Organization; FRRS, Forest Resources Reconnaissance Survey (peninsular Malaysia); IBDF, Instituto Brasileiro de Desenvolvimento Florestal (Brazil); IDESP, Instituto de Desenvolvimento Económico-Social do Pará (Brazil); IG, Instituto Geografico (Colombia); INDERENA, Instituto de Desarollo de lose Recursos Naturales Renovables (Colombia); JAPDEVA, Junta de Administración Portuaria y Desarollo de la Vertiente Atlántica (Costa Rica); LRD, Land Resources Division (United Kingdom); OAS, Organization of American States; ONF, Office National des Forêts (France); PIS, Preinvestment Survey of Forest Resources (India); PROFLAMA, Projetos Florestais da Amazônia (Brazil); RADAM, Radar da Amazônia (Brazil); SOGACEL, Societé Gabonaise de Cellulose (Gabon); SUDAM, Superintendência do Desenvolvimento da Amazônia (Brazil); SUFRAMA, Superintendência da Zona Franca da Manaus (Brazil); SWEDFOREST, Swedish Forest Service Consulting Firm.

[c]Values shown in parentheses derived from small-scale mapping exercises.

APPENDIX TABLE 2   Fertility Capability Soil Classification System, 1974 Version (Supplements Appendix D)

Type: Texture is average of plowed layer or 20 cm (8 in) depth, whichever is shallower.

S = Sandy topsoils: loamy sands and sands (USDA)
L = Loamy topsoils: <35% clay but not loamy sand or sand
C = Clayey topsoils: >35% clay
O = Organic soil: >30% O.M. to a depth of 50 cm or more

Substrata type: Used if textural change of hard root restricting layer is encountered within 50 cm (20 in).

S = Sandy subsoil: texture as in type
L = Loamy subsoil: texture as in type
C = Clayey subsoil: texture as in type
R = Rock or other hard root restricting layer

Conditioner modifiers: In plowed layer or 20 cm (8 in.), whichever is shallower, unless otherwise specified (*).

*g = (gley):	Mottles ≤2 chroma within 60 cm for surface and below all A horizons or saturated with H_2O for >60 days in most years
*d = (dry):	Ustic or xeric environment: dry >60 consecutive days per year within 20-60 cm depth
e = (low CEC):	<4 meq/100 g soil by Σ bases + unbuffered Al <7 meq/100 g soil by Σ cations at pH 7 <10 meq/100 g soil by Σ cations + Al + H at pH 8.2
*a = (Al toxic):	>60% Al saturation of CEC by Σ bases and unbuffered Al within 50 cm >67% Al saturation of CEC by Σ cations at pH 7 within 50 cm >86% Al saturation of CEC by Σ cations at pH 8.2 within 50 cm of pH < 5.0 in 1:1 H_2O except in organic soils
*h = (acid):	10-60% Al saturation of CEC by bases and unbuffered Al within 50 cm or pH in 1:1 H_2O between 5.0 and 6.0
i = (Fe-P fixation):	% free Fe_2O_2-clay >0.20 or hues redder than 5 YR and granular structure
x = (X-ray amorphous):	pH > 10 in 1 N NaF or positive to field NaF test or other indirect evidences of allophane dominance in clay fraction
v = (Vertisol):	Very sticky plastic clay, >35% clay and >50% of 2:1 expanding clays; COLE >0.09; severe topsoil shrinking and swelling
*k = (k deff):	<10% weatherable minerals in silt and sand fraction within 50 cm or exch. K <0.20 meq/100 g or K <2% of Σ of bases, if Σ of bases <10 meq/100 g
*b = (carbonate):	Free $CaCO_3$ within 50 cm (fizzing with HCl) or pH >7.3
*s = (salinity):	>4 mmhos/cm of saturated extract at 25° within 1 m
*n = (sodic):	>15% Na saturation of CEC within 50 cm
*c = (cat clay):	pH in 1.1 H_2O <3.5 after drying; Jarosite mottles with hues 2.5 Y or yellower and chromas 6 or more within 60 cm

APPENDIX TABLE 3   Climatic Subregions of the Amazon
(Supplements Appendix D)

Subregion	Climate[a]	Name	Millions of Hectares
A	WSPET >1,300 mm Wet season >9 months WSMT >23.5°C	Tropical rainforest	171
B	WSPET: 1,061–1,300 mm Wet season: 8–9 months WSMT: >23.5°C	Semievergreen seasonal forest	274
C	WSPET: 900–1,060 mm Wet season: 6–8 months WSMT >23.5°C	Savannas (isohyperthermic)	37
D	WSPET: 900–1,060 mm Wet season: 6–8 months WSMT >23.5°C	Savannas (isothermic)	2
TOTAL			482

[a]Terminology: WSPET = Total wet season potential evapotranspiration
Wet season = MAI (moisture availability index) >0.33
WSMT = Mean wet season air temperature

APPENDIX TABLE 4   Topography of Climatic Subregions of the
Amazon (Data Expressed in Millions of Hectares) (Supplements
Appendix D)

Subregion	Flat, Poorly Drained	Well Drained 0–8% Slope	8–30% Slope	>30% Slope	Total
A—Tropical rainforest	50	79	30	12	171
B—Semievergreen seasonal forests	47	142	69	16	274
C—Isohyperthermic savannas	12	19	4	2	37
D—Isothermic savannas	0	2	0	0	2
TOTAL	109	242	103	30	484
%	23	50	21	6	100

APPENDIX TABLE 5   Summary of Main Soil
Constraints in the Amazon Under Native Vegetation
(Supplements Appendix D)

Soil Constraint	Millions of Hectares	% of Amazon
Phosphorus deficiency	436	90
Aluminum toxicity	315	73
Loss potassium reserves	242	56
Poor drainage and flooding hazard	116	24
High phosphorus fixation	77	16
Low cation exchange capacity	64	15
High erodibility	39	8
No major limitations	32	6
Steep slopes (>30%)	30	6
Laterite hazard if subsoil exposed	21	4

APPENDIX TABLE 6   Methods for Assessing Humid Tropical
Ecosystems as a Basis for Development Planning (Supplements
Appendix E)

Protocol	Format	Time Frame	Zones	Characteristics
First	Detailed evaluation of soils, water resources, vegetation, successional stages, primary and secondary production, effects of ecosystem perturbation, key biogeochemical cycles, human use patterns	≥ 12 months	1,4	Critical and holding zones: previous critical ecological damage or adequate time available for study before alteration of landscape
Second	Minimal data inputs: soil, vegetational physiognomy and plant and animal diversity; Kikkawa–Webb data form used	≤ 3 months	2	Unique zones; preservation of natural features, unique flora, and fauna important
Third	Identify ecological indicators, potential effects of disturbances	≤ 6 months	3,5	Multipurpose and agroforestry/agriculture zones: nearly undisturbed to substantially disturbed environments

APPENDIX TABLE 7 Principal Leafy Vegetables Used as Food in the Humid Tropics (Limited to Vegetables Having Potential for Further Improvement)

Genus and Species	Common Name	Where Cultivated and Used
Annual hot-season leafy vegetables		
Amaranthus spp.	Amaranth	
Ipomoea aquatica Forsk. (syn. *I. reptans* (L.) Poir.)	Kangkong, water spinach	Southeast Asia and southern India
Corchorus olitorius L.	Jew's mallow, jute mallow, jute	Originated in southern China and taken to Indian subcontinent
Xanthosoma brasiliense (Desf.) Engl.	Calalou, yautia	Both originated in tropical South America *X. brasiliense* now mainly cultivated in South America, Caribbean, and Pacific islands for its leaves
Basella rubra L. (syn. *B. alba* L.)	Ceylon spinach, Malabar nightshade	Originated in southern Asia or South America; now pantropical
Solanum macrocarpon L. *Solanum aethiopicum* *Solanum incanum*	African eggplant	All three *Solanum* spp. originated in Africa and are cultivated there
Solanum nigrum L.	Black nightshade	Native region unknown, at present a cosmopolite weed that is cultivated
Talinum triangulare (Jacq.) Willd.	Water leaf, talinum	Probably originated in Central or South America or tropical Africa; cultivated in Brazil, West Indies, and West Africa
Celosia argentea L.	Quail grass, sokoyokoto	
Hibiscus sabdariffa L.	Roselle	Originated in Africa; now grown to a large extent in the drier parts of western and central Africa and India
Annual cool-season leafy vegetables		
Brassica campestris L. ssp. *chinensis* (L.) Makino	Pak-choi	Asia pantropical
Brassica campestris ssp. *pekinensis* (Lour.) Rupr.	Chinese cabbage	Asia pantropical

APPENDIX TABLE 7 *(Continued)*

Genus and Species	Common Name	Where Cultivated and Used
Brassica juncea (L.) Czern. & Cross	Chinese mustard	Asia pantropical
Brassica carcinata A. Br.	Ethiopian mustard	Asia pantropical
Brassica oleracea L.	Cabbage, kale	Asia pantropical
Lactuca sativa L.	Lettuce	*L. sativa* found mostly in
Lactuca indica L.	Indian lettuce	the Middle East, and *L. indica* in India, Japan, Philippines, and Indonesia where it is cultivated *L. sativa* is more popular in Latin America, Africa, and the Near East than in India and Southeast Asia
Beta vulgaris var. *cicla* L.	Swiss chard	Originated in the Mediterranean area; is becoming increasingly popular in cool tropical areas as a vegetable
Perennial vegetables		
Moringa oleifera Lam.	Drumstick tree, horseradish tree	Originated in India, very popular there and in Southeast Asia and West Africa
Vernonia amygdalina Delile	Bitterleaf	Originated in tropical Africa; popular in West Africa; other wild or cultivated *Vernonia* species are known in tropical lowlands of Asia, Africa, and America
Cnidoscolus Chayamansa McVaugh	Chaya, tree spinach	Grown in compounds in the Caribbean area and Central America
Sauropus androgynus Merr.	Sauropus	Grown in India, Malaysia, and Indonesia as a leaf vegetable in home gardens
Abelmoschus manihot (L.) Medik.	Aibika	India, Pakistan, through southern China to New Guinea and northern Australia; widely grown in Pacific islands

APPENDIX TABLE 7 *(Continued)*

Genus and Species	Common Name	Where Cultivated and Used
Leaves of food crops grown for other purposes		
Manihot esculenta Crantz	Cassava	Cassava originated in Central and South America; secondary gene centers almost certainly exist in Africa; cassava leaves are consumed in many countries, especially in West Africa, Indonesia, Malaysia, and parts of South America
Ipomoea batatas (L.) Lam.	Sweet potato	Originated in central and northern South America; now pantropical; the leaves are used as pot herbs in Southeast Asia, the Pacific, and Latin America
Colocasia esculenta (L.) Schott	Taro	Originated in Indo-Malaysia; spread eastward and westward; now pantropical
Vigna unguiculata (L.) Walp. subsp. *unguiculata*	Cowpea, yardlong bean	Found primarily in western and central Africa; introduced into the Indian subcontinent where subsp. *sequipedalis* (L.) Verdc. (yardlong bean) developed. The leaves of both cowpeas and yardlong beans are frequently consumed

SOURCE: D. H. van Sloten. 1981. Changing priorities—the genetic resources of leafy vegetables. Paper presented at FAO/UIVEP/IBPGR Technical Conference, April 1981, Rome. 13 p., mimeographed.

APPENDIX TABLE 8   Tropical Fruits Used as Food
in the Humid Tropics, by Region Where Cultivated and
Used (Limited to Fruits Having Potential for Further
Improvement)

Genus and Species	Common Name
CHINA	
Fortunella margarita (Lour.) Swingle	Swingle-kumquat
Fortunella japonica (Thunb.) Swingle	Swingle
Poncirus trifoliata Raf.	Trifoliate orange
Diospyros kaki L. F. and D. *chinensis* Bl.	Persimmon
Diospyros lotus L.	Date plum
Eriobotrya japonica Lindl.	Loquat
Clausena lansium Skeels.	Wampi
Myrica rubra S. and Z.	
Litchi chinensis Sonn.	Litchi
Nephelium longana (Lam.) Cambess.	Litchi
Rhodomyrtus tomentosa (Ait.) Hassk.	Hill gooseberry
SOUTHERN ASIA	
Averrhoa bilimbi L.	Bilimbi
Averrhoa carambola L.	Carambola
Carissa carandas L.	Karanda
Murraya exotica L., *M. koenigii* (L.) Ser.	
Morinda citrifolia L.	
Morinda citrifolia L.	Indian mulberry
Mimusops hexandra Roxb.	
Mangifera indica L.	Mango
Garcinia indica	
Mimusops elengi L.	Spanish cherry
Feronia elephantum Correa.-*F. limonia* (L.) Swingle	
Eugenia jambolana Lam.	Jambos or
(*E. jambos* L.)	jambolan plum
SOUTHEAST ASIA	
Nephelium mutabile Bl.	
Canarium pimela Koenig, *C. album* Roensch	
Erioglossum rubiginosum (Roxb.) Blume, *E. edule* Bl.	
Antidesma delicatulum Hutch., *A. hainanensis* Merr., *A. bunias* (L.) Spreng.	
Garcinia mangostana L., *G. dulcis* (Roxb.) Durz. (wild and cultivated)	Mangosteen

APPENDIX TABLE 8 (*Continued*)

Genus and Species	Common Name
Durio zibethinus Murr.	Durian
(Malay Archipelago)	
Lansium domesticum Corr.—	
(Malay Archipelago)	
Bouea macrophylla Griff.—	
(Malay Archipelago)	
Mangifera caesia Jack., *M. foetida* Lour.,	
M. odorata Griff.—(Malay Archipelago)	
Baccaurea racemosa (Bl.) Muell.	
(Java and the Philippines)	
Flacourtia rukam Zoll. and Mor.	
(wild and cultivated on Java)	
Pangium edule Reinw. and Bl. (wild and	
cultivated on the Sunda Islands)	
Pithecelobium lobatum Benth.	
(Sunda Islands)	
Cynometra caulifora L. (on islands)	
Sandoricum koetjape (Burm.) Merr. f. Wild	
and cultivated (Java)	
Eugenia aquea Burm. f., *E. cuminii* (L.)	Jambolan plum
Merr.	
E. jambos L.	Rose apple
E. javanica Lam.	
E. malaccensis L.	Malay apple
Nephelium lappaceum (L.) Wight.	
Salacca edulis Reinw.	Salacca palm
Rubus rosaefolius Smith—(introduced into	
cultivation in Java; also found wild on	
the Philippine Islands; extends as far	
as southern Japan)	

MEXICO AND CENTRAL AMERICA

Anona cherimolia Mill. (possibly a second-	
ary center), *A. reticulata* L., *A. squamosa*	
L., *A. muricata* L., *A. purpurea* Moc.	
and Sesse, *A. cinerea* Dun., *A. diver-*	
sifolia Safford, *A. glabra* L.	
Sapota achras Miller, *S. sapotilla* Coville	Sapodilla
Casimiroa edulis La Llave	White sapote
Calocarpum mammosum (L.) Pierre	
Calocarpum viride Pittier	
(*Archradelpha viridis* Cook)	
Lucuma salicifolia H.B.K.	Yellow sapote
Carica papaya L.	Papaya

APPENDIX TABLE 8   (*Continued*)

Genus and Species	Common Name
Persea schiedeana Nees and *P. americana*	
Mill. (*P. gratissima* Gaertn.)	Avocado
Psidium guajava L.	Guava
Psidium friedrichsthalianum (Berg) Niedenzu,	
P. sartorianum (Berg) Niedenzu	Guava
Spondias mombin L.	Yellow mombin
S. purpurea L.	Purple mombin
Diospyros ebenaster Retz.	Black sapote
Chrysophyllum cainito L. (found chiefly on	Star apple
on the Antilles Islands, in Jamaica, in	
Panama, both in wild and cultivated	
form)	
Anacardium occidentale L.	Cashew
(Antilles, Panama)	

WESTERN SOUTH AMERICA

Passiflora ligularis Juss., *P. quadrangularis* L.	Passion flower
Carica candamarcensis Hoo., *C.*	
chrysopetala Heilborn, *C. pentagona*	
Heilborn—three Ecuadorean species; *C.*	
pubescens (A. DC.) Solms Laub. and *C.*	
candicans A. Gray—two Peruvian species	
Lucuma obovata H.B. & K., *L. caimito*	
A.c.X.C. (wild and cultivated)	
Psidium guajava L. (wild and cultivated)	Guava
Anona cherimolia Mill. (one of the centers)	
Inga feuillei DC.	
Bunchosia armeniaca DC.	
Matisia cordata Humb. & Bonpl.	
Caryocar amygdaliferum Cav.	
Guilielma speciosa Mart.	Peach palm
Malpighia glabra L.	
Solanum quitoense Lam.	

EASTERN SOUTH AMERICA

Eugenia uniflora L., *E. uvalha* Cambess.,	Surinam cherry
E. dombeyi Skeels-*E. brasiliensis*,	Grumixameira tree
E. tomentosa-Myrcia tomentosa Cambess	
(all of these are cultivated)	
Myrciaria joboticaba Berg., *M. cauliflora*	
(DC.) Berg.	Jaboticaba
Ananas comosa (L.) Merr. (on dry soils)	Pinapple
Feijoa sellowiana Berg.	
Passiflora edulis Sims	Purple granadilla

APPENDIX TABLE 9   Significant (Mostly Food) Plants of the Humid
Tropics

Scientific Name	Common Name	Use	Region Where Most Frequently Encountered
ALLIACEAE	I. MONOCOTYLEDONS		
Allium			
cepa L.			
var. *aggregatum* G. Don	Shallot	vegetable	Western Asia
var. *cepa*	Common onion	vegetable	Western Asia
chinense G. Don	Rakkyo	vegetable	China
galanthum Kar. & Kir. var.			
porrum (L.) Gay			
sativum L.	Garlic	condiment	Central Asia
schoenoprasum L.	Chives	vegetable	Circumpolar
tuberosum Rottl. ex Spreng.	Chinese onion	vegetable	Eastern Asia
ARACEAE			
Alocasia			Southeast Asia
indica (Roxb.) Schott		root crop	Southeast Asia
macrorrhiza (L.) Schott	Giant alocasia	root crop	Southeast Asia
Amorphophallus			Africa–Asia
campanulatus (Roxb.) Blume	Elephant yam	root crop	Southeast Asia
rivieri Durieu		root crop	China
Colocasia			Southeast Asia
esculenta (D.) Schott			Southeast Asia
var. *antiquorum* (Schott) Hubbard & Rehder	Eddoe	root crop	Southeast Asia
	Dasheen, taro, cocoyam	root crop	Southeast Asia
var. *globulifera* Engl. & Krause = var. *antiquorum* (Schott) Hubbard & Rehder			
Cyrtosperma			Malaysia
chamissonis (Schott) Merr.	Giant taro	root crop	Pacific
Monstera			Tropical America
deliciosa Liebm.	Ceriman	edible fruit	Mexico
Xanthosoma			Tropical America
atrovirens Koch & Bouche	Tannia	root crop	Tropical America
belophyllum Kinth	Tannia	root crop	Tropical America
brasiliense (Desf.) Engl.		pot herb	South America
caracu Koch & Bouche	Tannia	root crop	Tropical America
jacquinii Schott	Tannia	root crop	Mexico
mafaffa Schott	Tannia	root crop	South America
sagittifolium (L.) Schott	Tannia	root crop	Tropical America
violaceum Schott			

APPENDIX TABLE 9 *(Continued)*

Scientific Name	Common Name	Use	Region Where Most Frequently Encountered
BROMELIACEAE			
Ananas			South America
ananassoides (Bak.) L.B. Smith	Wild pineapple	breeding	South America
bracteatus (Lindl.) Schultes	Wild pineapple	breeding	South America
comosus (L.) Merr.	Pineapple	edible fruit	Americas
erectifolius L.B. Smith	Wild pineapple	breeding	South America
sativus Schult. f. = *A. comosus* (L.) Merr.			
CANNACEAE			
Canna edulis Ker.	Edible canna	edible rhizome	South America
CYPERACEAE			
Cyperus	Sedge,	weeds,	Pantropical
esculentus L.	tiger	root crop	Asia
DIOSCOREACEAE			
Dioscorea	Yams	root crop	Pantropical
alata L.	Greater yam	root crop	Southeast Asia
batatus Decne = *D.*			
opposita Thunb.	Aerial yam	edible bulbils	Africa, Asia
cayennensis Link	Yellow Guinea yam	root crop	Western Africa
dumetorum (Kunth) Pax	African bitter yam	root crop	Africa
esculenta (Lour.) Burk.	Lesser yam	root crop	Southeast Asia
floribunda Mart. & Gal.	Wild yam	drug	Mexico
hamiltonii Hook.	Wild yam		Southeast Asia
hispida Dennst.	Asiatic bitter yam	edible roots	Asia
nummularia Lam.	Yam	root crop	Southeast Asia
opposita Thunb.	Chinese yam	root crop	China
pentaphylla I.	Yam	root crop	Southeast Asia
persimalis Prain & Burk.	Bush yam	edible roots	Western Asia
rotundata Poir.	White Guinea yam	root crop	Western Africa
sansibarensis Pax	Wild yam	edible roots	Tropical Africa
trifida L.	Cush-cush yam	root crop	South America
EBENACEAE			
Diospyros ebenaster L.	Black sapote	edible fruit	Central America

APPENDIX TABLE 9 *(Continued)*

Scientific Name	Common Name	Use	Region Where Most Frequently Encountered
GRAMINEAE			
Bambusa			Pantropical
vulgaris Schrad. ex. Wendland	Bamboo	many	Asia
Brachiaria			Pantropical
decumbens Stapf	Surinam grass	pasture	Tropical Africa
·deflexa (Schumach) C.E. Hubbard ex Robyns		cereal	Tropical Africa
Coix			
lachryma-jobi L.	Job's tears	cereal	Pantropical
Dendrocalamus			
asper (Schult.) Backer ex Heyne	Bamboo	edible shoots	Southeast Asia
Digitaria			
exilis (Kippist) Stapf	Hungry rice	cereal	Western Africa
iburua Stapf	Hungry rice	cereal	Nigeria
longiflora (Retz.) Pers.		grass	Pantropical
scalarum (Schweinf.) Chiov.	African couch	weed	Eastern Africa
Echinochloa			
crus-galli (L.) Beauv.	Barnyard millet	cereal	Cosmopolitan
frumentacea (Roxb.) Link	Japanese barn- yard millet	cereal	Eastern Asia
Eleusine			
africana Kennedy-O-Byrne		weed	Eastern Africa
coracana (L.) Gaertn.	Finger millet	cereal	Eastern Africa, Western Africa, India
indica (L.) Gaertn.	Fowl foot grass	weed	Africa–Asia
Eragrostis			
abysinnica (Jacq.) Link = E. tef (Zucc.) Trotter			
tef (Zucc.) Trotter	Teff	cereal	Ethiopia
Gigantochloa			
apus (Schult.) Kurz	Bamboo	building	Java
verticillata (Willd.) Munro.	Bamboo	edible shoots	Java
Oryza			
breviligulata A. Chev. & Roehr. = O. barthii A. Chev.	Wild rice	weed	Western Africa
glaberrima Steud.	African rice	cereal	Western Africa
officinalis Wall. = O. minuta Pres. O.	Wild rice	weed	India–Southeast Asia

APPENDIX TABLE 9   (*Continued*)

Scientific Name	Common Name	Use	Region Where Most Frequently Encountered
perennis Moench =			
O. rufipogon	Wild rice	weed	Pantropical
rufipogon Griff.	Wild rice	weed	Pantropical
sativa L.	Rice	cereal	Southeast Asia
subsp. *indica* Kato	Tropical rice	cereal	India
subsp. *japonica* Kato	Temperate rice	cereal	China
Panicum			
miliaceum L.	Common millet	cereal	Pantropical
repens L.		weed	
spontaneum Lyssov & Zukovskij		weed	Central Asia
sumatrense Roth ex Roem & Schult.	Little millet	cereal	India–Southeast Asia
psilopodium Trin.		weed	Southeast Asia
Paspalum scrobiculatum L.			
var. *scrobiculatum*	Kodo millet	cereal	India
vaginatum Sw.		weed	Pantropical
Pennisetum			
cinereum Stapf & Hubbard	Bulrush millet	cereal	Ghana
nigritarum (Schlechld.) Durand & Schinz	Bulrush millet	cereal	Nigeria
typhoids (Burm. f.) Stapf & Hubbard	Bulrush millet	cereal	Western Africa
All cultivars of *Pennisetum glaucum* (L.) R.Br. [syn. *P. americanum* (L.) Lecke]			
Saccharum	Sugar cane	sugar	Asia, Pacific islands
barberi Jeswiet	Sugar cane	sugar	India
edule Hassk.		edible inflorescence	New Guinea
officinarum L.	Noble sugar cane	sugar	New Guinea
robustum Brandes & Jeswiet	Wild sugar cane		New Guinea
sinense Roxb.	Sugar cane	sugar	Eastern Asia
spontaneum L.	Wild sugar cane	breeding	Asia
Setaria			
italica (L.) Beauv.	Foxtail millet	cereal	Eastern Asia
sphacelata (schum.) Stapf & Hubbard	Gold timothy	pasture weed	Tropical Africa, Old World tropics

APPENDIX TABLE 9 (*Continued*)

Scientific Name	Common Name	Use	Region Where Most Frequently Encountered
Sorghum			
arundinaceum (Desv.) Stapf	Wild sorghum	fodder	Africa
bicolor (L.) Moench	Sorghum	cereal	Africa
caffrorum Beauv.	Kafir corn	cereal	South Africa
cernuum Host	Feterita	cereal	Sudan
dochna (Forsk.) Snowden	White durra	cereal	Asia
drummondii (Steud.)	Broomcorn	brooms	Asia
Millsp. & Chase	Chicken corn	grain	Western Africa
durra Stapf	Durra	cereal	Sudan, India
guinese Stapf	Guinea corn	cereal	Western Africa
halepense (L.) Pers.	Johnson grass	fodder	Mediterranean
nervosum Bess. ex. Schult	Kaoliang	cereal	China
nigricans (Ruiz & Pavon)			
Snowden	Beer sorghum	beer	Africa
propinquum (Runth) Hitchc.	Wild sorghum	fodder	China
roxburghii Stapf	Shallu	cereal	East Africa
Zea			
mays L.	Maize	cereal	Central America
mexicana (Schrad.) Reeves &			
Mangelsd. = *Euchlaena*			
mexicana Schrad.	Teosinte	weed	Central America
MARANTACEAE			
Calathea			
allouia (Aubl.) Lindl.	Topee tambu	root crop	Caribbean
lutea G.F.W. Mey	Cauassu	wax	Brazil
Maranta arundinacea L.	Arrowroot	starch	Caribbean
MUSACEAE			
Ensete			
glaucum (Roxb.) Cheesm.			Asia
ventricosa (Welw.) Cheesm.	Ensete	edible stems	Tropical Africa
Musa			
acuminata Colla	Banana	edible fruit	Southeast Asia
subsp. *banksoil* (F. Muell.)		breeding	Pacific
subsp. *burmannica*			
Simmonds		breeding	Burma
subsp. *malaccensis* (Ridl.)		breeding	Malaya
Simmonds			
subsp. *siamea* Simmonds		breeding	Indochina
angustigemma Simmonds		breeding	New Guinea
balbisiana Colla	Wild banana	breeding	Southeast Asia
beccarii Simmonds	Wild banana		Sabah

APPENDIX TABLE 9   (*Continued*)

Scientific Name	Common Name	Use	Region Where Most Frequently Encountered
cavendishii Lambert = *M.*			
cv. AAA group			Malaya
corniculata Lour. = *M.*			
cv. AAB group	Banana	edible fruit	Southeast Asia
ensete Gmel. = *Ensete*			
ventricosa (Welw.) Cheesm.			
fehi Bert. ex Vieill.	Fe'i banana	edible fruit	Solomons
flaviflora Simmonds	Wild banana	breeding	Assam
ingens Simmonds	Wild banana		New Guinea
lododensis Cheesm.		breeding	Indonesia
maclayi F. Muell.	Wild banana		New Guinea
nana Lour. = *M.*			
cavendishii Lambert ×			
paradisiaca L.	Plantain	edible fruits	Southeast Asia
var. *sapientum* (L.)			
Kuntz = *M.* cv.		breeding	New Ireland
peekelii Lauterb.			
ORCHIDACEAE			
Vanilla			Pantropical
fragrans (Salisb.) Ames	Vanilla	spice	Mexico
phaentha Rchb.f.			Tropical America
planifolia Andrews = *V.*			
fragrans (Salisb.) Ames			
pompona Schiede	W. Indian vanilla	spice	Tropical America
tahitensis J.W. Moore	Tahitian vanilla	spice	Tahiti
PALMAE			
Areca			Asia
catechu L.	Areca palm	masticatory	Asia
triandra Roxb.		masticatory	Asia
Arenga			Southeast Asia
pinnata (Wurmb.) Merr.	Sugar palm	sugar	
saccharifera Labill = *A.*			
pinnata (Wurmb.) Merr.			
Astrocaryum			Americas
murumuru Mart.	Murumuru palm	oil	Brazil
tucumu Mart.	Tucuma palm	oil	South America
vulgare Mart.			South America, tropical America
Borassus			Africa–Asia
aethiopicum Mart.	African fan palms	edible fruit	Tropical Africa

APPENDIX TABLE 9 (*Continued*)

Scientific Name	Common Name	Use	Region Where Most Frequently Encountered
flabellifer L. var. *aethiopicum* Warb. = B. *aethiopicum* Mart.	Palmyra palm	sugar	Asia
Caryota			
urens L.	Fish-tail palm	palm wine	Asia
Cocos			
nucifera L.	Coconut	oil	Pacific islands
Corypha			
elata Roxb.	Gebang palm	palm wine	Asia
umbraculifera L.	Talipot	palm wine	Ceylon
Elaeis			
guineensis Jacq.	Oil palm	oil	Western Africa
Eugeissona			
thebaica (L.) Mart.		sago	Borneo
Hyphaene			
thebaica (L.) Mart.	Dum palm	edible fruit	Tropical Africa
Lodoicea			
maldivica (Gmel.) Pers.	Double coconut	medicinal	
Metroxylon			
rumphii Mart.	Rough sago palm	sago	Malaysia
sagus Rottb.	Smooth sago palm	sago	Malaysia
Nypa			
frutican Wurmb.	Nipa palm	Palm wine, sugar	Malaysia
Orbignya			
cohune (Mart.) Dahlgren	Cohune palm	oil	Mexico
martiana Barb. Rodr.	Babacu palm	oil	Brazil
olifera Burret	Babacu palm	oil	Brazil
Phoenix			
dactylifera L.	Date palm	edible fruit	Middle East
reclinata Jacq.	Wild date palm	fiber	Tropical Africa
sylvestris Roxb.	Wild data palm	palm wine	India
Raphia			Tropical Africa
hookeri Mann & Wendl.	Wine palm	palm wine	Western Africa
humilis A. Chev.			Dahomey
Salacca			
edulis Reinw.	Salak palm	edible fruit	Malaysia
PANDANACEAE			
Pandanus			
andamanensium Kurz	Screw pine	edible fruit	Andamans
brosimos Merr. & Perry	Screw pine	edible seeds	New Guinea

APPENDIX TABLE 9   *(Continued)*

Scientific Name	Common Name	Use	Region Where Most Frequently Encountered
fascicularis Lam. = *P. odoratissimus* L.f.			
houlletii Carr	Screw pine	edible fruit	Malaya
julianetii Mart.	Screw pine	edible seeds	New Guinea
TACCACEAE			
Tacca			
leontopodiodes (L.) Kuntze	Tahiti arrowroot	starch	Africa-Asia
ZINGIBERACEAE			
Aframomum			Africa
angustifolium K. Schum.	Madagascar cardamom	spice	Madagascar
daniellii K. Schum.	Camerouns cardamom		Western Africa
granum-paradisi K. Schum.		spice	Western Africa
hanburyi K. Schum. = *A. daniellii* K. Schum.			
korarima Pereira	Korarima cardamom	spice	Ethiopia
melegueta (Rosc.) K. Schum.	Grains of paradise	spice	Western Africa
Aninyn			Pantropical
aromaticum Roxb.	Bengal cardamom	spice	India
kepulaga Sprague & Burkill	Round cardamom	spice	Java
krervahn Pierre	Cambodian cardamom	spice	Southeast Asia
subulatum Roxb.	Nepal cardamom	spice	India
Curcuma			
amada Roxb.	Mango ginger	spice	India
angustifolia Roxb.	Indian arrowroot	starch	India
domestica Val.	Turmeric	dye spice	India
longa Koenig non *L.* = *C. domestica* Val.			
mangga Val. & van Zijp		spice	Malaysia
Elettaria			
cardamomum Maton	Cardamom	spice	India
var. *cardamomum*	Cardamom	spice	India
var. *major* Thw.	Wild cardamon	spice	India

APPENDIX TABLE 9 (*Continued*)

Scientific Name	Common Name	Use	Region Where Most Frequently Encountered
minor Watt = var. *cardamomum*			
minuscula Burkill = var. *cardamomum*			
Kaempferia			
galanga L.		spice	Southeast Asia
rotunda L.		spice	Southeast Asia
Languas			
galanga (L.) Stuntz	Greater galangal	spice	Southeast Asia
officinarum (Hance) Farwell	Lesser galangal	spice	China
Phaeomeria			Asia
speciosa (Bl.) Merr.		spice	Southeast Asia
Zingibar			
officinale Rosc.	Ginger	spice	Southeast Asia
AMARANTHACEAE	II. DICOTYLEDONS		
Amaranthus			
caudatus L.	Grain amaranth	grain	South America
cruentus L.	Grain amaranth	grain	Central America
dubius Mart. ex Thell.		pot herb	Tropics
gangeticus L.		pot herb	Asia
hybridus L.		pot herb	Tropics
leucocarpus S. Wats.	Grain amaranth	grain	Mexico
paniculatus		pot herb	Asia
ANACARDIACEAE			
Anacardium			
occidentale L.	Cashew	edible nut	Tropical America
Bouea Meiss.		edible fruit	Asia
Buchanania			
lanzan Spreng.		edible nut	India
Dracontomelon			
mangiferum Blume	Argus pheasant tree	edible fruit	Indo–Malay
Mangifera			
caesia Jack		edible fruit	Tropical Asia
foetida Lour.		edible fruit	Tropical Asia
indica L.	Mango	edible fruit	Indo-Burma
lagenifera Griff.		edible fruit	Tropical Asia

APPENDIX TABLE 9   (*Continued*)

Scientific Name	Common Name	Use	Region Where Most Frequently Encountered
odorata Griff.		edible fruit	Tropical Asia
zeylanica Hook.f.		edible fruit	Tropical Asia
Spondias			
cytherea Sonn.	Golden apple	edible fruit	Polynesia
mombin L.	Hog plum	edible fruit	Tropical America
purpurea L.	Red mombin	edible fruit	Tropical America
ANNONACEAE			
Annona			
cherimolia Mill.	Cherimoya	edible fruit	South America
diversifolia Saff.	Ilama	edible fruit	Tropical America
montana Macfad.	Mountain soursop	edible fruit	Central America
muracata L.	Soursop	edible fruit	Tropical America
reticulata L.	Bullock's heart	edible fruit	Tropical America
squamosa L.	Sugar apple	edible fruit	Tropical America
APOCYNACEAE			
Carissa			
carandas L.		edible fruit	Tropical India
edulis Vahl		edible fruit	Tropical Africa
grandiflora A. DC.	Natal plum	edible fruit	South Africa
BASELLACEAE			
Basella alba L.	Indian spinach	pot herb	Tropical Asia
Ullucus			
tuberosus Caldas	Ullucu	edible tuber	Andes
BIGNONIACAE			
Crescentia			
cujete L.	Calabash	utensils	Tropical America
Parmentiera			
edulis DC.	Cuachilote	edible fruit	Central America
BOMBACACEAE			
Adansonia			
digitata L.	Baobab	edible fruit	Africa
Durio			
zibethinus Murr.	Durian	edible fruit	Malaysia
CARICACEAE			
Carica			
candamarcensis Hook.f.	Mountain papaya	edible fruit	South America

APPENDIX TABLE 9 (*Continued*)

Scientific Name	Common Name	Use	Region Where Most Frequently Encountered
papaya L.	Papaya	edible fruit	Central America
peltata Hook. & Arn.	Wild papaya		Central America
COMPOSITAE			
Guizotia			
abyssinica (L.f.) Cass.	Niger seed	oil seed	Tropical Africa
Lactuca			
indica L.		vegetable	China
sativa L.	Lettuce	salad vegetable	Eurasia
CONVOLVULACEAE			
Impomoea			
aquatica Forsk.		pot herb	Tropics
batatas (L.) Lam.	Sweet potato	edible tuber	Tropical America
eriocarpa		pot herb	India
titiacea (Willd.) Choisy			
CRUCIFERAE			
Brassica			
campestris L.	Field mustard	oil seed	India
var. *sarson* Prain	Indian colza	oil seed	India
var. *toria* Duthie & Fuller	Indian rape	oil seed	India
caulorapa Pasw. = *oleracea* L. var. *gongylodes* L.			
chinensis L.	Chinese cabbage	vegetable	Asia
var. *pekinensis* (Rupr.) Sun.	Pe-tsai	salad	China
harta Moench. = *B. alba* (L.) Rabenh.			
juncea (L.) Czern. & Cross var. *napobrassica* (L.) Rchb. = *B. napobrassica* (L.) Rchb.	Indian mustard	oil seed	Africa
Raphanus			
caudatus L.	Rat-tailed radish	vegetable	India
sativus L.	Radish	salad	Western Asia
var. *longipinnatus* Bailey	Japanese radish	vegetable	Eastern Asia

APPENDIX TABLE 9 *(Continued)*

Scientific Name	Common Name	Use	Region Where Most Frequently Encountered
CUCURBITACEAE			
Benincasa			
hispida (Thunb.) Cong.	Wax gourd	vegetable	Java
Citrullus			
lanatus (Thunb.) Mansf.	Watermelon	edible fruit	Africa
var. *fistulosus* (Stocks) Duthie & Fuller		vegetable	India
Cucumis			
anguria L.	West Indian gherkin	vegetable	Tropical Africa
hardwickii Royle	Wild cucumber		India
melo L.	Melon	edible fruit	Africa
sativus L.	Cucumber	salad vegetable	India
Cucurbita			
andreana Naud.	Wild pumpkin		Argentina
ficifolia Bouche	Malabar gourd	edible fruit	Tropical America
maxima Duch. ex Lam.	Pumpkin	vegetable	South America
var. *maxima*	Winter squash	vegetable	
var. *turbaniformis* Alef.	Turban squash	vegetable	
mixta Pang.	Pumpkin	vegetable	Mexico
moschata (Such. ex Lam.) Duch. ex Prior.	Pumpkin	vegetable	Central America
pepo L.	Marrow	vegetable	Mexico
var. *medullosa* Alef.	Vegetable marrow	vegetable	
var. *melopepo* Alef.	Bush squash		
var. *ovifera* Alef.	Ornamental gourd	ornamental	Tropical America
Cyclanthera			
pedata Schrad.			
var. *edulis* Schrad.	Wild cucumber	edible fruit	Central America
Lagenaria			
siceraria (Molina) Standl.	Bottle guard	containers	Africa
Luffa			
acutangula (L.) Roxb.	Angled loofah	edible fruit	India
cylindrica (L.) M.J. Roem.	Smooth loofah	sponges	Tropical Asia
Momordica			
balsamina L.	Balsam apple	vegetable	Tropics

APPENDIX TABLE 9 *(Continued)*

Scientific Name	Common Name	Use	Region Where Most Frequently Encountered
charantia L.	Bitter gourd	vegetable	Tropics
cochinchinensis Spreng.		vegetable	Tropical Asia
dioica Roxb. ex Willd.		vegetable	Tropical Asia
Sechium			
edule (Jacq.) Swartz	Choyote	vegetable	Mexico
Sicana			
odorifera (Vell.) Naud.		vegetable	South America
Trichosanthes			
cucumerina L.	Snake gourd	vegetable	Tropical Asia
EUPHORBIACEAE			
Aleurites			
fordii Hemsel.	Tung	oil	China
moluccana (L.) Willd.	Candlenut	oil	Malaya
montana (Lour.) Willd.	Tung	oil	China
trisperma Blanco		oil	Philippines
Antidesma			
bunius (L.) Spreng.	Bignay	edible fruit	Asia
Baccaurea			
motleyana Muell.-Arg.	Rambai	edible fruit	Southeast Asia
sapida Muell.-Arg.		edible fruit	Southeast Asia
Croton			
tiglium L.	Purging croton	croton oil	Southeast Asia
Manihot			
catingae Ule			Tropical America
dulcis Pax			
= *M. esculentus* Crantz			
esculentus Crantz	Cassava	edible tuber	Tropical America
melanobasis Muell.-Arg.			Tropical America
tristis Muell.-Arg.			Tropical America
ssp. *saxicola* (Lanj) Rogers & Appan.			
Micrandra			
spp.		edible seeds	South America
Phyllanthus			
acidus (L.) Skeels	Otaheite gooseberry	edible fruit	Madagascar
emblica L.	Emblic	edible fruit	Tropical Asia
Ricinus			
communis L.	Castor	oil	Africa
Vupesia			
cataractarum R.E. Schultes		edible seeds	South America

APPENDIX TABLE 9   (*Continued*)

Scientific Name	Common Name	Use	Region Where Most Frequently Encountered
GUTTIFERAE			
Garcinia			
dulcis (Roxb.) Durz		edible fruit	Tropical Asia
livingstonei T. Anders		edible fruit	East Africa
mangostana L.		edible fruit	Malaysia
xanthochymus Hook.f.		edible fruit	Tropical Asia
Mammea			
americana L.	Mammey apple	edible fruit	Tropical America
LABIATAE			
Coleus			
amboinicus Lour.	Indian borage	herb	Indonesia
parviflorus Benth.		edible tuber	India
Hyptis			
spicigera Lam.		oil seed	Tropical Africa
Ocimum			
americanum L. = *O.*			
basilicum L.			
basilicum L.	Sweet basil	cultivated herb	Tropics
canum Sims	Hoary basil	cultivated herb	Tropics
sanctum L.	Holy basil	holy herb	India
Plectranthus			
esculentus N.E. Br.	Hausa potato	edible tubers	Tropical Africa
LAURACEAE			
Cinnamomum			
burmanni (Nees) Blume	Padang cassia	spice	Indonesia
camphora (L.) Nees & Eberm.	Camphor	oil	Eastern Asia
cassia (Nees) Nees ex Blume	Cassia	spice	Burma
massoia Schewe	Massoia bark	spice	New Guinea
oliveri Bailey	Oliver's bark	spice	Australia
tamala (Buck.-Ham.) Nees & Eberm.	Indian cassia	spice	India
zeylanicum Blume	Cinnamon	spice	Ceylon
Persea			
americana Mill.	Avocado	edible fruit	Central America
var. *drymifolia* Mez	Avocado		Mexico
LECYTHIDACEAE			
Bertholletia			
excelsa Hbk. & Bonpl.	Brazil nut	edible nut, oil	South America

APPENDIX TABLE 9 (*Continued*)

Scientific Name	Common Name	Use	Region Where Most Frequently Encountered
Lecythis			
elliptica Kunth	Sapucaia nut	edible nut	Tropical America
ollaria L.	Sapucaia nut	edible nut	Tropical America
usitatis Miers	Sapucaia nut	edible nut	Tropical America
zabucajo Aubl.	Sapucaia nut	edible nut	South America
LEGUMINOSAE			
Acacia	Cutch		
	Silver wattle		
	Green wattle		
farnesiana (L.) Willd.	Cassie flower	perfume	Tropical America
mearnsii DeWild.	Black wattle	tannin	Australia
nilotica (L.) [Willd. ex] Del.	Babul	tannin, gum	Africa
pycnantha Benth.	Golden wattle	tannin	Australia
senegal (L.) Willd.	Gum arabic	gum	Africa
seyal Del.	Shittim	gum	Africa
spp.		browse	Africa
Arachis			
hypogaea L.	Groundnut	oil seed	South America
Cajanus			
cajan (L.) Druce	Pigeon pea	pulse	Africa, India
Canavalia			
ensiformis (L.) DC.	Jack bean	pulse	Central America
gladiata (Jacq.) DC.	Sword bean	pulse	Old World
maritima (Aubl.) Thou.		stand plant	Tropics
plagiosperma Piper		pulse	South America
rosea (Sw.) DC. = C.			
maritima (Aubl.) Thou.			
virosa (Roxb.) Wight & Arn.			Tropical Asia
Cicer			
arietinum L.	Chick pea	pulse	Tropical Asia
Cyamopsis			
tetragonolobus (L.) Taub.	Cluster bean	edible pods	India
Dipteryx			
odorata (Aubl.) Willd.	Tonka bean	flavoring	South America
opporitifolia (Aubl.) Willd.	Tonka bean	flavoring	South America
punctata Blake		flavoring	South America
rosea Spruce		flavoring	South America
Glycine			
gracilis Skvortzor		oil seed	Eastern Asia
max (L.) Merr.	Soya bean	pulse	Eastern Asia
tomentosa Benth.	Wild soya bean		South China
ussuriensis Regal & Maack	Wild soya bean		Eastern Asia

APPENDIX TABLE 9   (*Continued*)

Scientific Name	Common Name	Use	Region Where Most Frequently Encountered
Kerstingiella			
geocarpa Harms.	Lersting's groundnut	pulse crop	Western Africa
Lablab			
niger Medik.	Hyacinth bean	pulse crop	Tropical Asia
Pachyrrhizus			
ahipa (Wedd.) Peroki	Yam bean	edible tuber	Bolivia
erosus (L.) Urban	Yam bean	edible tuber	Mexico
tuberosus (Lam.) Spreng.	Yam bean	edible tuber	South America
Parkia			
filicoidea Wels. ex Oliv.	African locust bean	edible fruit	Western Africa
speciosa Hassk.		flavoring	Malaysia
Phaseolus			
aconitifolius Jacq.	Mat bean	pulse	Asia
acutifolius Gray var.			
latifolius Freem.	Tepary bean	pulse	Mexico
angularis (Willd.) Wight	Adzuki bean	pulse	Japan
arborigeus Brukhart			Tropical America
aureus Roxb.	Green gram	pulse	India
calaratus Roxb.	Gice bean	pulse	Asia
coccineus L.	Scarlet runner bean	pulse	Central America
lathyroides L.		cover crop	Tropical America
lunatus L.	Lima bean	pulse crop	Tropical America
metcalfei Wood. & Standl.		cover crop	Tropical America
mungo L.	Black gram	pulse crop	India
radiatus L.			India
sublobatus Roxb.			India
trinervius Heyne			India
vulgaris L.	Common bean	pulse crop	Tropical America
Pisum			
arvense L.			
= *P. sativum* L.			
elatius Steven	Wild pea	weed	Eurasia
hortense Ashers & Graegn.			
= *P. sativum* L.			
palustris Desv.		edible pods	Tropical Africa
sativum L.	Pea	pulse crop	Europe
subsp. *arvense* (L.) Poir			
= *P. sativum* L.			
subsp. *hortense* Poir			
= *P. sativum* L.			

APPENDIX TABLE 9 (*Continued*)

Scientific Name	Common Name	Use	Region Where Most Frequently Encountered
var. *humile* Poir			
= *P. sativum* L.			
var. *macrocarpon* Ser.			
= *P. sativum* L.		edible pods	Tropical Africa
tetragonolobus (L.) DC.	Goa bean	vegetable	Tropical Asia
Pueraria			
phaseoloides (Roxb.) Benth.	Tropical kudzu	cover crop	Malaysia
thunbergiana (Sieb. & Zucc.)	Kudzu	cover crop	China
Benth. (possible synonym			
of *P. lobata* (Willd.))			
Sesbania			
grandiflora Poir.		edible flower	India
Tamarindus			
indica L.	Tamarind	edible fruit	Tropical Africa
Vigna			
sesquipedalis (L.) Fruw.	Asparagus pea	vegetable	Tropical Africa
sinensis (L.) Savi ex Hassk.	Cowpea	pulse crop	Tropical Africa
unguiculata (L.) Walp.	Cowpea	pulse crop	Tropical Africa
vexillata (L.) A. Rich.		edible tuber	Tropical Africa
Voandzeia			
subterranea (L.) Thouars	Bambara groundnut	pulse crop	Western Africa
MALPIGHIACEAE			
Malpighia			
glabra L.	Barbados cherry	edible fruit	Tropical America
MALVACEAE			
Hibiscus			
esculentus L.	Okra	vegetable	Tropical Africa
manihot L.		pot herb	Eastern Asia
sabdariffa L.	Rosell	soft drink	Western Africa
MORACEAE			
Artocarpus			
altilis (Park.) Fosberg	Breadfruit, breadnut	edible fruit	Polynesia
champeden (Lour.) Spreng.	Champedak	edible fruit	Malaya
communis Forst. = *A.*			
altilis (Park.) Fosberg			
heterophyllus Lam.	Kackfruit	edible fruit	India
hirsuta Lam.			India
mariannensis Trec.	Wild grapefruit	edible fruit	Micronesia
rigida Blume	Monkey jack	edible fruit	Malaysia

APPENDIX TABLE 9   (*Continued*)

Scientific Name	Common Name	Use	Region Where Most Frequently Encountered
Brosiumum			
alicastrum Sw.		edible fruit	Mexico
Ficus			
carica L.	Fig	edible fruit	Asia
Morus			
alba L.	White mulberry	edible fruit	China
nigra L.	Black mulberry	edible fruit	Asia
Treculia			
africana Decne	African breadfruit	edible fruit	Western Africa
MORINGACEAE			
Moringa			
oleifera Lam.	Horseradish tree	condiment	India
MYRISTICACEAE			
Myristica			
argentea Warb.	Papua nutmeg	adulterant	New Guinea
fragrans Houtl.	Nutmeg	spice	Moluccas
malabarica Lam.	Bombay nutmeg	adulterant	India
MYRTACEAE			
Eugenia			
aquea Brum. f.	Watery rose apple	edible fruit	India
caryophyllus (Sprengel) Bullock & Harrison	Clove	spice	Moluccas
cuminii (L.) Druce	Jambolan	edible fruit	Brazil
jambos L.	Rose apple	edible fruit	Indo–Malaya
javanica Lam.	Java apple	edible fruit	Malaysia
malcaccensis L.	Pomerac	edible fruit	Malaysia
uniflora L.	Pitanga cherry	edible fruit	Brazil
Feijoa			
sellowiana Berg.	Feijoa	edible fruit	South America
Melaleuca			
leucadendron L.	Punk tree	cajeput oil	Malaysia
Myrciaria			
caulifera (DC.) Berg.	Jaboticaba	edible fruit	Brazil
Pimenta			
acris Kostel. = *P. racemosa* (Mill.) J.W. Moore			

APPENDIX TABLE 9 (*Continued*)

Scientific Name	Common Name	Use	Region Where Most Frequently Encountered
dioica (L.) Merr.	Pimento	spice	Jamaica
officinalis Lindl. = *P. dioica* (L.) Merr.			
racemosa (Mill.) J.W. Moore	Bay	essential oil	West Indies
Psidium			
cattleianum Savine = *P. littorale* Raddi			
friedrichsthalianum (Berg.) Mied.		edible fruit	Central America
guajava L.	Guava	edible fruit	Tropical America
guineense Sw.		edible fruit	Tropical America
littorale Raddi	Strawberry guava	edible fruit	Brazil
var. *lucidum* Degener	Strawberry guava (yellow)		
microphyllum Britton		edible fruit	Puerto Rico
montanum Sw.	Wild guava	edible fruit	Jamaica
OXALIDACEAE			
Averrhoa			
bilimbi L.	Bilimbi	edible fruit	Malaya
carambola L.	Carambola	edible fruit	Indonesia
Oxalis			
tuberosa Mol.	Oca	edible tuber	South America
Passiflora			
antioquiensis Karst.	Banana passion fruit	edible fruit	Colombia
edulis Sims	Passion fruit	edible fruit	Brazil
f. *edulis*	Purple passion fruit	edible fruit	South America
f. *flavicarpa* Degener	Yellow passion fruit	edible fruit	South America
foetida L.	Wild passion fruit		Tropical America
laurifolia L.	Water lemon	edible fruit	South America
ligularis Juss.	Sweet granadilla	edible fruit	Tropical America
mollissima (HBK) Bailey	Banana passion fruit	edible fruit	Andes
quadrangularis L.	Giant granadilla	edible fruit	South America
van-volxemii (Lem.) Triana & Planch. = *P. antioquiensis* Karst.			

APPENDIX TABLE 9   (*Continued*)

Scientific Name	Common Name	Use	Region Where Most Frequently Encountered
PEDALIACEAE			
Ceratotheca			
sesamoides Endl.		oil seed	Tropical Africa
Sesamum			
alatum Thonn.		oil seed	Tropical Africa
indicum L.	Sesame	oil seed	Tropical Africa
prostratum Retz.			India
radiatum Schum. & Thonn.		oil seed	Tropical Africa
PIPERACEAE			
Piper			
betle L.	Betel pepper	masticatory	Malaysia
clusii DC.		pepper substitute	Tropical Africa
cubeba L.f.	Cubeb	spice	Indonesia
guineense Schum. & Thonn.		pepper substitute	Tropical Africa
longifolium Ruiz & Pavon		pepper substitute	Tropical America
longum L.	Indian long pepper	spice	India
methysticum Forts.	Kava	beverage	Polynesia
nigrum L.	Pepper	spice	India
retrofractum Vahl	Javanese long pepper	spice	Malaysia
saigonense DC.		pepper substitute	Vietnam
PROTEACEAE			
Macadamia			
ternifolia F. Muell.	Macadamia nut	edible nut	Australia
tetraphylla L.A.S. Johnson	Macadamia nut	edible nut	Australia and Hawaii
RHAMNACEAE			
Zizyphus			
jujuba Mill.	Chinese jujube	edible fruit	China
mauritiana Lam.	Indian jujube	edible fruit	Africa, Asia
RUBIACEAE			
Coffea			
arabica L.	Arabica coffee	beverage	Ethiopia
bengalensis Heyne & Willd.	Coffee	beverage	India

APPENDIX TABLE 9   (*Continued*)

Scientific Name	Common Name	Use	Region Where Most Frequently Encountered
canephora Pierre ex Froehner	Robusta coffee	beverage	Tropical Africa
congensis Froehner	Coffee	beverage	Congo
dewevrei De Wild & Th. Dur. var. *excelsa* A. Chev.	Coffee	beverage	Western Africa
eugenioides S. Moore	Coffee	beverage	East Congo
excelsa A. Chev.	Coffee	beverage	Western Africa
liberica Bull. ex Hiern	Liberica coffee	beverage	Liberia
stenophylla G. Don	Coffee	beverage	Western Africa
RUTACEAE			
Aegle			
marmelos (L.) Corrêa	Indian bael	edible fruit	India
Casimiroa			
edulis Llave & Lex.	White sapote	edible fruit	Central America
Citrus			
aurantifolia (Christm.) Swing.	Lime	edible fruit	East Indies
aurantium L.	Sour orange	edible fruit	Southeastern Asia
subsp. *bergamia* (Risso & Poit.) Wight & Arn.			
var. *myrtifolia* Ker-Gawl.			
var. *sinensis* L.			
= *C. sinensis* (L.) Osbeck			Philippines
celebica Koord.			
decumana L. = *C. grandis* (L.) *Osbeck*			
grandis (L.) Osbeck	Pummelo	edible fruit	Malaysia
hystrix DC.			Southeastern Asia
ichangensis Swing.			China
indica Tan.			India
japonica Thunb.			
latipes (Swing.) Tan.			India
limon (L.) Burm. f.	Lemon	edible fruit	Southeastern Asia
macroptera Montr.			Southeastern Asia
margarita Lour. = *Fortunella margarita* (Lour.) Swing			
maxima (Burm.) Merr. = *C. grandis* (L.) Osbeck			
medica L.	Citron	edible fruit	Southeastern Asia
var. *ethrog* Engl.	Etrog citron		
var. *sarcodactylis* (Noot.) Swing.	Fingered citron		
micrantha Wester			Philippines
nobilis Andrews non Lour. = *C. reticulata* Blanco			

APPENDIX TABLE 9   (*Continued*)

Scientific Name	Common Name	Use	Region Where Most Frequently Encountered
paradisi Macfad.	Grapefruit	edible fruit	West Indies
reticulata Blanco	Mandarin	edible fruit	China
var. *austera* Swing.	Sour mandarin		
reticulata × *C. sinensis*	Tangor	edible fruit	
reticulata × *C. paradisi*	Tangelo	edible fruit	
sinensis (L.) Osbeck	Sweet orange	edible fruit	South China
tachibana (Mak.) Tan.	Tachibana orange	edible fruit	China
Clausena			
dentata (Willd.) Roem.		edible fruit	India
lansium (Lour.) Skeels		edible fruit	South China
Feronia			
limonia (L.) Swing.	Indian wood apple	edible fruit	India
Fortunella			
japonica (Thunb.) Swing.	Round kumquat	edible fruit	China
margarita (Lour.) Swing.	Oval kumquat	edible fruit	China
polyandra (Ridl.) Tan.	Kumquat	edible fruit	Malaya
spp.	Kumquats	edible fruit	Eastern Asia
Microcitrus	Australia wild limes	edible fruit	Australia
Murraya			
koenigii (L.) Spreng.	Curry-leaf tree	flavoring	India
Poncirus			
trifoliata × *Citrus* sinensis	Citrange	edible fruit	
Triphasia			
trifolia (Burm. f.) P. Wils.	Limeberry	edible fruit	Southeastern Asia
SAPINDACEAE			
Blighia			
sapida Koenig	Akee	edible aril	Western Africa
Nephelium			
lappaceum L.	Rambutan	edible aril	Malaysia
mutabile Bl.	Pulasan	edible aril	Malaysia
Litchi			
chinensis Sonn.	Litchi	edible aril	China
Paullinia			
cupana Kunth	Guarana	beverage	South America
yoyo Schultes & Killip	Yoco	beverage	Colombia
Schleichera			
oleosa (Lour.) Merr.	Lac tree	edible oil	India

APPENDIX TABLE 9 *(Continued)*

Scientific Name	Common Name	Use	Region Where Most Frequently Encountered
SAPOTACEAE			
Butyrospermum			
paradoxum (Gaertn. f.) Hepper			
subsp. *nilotica* (Kotschy) Pierre ex. Engl.	Shea butter	edible fat	Uganda
subsp. *parkii* (G. Don) Hepper	Shea butter	edible fat	Western Africa
parkii (G. Don.) Kotschy = *B. paradoxum* (Gaertn. f.) Hepper			
cainito L.	Star apple	edible fruit	Central America
Lucuma			
bifera Molina	Egg fruit	edible fruit	Peru
nervosa A. DC.	Egg fruit	edible fruit	South America
salicifolia Kunth	Egg fruit	edible fruit	Mexico
Manilkara			
achras (Mill.) Fosberg	Sapodilla	edible fruit	Central America
SOLANACEAE			
Capsicum L.			
annuum L.	Chilli	condiment, spice	Tropical America
baccatum var. *pendulum* (Willd.) Eshb.	Chilli	spice	South America
frutescens L.	Bird pepper	condiment	Tropical America
pubescens Ruiz & Pav.	Chilli	spice	Central and South America
Cyphomandra			
crassifolium Ort.	Tree tomato	edible fruit	Peru
Lycopersicon			
cheesmanii Riley	Wild tomato		Galapagos
esculentum Mill.	Tomato	edible fruit	Tropical America Ecuador
glandulosum C.H. Muller			South America
hirsutum			South America
peruvianum Mill.			South America
pimpinellifolium (Jusl.) Mill.	Currant tomato	edible fruit	South America
Physalis			
peruviana L.	Cape gooseberry	edible fruit	Tropical America
Solanum			
aethiopicum L.		vegetable	Tropical Africa
lasiocarpum Dun.		vegetable	Southeast Asia
gilo Raddi		vegetable	Tropical Africa

APPENDIX TABLE 9   (*Continued*)

Scientific Name	Common Name	Use	Region Where Most Frequently Encountered
incanum L.		vegetable	Tropical Africa
indicum L.		vegetable	Africa, India
lycopersicum L. = Lycopersicon esculentum Mill.			
macrocarpon L.		vegetable	Tropical Africa
melongena L.	Egg plant	vegetable	Warm temperate and tropics
muricatum Ait.	Papino	edible fruit	Peru
nigrum L.		pot herb	Tropics
quitoense Lam.	Naranjilla	edible fruit	Ecuador
scabrum Milli		fruits	Africa
sessiliflorum Dun.	Cocona	edible fruit	South America
sparsipilum (Bitt.) Juz. and Buk.			South America
stenotomum Juz. and Buk.			South America
torvum Sw.		vegetable	Tropics
tuberosum L.	Potato	edible tuber	Andes
vernei Juz. & Buk.			South America
wendlandii Hook.f.		ornamental	Tropical America
STERCULIACEAE			
Theobroma			
angustifolium Moc. & Sesse		edible pulp	Mexico
bicolor H. & B.		edible pulp	Mexico
cacao L.	Cocoa	beverage	South America
subsp. *cacao*			
f. *cacao*	Central American criollo cocoa	beverage	Central America
f. *lacandonense* Cuatr.			Mexico
f. *leiocarpum* (Bern.) Ducke		beverage	Guatemala
f. *pentagonum* (Bern.) Cuatr.	Alligator cocoa	beverage	Central America
subsp. *sphaerocarpum* (Chev.) Cuatr.	Amazonian forestero cocoa	beverage	South America
grandiflorum (Willd. ex Spreng.) L. Schum.		edible pulp	Brazil
sphaerocarpum (Chev.) Cuatr.			

APPENDIX TABLE 9 (*Continued*)

Scientific Name	Common Name	Use	Region Where Most Frequently Encountered
THEACEAE			
Camelia			
sasanqua Thunb.		oil	China
sinensis (L.) O. Kuntze	Tea	beverage	Burma
var. *assamica* (Mast.) Pierre	Assam tea		
var. *macrophylla* Makino	Tetraploid tea		
var. *sinensis*	China tea		
TILIACEAE			
Corchorus			
aestuans L.		pot herb	Tropical Africa
tridens L.		pot herb	Tropical Africa
trilocularis L.		pot herb	Tropical Africa
TROPAEOLACEAE			
Tropaeolum			
tuberosum Ruiz & Pav.			
UMBELLIFERAE			
Arracacha			
xanthorrhiza Bancr.	Arracacha	edible tuber	South America